# Archaeological Sciences 1999

Proceedings of the Archaeological Sciences
Conference, University of Bristol, 1999

Edited by

## Kate A. Robson Brown

BAR International Series 1111
2003

Published in 2016 by
BAR Publishing, Oxford

BAR International Series 1111

*Archaeological Sciences 1999*

ISBN  978 1 84171 489 9

BAR Publishing is the trading name of British Archaeological Reports (Oxford) Ltd.
British Archaeological Reports was first incorporated in 1974 to publish the BAR
Series, International and British. In 1992 Hadrian Books Ltd became part of the BAR
group. This volume was originally published by Archaeopress in conjunction with
British Archaeological Reports (Oxford) Ltd / Hadrian Books Ltd, the Series principal
publisher, in 2003. This present volume is published by BAR Publishing, 2016.

Printed in England

# BAR
PUBLISHING

BAR titles are available from:

       BAR Publishing
       122 Banbury Rd, Oxford, OX2 7BP, UK
EMAIL   info@barpublishing.com
PHONE  +44 (0)1865 310431
FAX    +44 (0)1865 316916
       www.barpublishing.com

# Contents

# Introduction

The Bristol Archaeological Research Group (BASRG) was set up in 1994 to bring together the various strands of archaeological science developing within the University of Bristol, fostering a culture of collaborative research and support. Today BASRG has a large membership of University staff, graduate students and undergraduates drawn form the Departments of Archaeology, Chemistry, Earth Sciences, Computer Science, Anatomy, Medicine, Interface Analysis, Geographical Sciences, Psychology, and the Bristol City Museum and Art Gallery. During term the Research Group runs weekly open seminars and discussion sessions presented by both members and invited speakers. Many BASRG members are currently or have been recently involved in collaborative research projects developing out of this organisation.

The Archaeological Sciences 1999 conference hosted by BASRG at the University of Bristol brought together scientists from throughout the UK, and also international participants from France, Germany, Poland and Egypt. The papers presented provided a valuable insight into the exciting new avenues for research opening up to archaeological science within the UK. This volume is representative of the very broad range of research themes addressed during the conference, so to simply the structure of the collection, the papers are arranged in alphabetical order.

Many colleagues deserve thanks for their help and support during the period of conference organisation and also for the preparation of this volume. Many thanks must go to the whole BASRG committee (Dr Alan Chalmers, Dr Mary Benton, Dr Ticca Ogilvie, Dr Vanessa Straker, Prof Richard Evershed, and Dr Larry Barham) for their organisation of the conference itself. In particular Dr Vanessa Straker and Matthew Gordon deserve special mention for their advice and effort during the editing of the papers presented here. Heartfelt thanks goes also to all the authors who have contributed to this volume, and who have waited patiently for the publication of their work.

This volume is dedicated to the memory of Dr Juliet Rogers, founder member of BASRG, colleague, and friend.

# Electron Microscopical (S.E.M.) studies on biodeteriorated archaeological Egyptian textiles

Omar Abdelkareem*, Jadwiga Szostak-Kotowa **

*Microbiology Dept., Cracow Univ. of Economics, ul. Sienkiewicza 5, 30-033 Kraków, Poland
Permanent address: Conservation Dept., Faculty of Archaeology, Cairo Univ., Egypt
** Microbiology Dept., Cracow Univ. of Economics, ul. Sienkiewicza 5, 30-033 Krakow, Poland

## Abstract

In this work valuable, but deteriorated, ancient Egyptian samples were observed by the scanning electron microscope. These samples, which belong to different Egyptian historical periods, were obtained from different Egyptian museums and excavations. The surface features and morphological characters of each fungus together with their damage effects were recorded and illustrated. The results obtained show that the most dominant isolated fungi on archaeological Egyptian textiles, belong to the *Aspergillus*, *Penicillium*, *Alternaria* and *Chaetomium* genera. The study shows that all kinds of archaeological Egyptian textile fibres are liable to fungal attack, and that cellulosic fibres are more liable to fungal attack than animal fibres. Linen textiles appear to be more liable to fungal deterioration than cotton textiles. The results also show that fungal species which dominate the wool fibres which are in contact with linen fibres, are less common on wool fibres that are not in contact with other fibres. This study demonstrates scanning electron microscopy is a very useful, non-destructive, technique for the identification of fungi directly, and for developing an understanding of fibre deterioration.

## Introduction

Archaeological Egyptian textiles were made from natural animal and vegetable products. Linen, cotton, wool and silk were the most important fibres used in the different Ancient Egyptian periods (Hall 1990; Coptic Encyclopaedia; 1991; Abdelkareem; 1995). These ancient textiles are organic substances in nature and hence they are liable to deterioration (Landi 1985). Microorganisms such as bacteria, actinomyceties and fungi (Kowalik 1980) cause the most serious damage to textiles. Fungi are very often found in museum storage conditions (Giuliani and Nugari 1993). Fungal deterioration can appear in several forms; different kinds of staining may be observed and the textile may undergo a loss of strength and material (Kowalik 1980; Vigo 1980; Sagar 1987; Raschle 1989; Nair 1991; Caneva *et al* 1991). Heavy infection results in rotting, involving a structural breakdown of the fibres and deterioration of the physical properties of the fibres (Aranyanak, 1995).

Many reports on the use of the scanning electron microscope to study biodeteriorated textiles, have been published (Kenjo *et al* 1987; Greaves and McCarthy 1991; Agrawal 1995; Aranyanak 1995; Ghawana and Shrivastava 1995; Suwanarit 1995; Peacock 1996). In a literature review of micromorphological aspects of cotton degradation by microorganisms, various structural changes in the fibre were reported, notably transverse cracking, segmentation and

segmentation planes. Irregular transverse segmentation in biodegraded linen was also observed. Studies of microbiological degradation of cellulosic fabrics and fibres conclude that fibres are subjected to attack from both the lumen proceeding outwards and from the outside surface proceeding inward. Lewis (1981) reported that in the early stages of an attack on wool by microorganisms, the distal scale edges exhibit marked morphological change and damaged fibre ends adopt a frayed appearance as cortical cells become disaggregated.

One of the main problems in biodeterioration studies is the difficulty in analysing the causal agents and the deterioration processes. Conventional methods of investigation include light microscopic examination and the use of the laboratory media for the isolation and identification of the fungi. The use of laboratory substrates for isolation is not only costly but also time consuming. In addition, the fungi cultured on laboratory substrates may be different from those are actually growing on the artefact itself. Some isolates result from spores present as contaminates on the artefact. Laboratory media sometimes permit the development of forms unable to grow on the original sample. Moreover the structure of the conidial fructification in the culture may be quite different from that which characterises the species when it is grown on its natural substrates (Aranyanak 1995).

The conservation literature describing fungal biodeterioration on Egyptian ancient textiles, is very limited. The main aim of this work is to investigate the possibility of using scanning electron microscopy for identification of fungal growth commonly found on biodeteriorated, archaeological Egyptian textiles. In addition the surface morphology of biodeteriorated, ancient Egyptian textiles is described, to provide textile conservators with details of the nature of degradation on these textiles.

## Materials and Methods

Biodeteriorated ancient Egyptian textile samples were obtained from a number of different Egyptian museums and excavations. These samples belong to different Egyptian historical periods. These collected samples were placed in sterilised petri dishes for further testing.

Samples No.1 to 10 were obtained from the Faculty of Archaeology excavation in the Saqara area. They represent several Pheronic periods.

Samples No.11 to 20 were obtained from the Fayom excavation. They date to the second and the third centuries A.D..

Samples No.21 to 25 were obtained from the Tal-Abomandor excavation in Rashid. They date from the Romanic period (the fourth century B.C.).

Samples No.26 to 35 were obtained from the Egyptian Museum in the Faculty of Archaeology, Cairo University. They date from the Coptic period, Tal-Elgabal excavation.

Samples No.36 to 45 were obtained from the Islamic Art Museum in the Faculty of Archaeology, Cairo University. They date from the Fatimid period (969-1171 A.D.).

Samples No.46 to 50 were obtained from the Tanta Museum in Tanta, and are variable in date. (a) Samples No.46 to 48 belong to the Sawy period. (b) Samples No.49, 50 belong to Mameluke period (1250-1517 A.D.).

## Identification of fibres
Textile fibres were identified microscopically by examining the surface morphology. Small fragments of weft and warp threads were transferred to slides and examined microscopically, using a transmitted light microscope according to the standard methods (Abdelkareem 1995). Wool, linen and cotton were identified from all samples. Some samples contained 2 different kinds of fibres (cotton and wool or linen and wool). These were separated from each other.

## Incubation
The samples were washed in sterilised distilled water and were transferred using sterilised tweezers onto a solid medium (Czapek-Dox agar modified) (Booth 1971; Kowalik 1980; Abdelkareem *et al* 1997), in petri dishes. These prepared cultures were incubated at 28° C for one to three weeks (until growth of colonies was observed).

Method of observation

A JSM-400 Scanning Electron Microscope was used to study the surface morphology of the biodeteriorated archaeological Egyptian textiles. Small pieces of the biodeteriorated samples were attached to a metal stub, then coated with a gold layer of about 20 nm thick. Coated samples were examined in order to detect possible morphological indication of the ability of fungi to deteriorate archaeological Egyptian textile fibres and to identify of fungal growth on archaeological Egyptian textile fibres directly.

## Results and Discussion

When considering the S.E.M. photographs of the obtained biodeteriorated archaeological Egyptian wool, (Figures 1,2 of the Appendix), linen (Figure 3 of the Appendix), and cotton (Figure 4 of the Appendix) samples, it is clear that the scanning electron microscope is a useful tool in the identification of fungal groups that are dominant on these samples. Species of *Aspergillus* are the most frequent fungi identified. *Aspergillus* can be observed in Figures 1, 3, and 4 of the Appendix. *Aspergillus* genera are characterised by the

head-like termination of the conidiophores. The shape, size and arrangement of various parts of the conidial heads are diagnostic of the species concerned. The conidiophore grows directly from the substrate or from aerial hypha. The results also show that *Chaetomium* is abundant on all kind of archaeological Egyptian textiles. Figures 2-4 of the Appendix demonstrate that species of *Chaetomium* typically produce perithecia on the surface of the hyphal mat. Perithecia are spherical, subglobose, elongated or vase-shaped. The perithecial wall is membranaceous, fragile, and distinctly cellular-ornamented with appendages in the form of diversity modified hairs. The mycelium consists of sparsely or densely branching fungus threads radiating in a network from the point of origin. The terminal hairs arise from the region of the neck around the ostiole. The ascospores are oval or roughly egg-shaped. The results also show also that species of *Penicillium* are abundant on archaeological Egyptian textiles (Figures 2-4 of the Appendix). Species of *Penicillium* are characterised by straight, aerial, septate, stalk-hypha branching above and finally producing a group of parallel terminal spore-forming cells (phialides). Each of these gives rise to a chain of conidia (phialospores). The results show that species of *Alternaria* are also present on the biodeteriorated archaeological Egyptian linen samples. Figure 3 of the Appendix illustrates that conidiophores of *Alternaria sp.*, are characterised by their simple chain-of-pearl appearance.

## Observation of the surface morphology of the obtained biodeteriorated, archaeological, Egyptian textile samples

### Wool samples
When considering the S.E.M. photographs of the biodeteriorated wool samples (Figure 5 of the Appendix) we may notice that the wool fibres are broken and fibrillated, with transverse cracking and longitudinal splitting, and the beginning of breakdown into the cortical cells. The damaged surfaces exhibit loss of scale structure, which may cause conservators to encounter difficult in identification of the fibres. The results show also that the mycelia and spores of fungi cover the surface of biodeteriorated samples, making the fibre surfaces opaque and causing a loss of definition of the fabric surface. These results are in agreement with other microscopic analyses of microbiological degraded wool (Lewis 1981; Greaves and McCarthy 1991; Ghawana and Shrivastava 1995; Peacock 1996).

### Linen samples
S.E.M. photographs of the observed biodeteriorated linen samples (Figure 6 of the Appendix) show surfaces covered with fungal mycelia and conidial heads. The attacked surfaces are rough and characterised by small scratches, large slits and holes. Fungal mycelia and spores are clearly observed in Figure 6 of the Appendix (A,B,C). Figure 6 (D,E, and F), also shows that the biodeteriorated surface without fungal growth has an extremely roughened, damaged surface. Since the fungal mycelia made holes, fungi clearly grow not only on the surface but also within the linen fibres.

*Cotton samples:*
When considering the S.E.M. photographs of the biodeteriorated cotton textile samples (Figure 7 of the Appendix) we may notice severe fibre surface damage caused by fungi. The surfaces of fibres are opaque and rough. Mycelia and spores of fungi cover the biodeteriorated samples, causing a loss of definition of the fabric surface. This may cause difficulties for textile conservators attempting to identify such fibres. The results in Figure 7 of the Appendix also show that the yarns are composed of collapsed, extensively pitted and corroded fibres that have latched together forming a smeared surface over the yarns. There is longitudinal splitting, cracking and loosening of the fibrils.

This study revealed that fungal species which attack ancient Egyptian textile belong to the *Aspergillus*, *Penicillium*, *Alternaria* and *Chaetomium* genera. These species are very dangerous because most of them belong to the class *Deuteromycetes*, which are capable of rapid growth when the environmental conditions are favourable, and which are also able to survive under unfavourable conditions.

It can be concluded from the results obtained, that several fungal species appear on ancient Egyptian textiles. This may be this due to the environmental conditions in Egypt, which promote fungal growth. The relative humidity (R.H.) and the air temperature in Egypt are high, and many types of pollutants are present in the atmosphere (Abdelgany 1992). Another factor which may promote fungal growth is the chemical composition of ancient Egyptian textiles. The major constituents of archaeological Egyptian textiles are cellulose, proteins and other carbohydrates (Abdelkareem 1995). Also most dyes present in these ancient textiles are acid dyes, so that ancient Egyptian textiles are mostly acidic, thus providing favourable conditions for fungal growth (Abdelkareem *et al*, 1997; Aranyanak 1995).

The results presented show that all kind of ancient Egyptian textile fibres are liable to fungal attack. This is in line with the work of other investigators who mentioned that cellulosic fibres are more liable to fungal attack than animal fibres (Montegut *et al* 1991; Aranyanak 1995). The results suggest that linen fibres are more liable to fungal attack than cotton fibres. The results also show that fungal species that dominate the wool fibres which are in contact with linen fibres, are less common on wool fibres that are not in contact with other fibres. These results are in agreement with those obtained by Greaves and McCarthy (1991), and Lewis (1981), who reported that contact of wool with jute, cotton and other cellulosic fibres, e.g. in packaging, or in carpets, can also promote biodeterioration because of the enhanced liability of wool to become mildewed in the presence of these less resistant fibres.

The morphological characteristics of all kinds of biodeteriorated archaeological Egyptian fibres indicate that the damage of the fibres surfaces arising from effect of fungi is extreme. So, maybe the archaeological Egyptian textiles suffer from loss of fibre strength and actual material failure. It is demonstrated that the loss in the mechanical properties is directly proportional to the damage on the surface morphology of deteriorated linen fibres. The results show that all the biodeteriorated fibres exhibited extremely marked morphological changes, and extremely damaged fibres, which may make fibre identification difficult.

The results show that the scanning electron microscope is a very useful tool for detecting morphological changes which may indicate damage to textile fibres by microorganisms, and so to identify the fungal growth commonly on them. This may be because that observation using scanning electron microscopy can reveal surface details that cannot be revealed by the ordinary microscopes. In addition this analysis is relatively non-destructive for archaeological Egyptian textiles. The authors recommended its use in the field of archaeological textile conservation, because the main target of this field is to preserve archaeological Egyptian textiles in order to pass them on to the future generations as complete as possible.

## Conclusion

The fungal species which are dominant on ancient Egyptian textiles, belong to the *Aspergillus*, *Penicillium*, *Alternaria* and *Chaetomium* genera.

All kinds of ancient Egyptian textile fibres are very liable to fungal attack, but cellulosic fibres are more liable to fungal attack than animal fibres.

Linen fibres are the most susceptible to fungal attack.

Scanning electron microscopy is a very useful technique for detecting possible morphological changes which indicate damage to ancient Egyptian textile fibres caused by microorganisms, and so to identifying the fungal growth present.

## References

Abdel-gany, A.R., (1992). *Environmental Conditions Prevailing at Helwan Region in Relation to Textile Deterioration. Unpublished* Masters Thesis, Cairo University 1992.

Abdelkareem , O.M.A., (1995). *Experimental and Applied Studies in Treatment and Conservation of Archaeological Textiles.* Unpublished Masters Thesis, Conservation and Restoration Dept., Faculty of Archaeology, Cairo University, Cairo.

Abdelkareem ,O.M.A., et al. (1997). *Fungal Biodeterioration of Ancient Egyptian Textiles, Part I: Surveying Study for The Most Dominant Fungi on Ancient Egyptian Textiles*, In: Drobnousreoje w srodowisku wystepowanie, Aktywnosc i Znachenie, AR Krakow, pp.279-290.

Agrawal, S.C. (1995). Biodeterioration of Wool: Efficacy of Some Fungicides in Controlling the Deterioration. In: *Biodeterioration of Cultural Property 3, Thailand*, July 4-7, pp. 203-209

Aranyanak,C. (1995). Microscopical Study of Fungal Growth on Paper and Textiles, In *Biodeterioration of Cultural Property 3, Thailand*, July 4-7, 1995, pp.83-101

Caneva,G., *et al* (1991). Biology in the Conservation of Works of Art, ICCROM, 1991, pp.41-70. *Coptic Encyclopaedia*, 1991,Vol.7.

Ghawana, V.K., and Shrivastava, J.N. (1995). Morphological Induced During the Biodeterioration of Wool by Soil-Borne Fungus, In: *Biodeterioration of Cultural Property 3, Thailand*, July 4-7, pp. 693-700.

Giuliani, M.R., and Nugari, M.P. (1993). A Case of Fungal Biodeterioration on an Ancient Textile, In *International Conference on Conservation and Restoration of Textiles ICOM Committee for Conservation*, 1993, pp. 305-307.

Greaves, P.H., and McCarthy, B.J. (1991). A Microscopical Study of Severe Biodeterioration in a Textile Floorcovering, A Case History, *Journal of Textile Inst* **82**, No.3, 291-295.

Hall, R . (1990). *Egyptian Textiles*, London: Shire Egyptology.

Kowalik, R., (1980). *Microbiodeterioration of Library Materials Part 2*, Restorer 4, Copenhagen.

Kenjo,T., et al. (1987). Application of Scanning Electron Microscope in Field of Conservation Science of Cultural Properties, *JEOL News*, **25E**, No.1, pp. 13-17.

Landi, S., (1998). *The Textile Conservator's Manual*. London: Butterworth.

Lewis, J., (1975). *The Biodeterioration of Wool by Microorganisms-Its Causes, Effects and Prevention*. In: Microbial Aspects of The Deterioration of Materials, London, pp. 153-186.

Montegut, D. *et al*, (1991). Fungal Deterioration of Cellulosic Textiles: a Review. *International Biodeterioration Bulletin* **28**, 1, pp. 209-226.

Nair, S.M., (1991). Problems of Biodeterioration in Natural History Museums. In O.P. Agrawal and S. Dhawan (Eds). *Biodeterioration of Cultural Property, Proceedings of The International Conference on Biodeterioration of Cultural Property, Lucknow, February 20-25 1989*, New Delhi, 1991, pp.35-44.

Peacock, E.E. (1996). Biodegradation and Characterisation of Water-degraded Archaeological Textiles Created for Conservation Research. *International Biodeterioration and Biodegradation*, **32**, 49-59.

Raschle, P., (1989). Microbial Influence on Cellulosic Textiles and Microbiological Testing. International Biodeterioration **25**, 237-244.

# Appendix

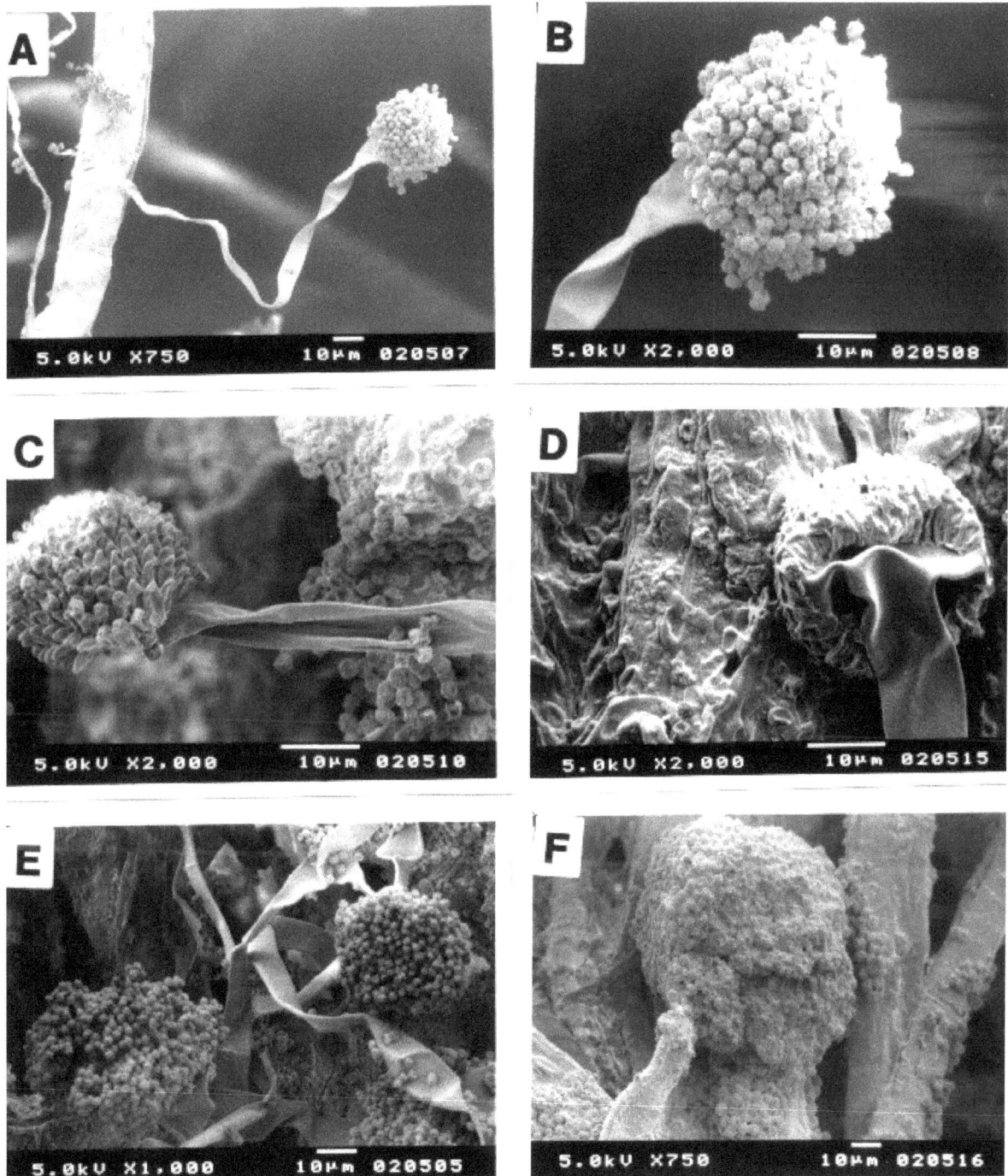

Figure 1. S.E.M. photographs of the fungal growth on the biodeteriorated archaeological Egyptian wool textiles samples, A) Conidiophores and conidia of *Aspergillus Sp.* B) High magnification of *Aspergillus Sp.* in (A) C) Conidiophores and conidia of *Aspergillus Sp.* D) Conidiophores and conidia of *Aspergillus Sp.* E) Conidiophores and conidia of *Aspergillus Sp.* F) Conidiophores and conidia of *Aspergillus Sp.*

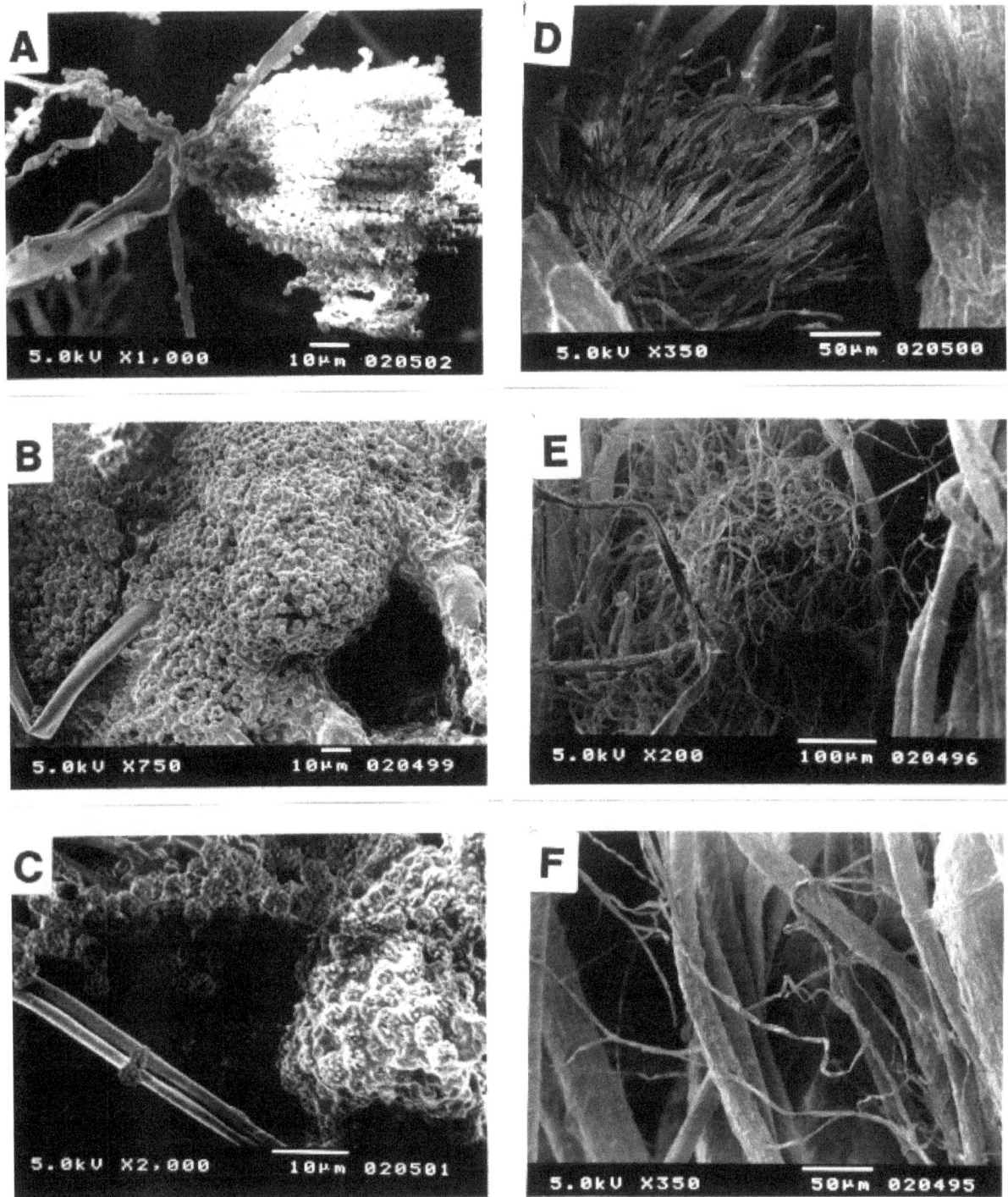

Figure 2. S.E.M.photographs of the fungal growth on the biodeteriorated archaeological Egyptian wool textiles samples, A) Conidiophores and conidia of *Penicillium sp., B)* Conidia of *Penicillium sp., C)* High magnification of conidia of *Penicillium sp.,* in (B), D) Perithecium and terminal hairs of *Chaetomium sp., E)* Perithecium and terminal hairs of *Chaetomium sp. F)* Terminal hairs of *Chaetomium sp.*

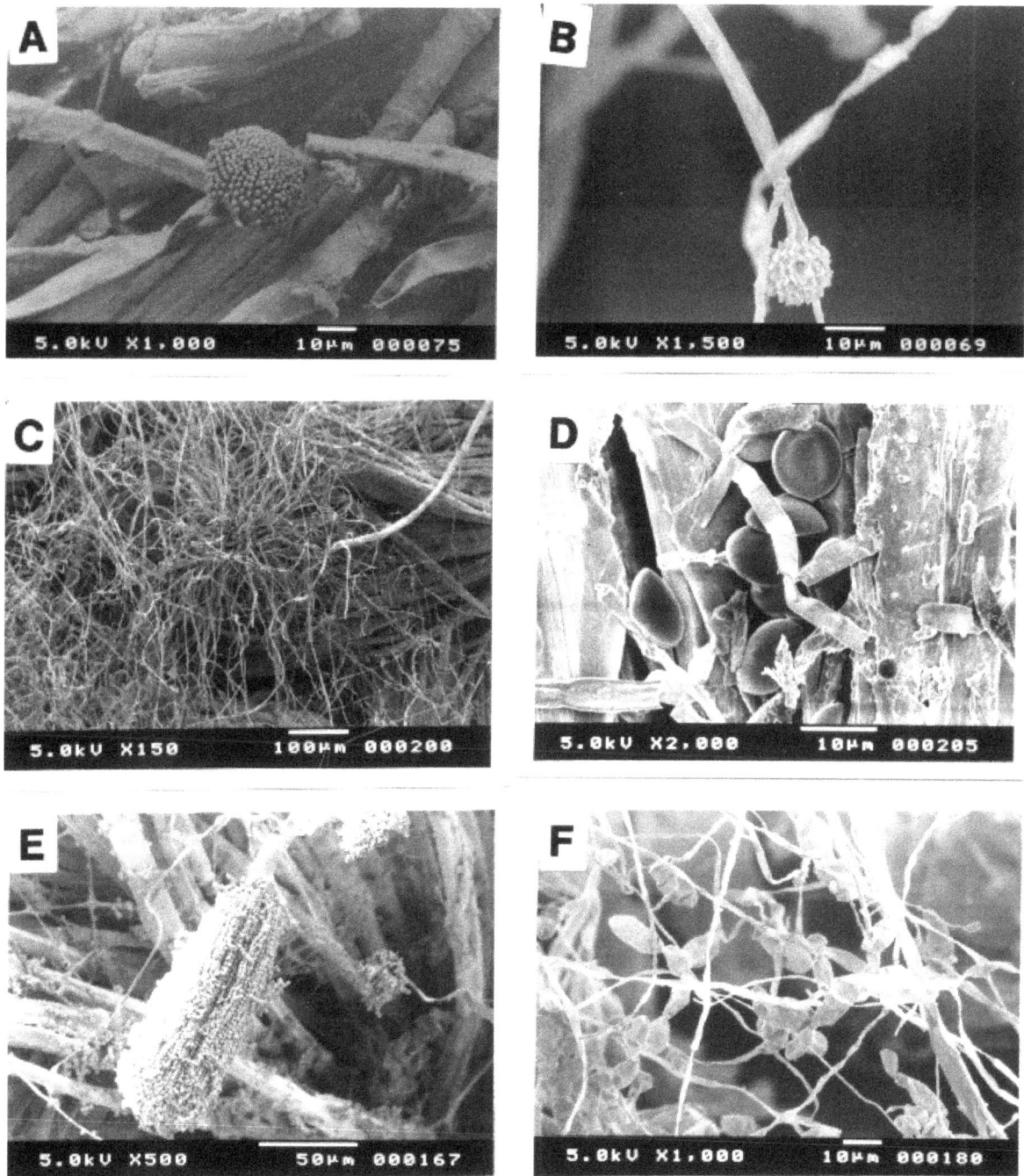

Figure 3. S.E.M. photographs of the fungal growth on the biodeteriorated archaeological Egyptian linen textiles samples, A) Conidiophores and conidia of *Aspergillus Sp.* B) Conidiophores and conidia of *Aspergillus Sp.*, C) Perithecium and terminal hairs of *Chaetomium sp.*, D) Ascospores of *Chaetomium Sp.*, E) Conidiophores and conidia of *Penicillium sp.*, F) Conidiophores and conidia of *Alternaria sp.*

Figure 4. S.E.M. photographs of the fungal growth on the biodeteriorated archaeological Egyptian linen textiles samples, A) Perithecium and terminal hairs of *Chaetomium sp.,* B) Perithecium and terminal hairs of *Chaetomium sp.,* C) Conidiophores and conidia of *Aspergillus Sp.* D) Conidiophores and conidia of *Aspergillus Sp.* E) Conidiophores and conidia of *Penicillium sp.,* F) Conidiophores and conidia of *Penicillium sp.*

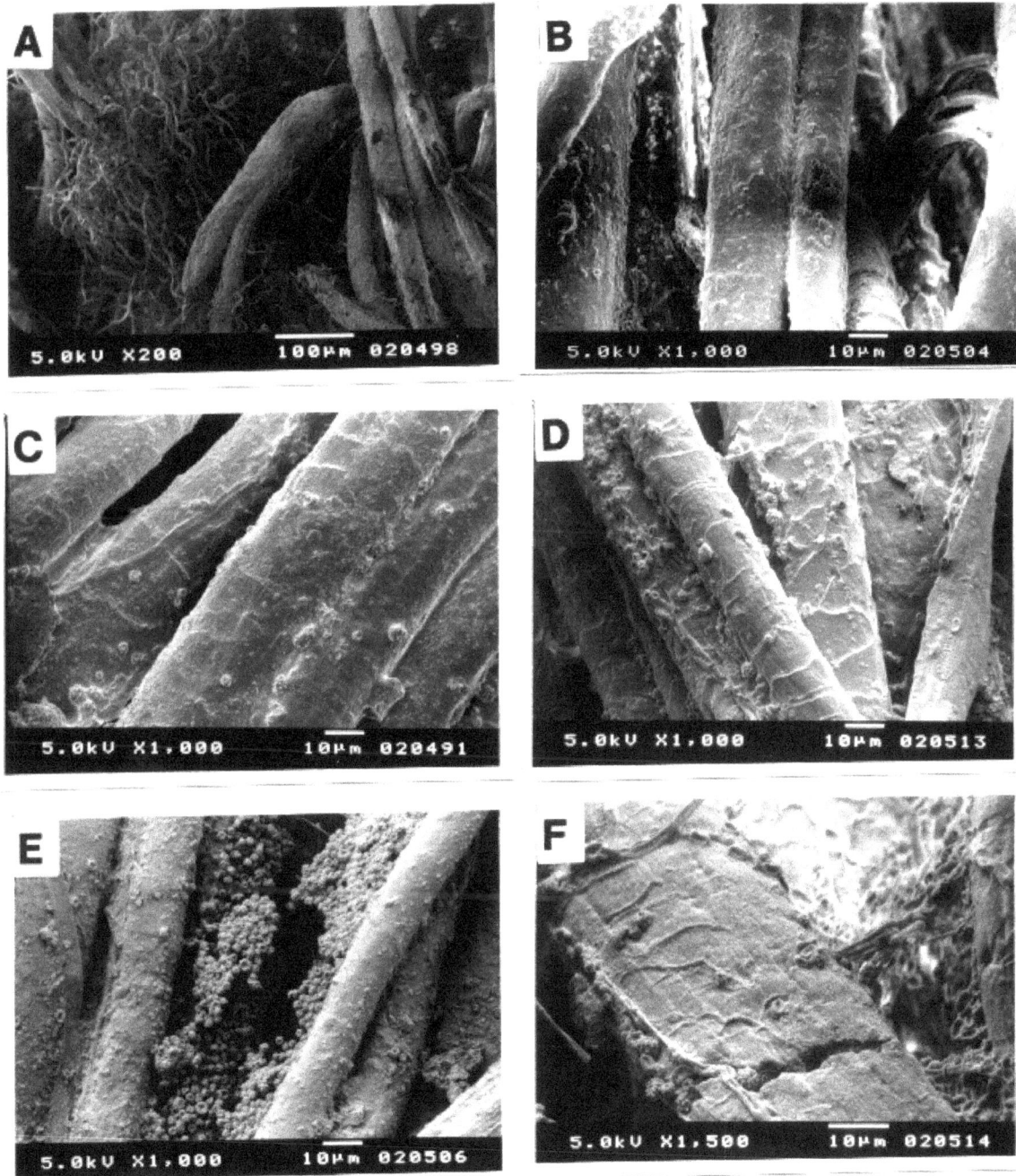

**Figure 5. S.E.M. photographs of the biodeteriorated surface of archaeological Egyptian wool textiles samples. It is notice that the damaged surfaces exhibit loose of the scale structure, and the wool fibers are broken and transverse cracking. Also it is notice that the mycelia and spores of fungi cover the surface of biodeteriorated samples, therefore the fiber surfaces are opaque and there is loss of definition of the fabric surface.**

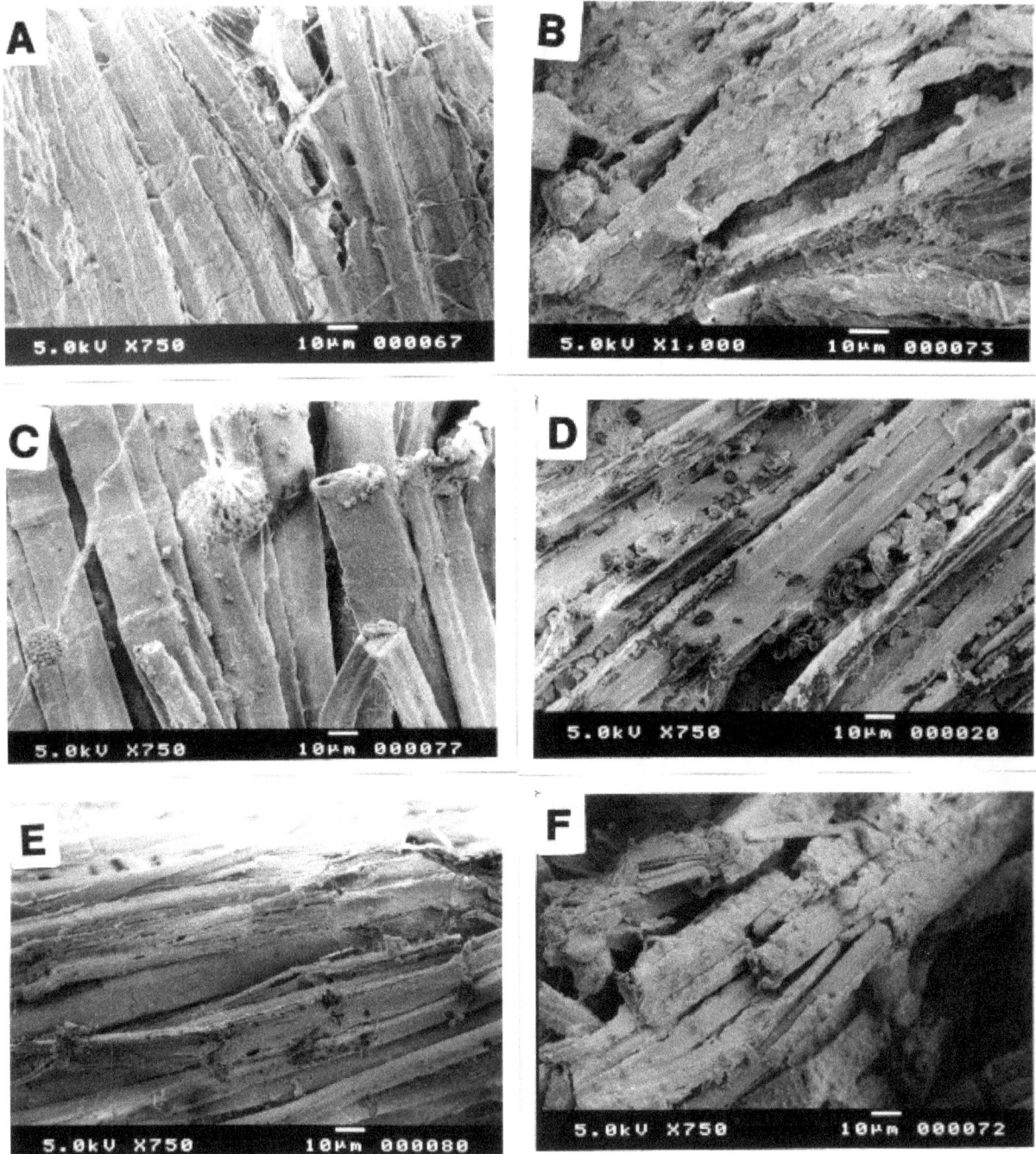

Figure 6. S.E.M. photographs of the biodeteriorated surface of archaeological Egyptian linen textiles samples. It is notice in photo (A,B,C), that the fungal mycelia and spores are observed, and in photo (D,E,F), that the attacked and roughened surface are clearly distinguished from the surface without fungal growth.

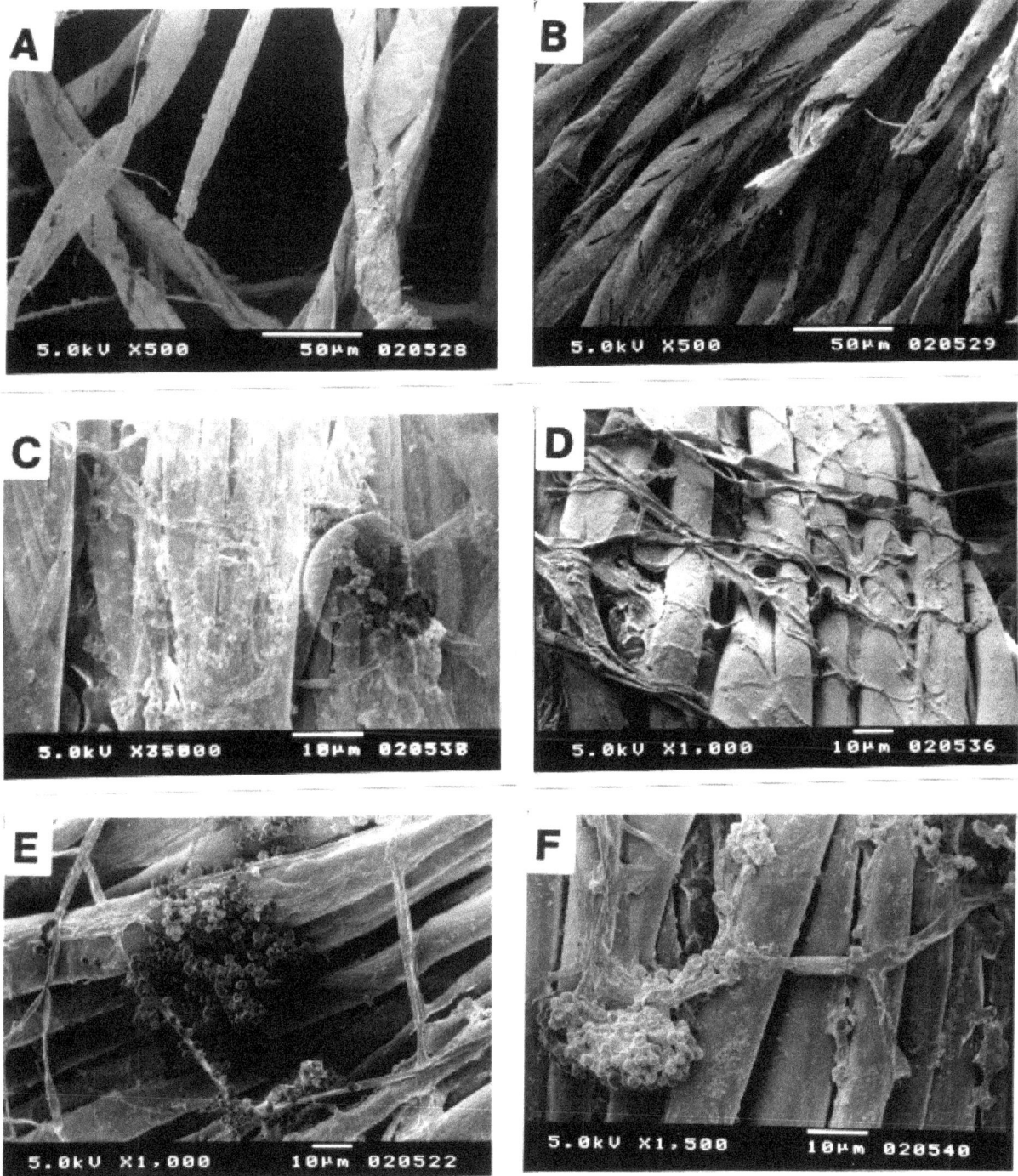

Figure 7. S.E.M. photographs of the biodeteriorated surface of archaeological Egyptian cotton textiles samples It is notice that the fiber surfaces are opaque and roughness. The mycelia and spores of fungi cover the surface of biodeteriorated samples. Therefore there is loss of definition of the fabric surface. Also it is notice that the yarns are composed of collapsed, extensively pitted and corroded fibers which have latched together forming a smeared surface over the yarns.

# Prehistoric crop husbandry and plant use in southern England: development and regionality

Gill Campbell[1] and Vanessa Straker[2]

[1] English Heritage, Centre for Archaeology, Fort Cumberland, Eastney, Portsmouth PO4 9LD
[2] School of Geographical Sciences, University Road, Bristol BS8 1SS

## Abstract

This paper seeks to provide a summary of our knowledge to date of the development of crop husbandry in southern England, from the Neolithic to the end of the Iron Age. It illustrates that there are considerable differences in the types of crop grown across the region and that there are still areas where there is little or no information. Context-related variation is briefly discussed as are issues concerning sampling and excavation programmes and the effects these have on interpretation of results. Areas and topics of potential for future research are suggested.

## Introduction

This paper arose as a result of work being carried out as part of English Heritage's review of archaeobotanical studies in southern region, which seeks to synthesise the results obtained from the analysis of plant macroscopic remains carried out in this area up to the late 1990's. For the purposes of the review the southern region was defined as the incorporating following counties: Oxfordshire, Gloucestershire, Berkshire, Kent, W and E Sussex, Surrey, Hampshire, the Isle of Wight, Wiltshire, Somerset. Dorset, Devon, Cornwall and the Isles of Scilly. Sites in London were also included. The review concentrates principally on published reports on plant macroscopic remains other than wood and charcoal. It covers not only the analysis of macroscopic plant remains preserved by charring, mineralisation and preservation in anoxic (i.e. waterlogged) conditions, but also reports on plant remains in pottery and fired clay.

Most the published reports were obtained through a search of the Environmental Archaeological Database (http://www.eng-h.gov.uk/EAB/ {accessed 1/10/2002}) which contains details of reports on environmental material up to and including those published in 1996, but is less comprehensive after this date. For the more recently published work, major journals, county archaeological journals, and monograph series such as Wessex Archaeological Reports were consulted. Archaeobotanists working in the region were also approached with regard to unpublished work and assessment reports. While coverage of archaeobotanical work in the region is comprehensive the review does not refer to every site where archaeobotanical remains have been found. Sites where the assemblages were very small, and/or the dating of the material suspect were often deliberately excluded.

The evidence considered in this paper dates from the Neolithic up to and including the late Iron Age. The discussion is divided into two broad periods: the Neolithic and early Bronze Age (c. 4000 to 1350 cal BC) looking at the evidence from the region with reference to the beginning and establishment of agriculture, and 1350 cal to cal AD50 with reference to the evidence for diversification and intensification. Archaeobotanical studies from different sites are not dealt with in detail, rather the quality and nature of the data are discussed along with the evidence for particular types of crop being grown. Possible regional differences are illuminated. The sites examined for each broad period are listed in tables 1 to 3, along with their grid references. Full bibliographical details are only included in the tables for sites not on the Environmental Archaeological Database.

## Neolithic and early Bronze Age c. 4000 to cal 1350 BC

This period includes both the Neolithic and early Bronze Age for as far as the crop record is concerned, the range of crops and associated weeds remains similar through out this long period despite major changes in other cultural aspects.

The macrofossil evidence reviewed is from around 40 sites in southern England, some of which have both Neolithic and Early Bronze Age phases. The records examined are for 32 Neolithic phases, 11 Early Bronze Age phases and 3 dated to Neolithic / Early Bronze Age. Although the individual reports distinguish between the early, middle or late Neolithic where possible, for the purposes of this summary all 3 periods are amalgamated as 'Neolithic'. There are few radiocarbon dates on the plant remains themselves, most dating relies on association with artefacts, particularly pottery. Most contexts examined are pits with others from ditches, middens/dumps, post pits, hearths, 2 palaeochannels and 1 waterhole.

### The evidence

The macrofossils were preserved by charring with the exception of those from the Neolithic palaeochannels at Anslow's Cottages (Carruthers, 1992), Runnymede (Greig, 1991) and Early Bronze Age waterhole at Abingdon (Pelling, unpublished) where preservation was by waterlogging. Because waterlogged preservation is so rare, as with the archaeobotanical record in general knowledge of the use of leafy plants is poor, despite the important contribution to diet and health they would have contributed by virtue of vitamins and trace elements. Plant impressions in pottery are also mentioned in the discussion but are not included on the location map unless they are significant assemblages or they are from sites where charred macrofossils are also present.

Where sufficient information is available, macrofossil density (concentration of items per litre sediment) was calculated and ranges from 0.1 to 39, with the average for most sites falling below 1 item per litre. The exceptions are a very rich context from the Neolithic causewayed enclosure at Stepleton, Dorset where Jones (Jones and Legge, in press) found c.50,000 spikelets of emmer wheat in the fill of one pit and the assemblage from Windmill Hill (Whittle et al, 2000). There was also a small cache of cleaned, predominantly naked barley on a buried ground surface at East Porth Samson, Isles of Scilly (Ratcliffe and Straker, 1996) which provided 144 items per litre sediment.

Sample sizes per context vary depending on the nature of the context and the sampling strategy ranging, for example, from under 2 litres at some sites to several hundred litres for the midden at Hazleton (Straker, 1990a) and c. 7000 litres from the settlement features at Yarnton (Robinson, 2000)

## Coverage of the region (Figure 1)

Most of the data comes from the central southern counties, particularly Dorset, Wiltshire, Hampshire and Oxfordshire. The south western counties of Cornwall, Devon and Somerset and south eastern counties of Kent and West and East Sussex have provided little data despite, for the south west, considerable attention to large-scale sampling and sieving programmes.

## The crops

The crops represented are principally emmer wheat (*Triticum dicoccum*) with hulled 6-row barley (the presence of hulled two-row barley is uncertain) and naked six- and two-row barley (*Hordeum vulgare*). There have been occasional identifications of einkorn (*Triticum monococcum* or cf. *monococcum*) for example at Stepleton, Dorset (Jones and Legge, in Press) and Hazleton, Gloucestershire (Straker, 1990a) and a free threshing wheat. These two species are presumed to have been minor contaminants. The free threshing wheat was usually identified as *Triticum aestivum or cf. aestivum* on the basis of grain morphology and in the absence of the more reliable rachis segments. In fact, subsequent observations (Hillman et al, 1995) suggest that distinction between wheat species on the basis of grain morphology alone can be unreliable, including the distinction between free threshing hexaploid wheat (bread wheat type) and tetraploid wheat (macaroni wheat type). While never presumed to be abundant, it is generally accepted that free threshing wheat, which sometime in the late Roman / early post Roman period became the main type to be cultivated in the British Isles, has probably been present as a minor element from early in the Neolithic. The only rachis internode of a free threshing wheat to be recovered is from Flagstones, Dorchester (Straker, 1997a). Probable grains of free threshing wheat were identified at 6 sites including Hazleton, Barton Court Farm, Oxfordshire (Jones, 1984) and Gravelly Guy (Moffett, 1989). Hulled wheat may be over

represented in comparison with free-threshing cereals, including barley and non cereal crops, owing to its more likely exposure to heat to facilitate dehusking.

Hulled and naked barley differ simply on the basis of a single recessive gene (Zohary and Hopf, 2000, 60) and in the early prehistoric period are often both found in the same assemblage. The Early Bronze Age cache at East Porth, Samson, Isles of Scilly differs in that its consists almost entirely of cleaned naked barley (Ratcliffe and Straker, 1996). Carruthers (1990) identified a cleaned deposit of naked and hulled barley (ratio of 3 naked:2 hulled) in an Early Bronze Age ditch fill at Coneybury henge and postulated ritual deposition.

There is a common view (e.g. Fairbairn, 2000) that wheat, in particular emmer wheat, was more commonly grown than barley in this early period. If presence of wheat and barley at each site, regardless of concentration is considered, then wheat is indeed more commonly found than barley at 67% compared with 47%.

The only evidence of oats (*Avena* sp.) is from rare grains at the Early Bronze Age site at Montefiore, Southampton (Hinton 1996a). Without floret bases it is not possible to determine whether the oats were domesticated or wild. They were probably a very minor crop contaminant whichever was the case.

The status of spelt wheat (*Triticum spelta*) in the British Neolithic has been discussed since the identification of spelt grains and chaff from the Neolithic causewayed camp at Hembury in Devon. Helbaek (1952) confirms the presence of spelt (originally identified by Percival) including chaff but casts doubt on the date of the context since it is overlain by contexts of Iron Age date. He considered that the grain and chaff was most likely to be intrusive. An attempt to resolve the question by submitting some spelt chaff for AMS dating was made by one of the authors (VS). Unfortunately none of the Hembury material viewed in the Royal Albert Museum in Exeter which holds the site archive proved to include spelt chaff (or likely spelt grain). Samples of material from British sites that Helbaek worked on which are housed in the National Museum of Denmark were also examined to no avail. Finally, the archive of Percival at Reading University was checked and did not include material from Hembury (Carruthers pers. comm). So for the present the possible presence of Neolithic spelt at Hembury is unresolved.

There is very limited evidence for the use of non-cereal domesticates. A few legumes identified as vetch, tare or pea were found at Flagstones (Straker, 1997a) and a possible pea was identified at Runnymede (Greig, 1991), the impression of a celtic bean (*Vicia faba*) was identified in Early Bronze Age pottery at Newbarn Down on the Isle of Wight (Scaife, 1981). As the processing of these protein-rich seeds does not involve exposure to fire, they may be under-represented in the crop record in a similar way to free-threshing cereals (see above).

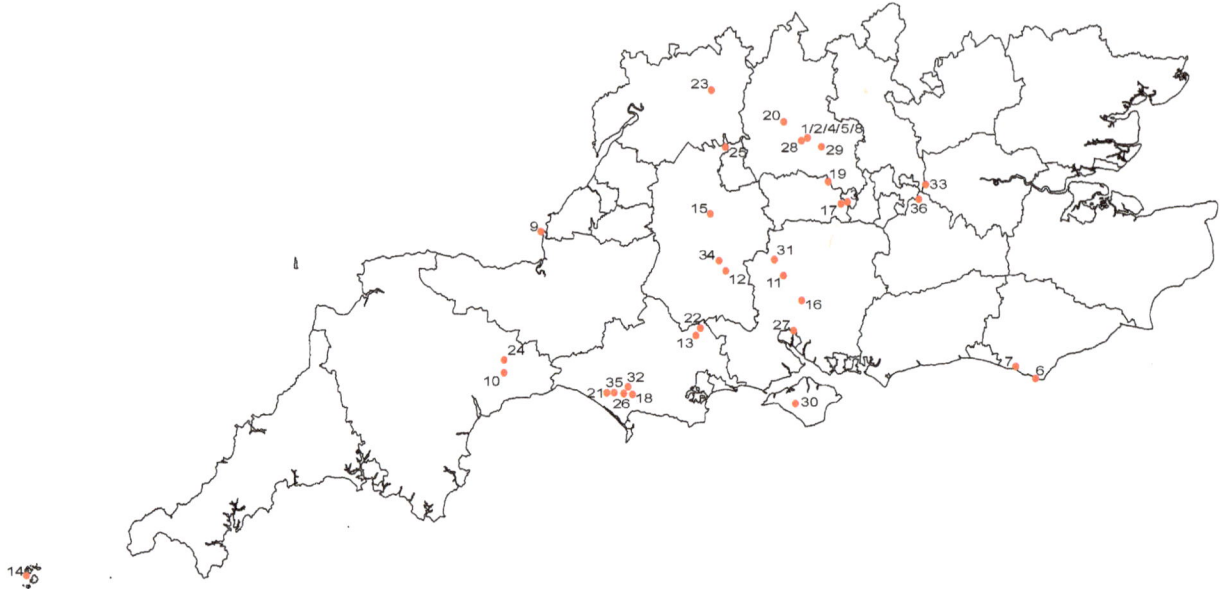

**Figure 1. Neolithic and early Bronze Age sites with archaeobotanical reports included in this study.**

| No. | Site |
|-----|------|
| 1 | Abingdon 63, Oxfordshire |
| 2 | Abingdon multiplex (Pelling unpubl.) |
| 3 | Anslows Cottages 85-6, Berkshire |
| 4 | Barrow Hillls, Oxfordshire |
| 5 | Barton Court Farm 72-6, Oxfordshire |
| 6 | Belle Tout 68-9, East Sussex |
| 7 | Bishopstone 72-5, East Sussex |
| 8 | Blewbury, Oxfordshire |
| 9 | Brean Down 83-7, Somerset |
| 10 | Castle Hill A30, Devon  (Clapham, 1999) |
| 11 | Chilbolton 86, Hampshire |
| 12 | Conebury, Wiltshire (Moffett et al, 1989; Carruthers, 1990) |
| 13 | Down Farm, Cranbourne Chase, Dorset |
| 14 | East Porth, Samson, Isles of Scilly (Ratcliffe & Straker, 1996) |
| 15 | Easton Down 91, Wlltshire |
| 16 | Easton Ln, Hampshire |
| 17 | Field Farm 85, Berkshire |
| 18 | Flagstones, Dorset (Straker, 1997a) |
| 19 | Gatehampton Farm 1985-92, Oxfordshire |
| 20 | Gravelly Guy AML 46/89, Oxfordshire |
| 21 | Greyhound Yard, Dorchester, Dorset (Jones & Straker 1993) |
| 22 | Handley Down, Dorset |
| 23 | Hazleton North 79-82, Gloucestershire |
| 24 | Hembury Fort, Devon (Helbaek 1952) |
| 25 | King Barrow Ridge 83, Wiltshire |
| 26 | Maiden Castle 85-6 (a), Dorset |
| 27 | Montefiore, Swaythling, Hampshire (Hinton, 1996a) |
| 28 | MG Abingdon, Oxfordshire |
| 29 | Mount Farm,  Oxfordshire |
| 30 | Newbarn Down AML 3501, Isle of Wight |
| 31 | Old Down Farm 74-7, Hampshire |
| 32 | Poundbury 66-8, Dorset |
| 33 | Prospect Park, Harmondsworth (Hinton, 1996) |
| 34 | Robin Hoods Ball 2, Wiltshire |
| 35 | Rowden 77-84, Dorset |
| 36 | Runnymede 78, Berkshire |
| 37 | Stepleton 81, Dorset |
| 38 | Stonehenge Environs 80-6, Wiltshire |
| 39 | Weir Bank Stud Farm, Bray, Berkshire (Clapham, 1995) |
| 40 | Wilsford Down, Wiltshire |
| 41 | Windmill Hill (Whittle et al, 2000) |
| 42 | Wytch Farm 87-90, Dorset |
| 43 | Yarnton, Oxfordshire (Robinson, 2000.) |

**Table 1. Neolithic and early Bronze Age sites with archaeobotanical reports included in this study**

## Plant impressions in pottery

In 1952 the Danish archaeobotanist Hans Helbaek published a major review of the evidence for early crops in Southern England which followed on from an earlier paper with Knud Jessen published in 1944 (Jessen and Helbaek, 1944). For the Neolithic and early Bronze Age the evidence was entirely derived from identification of 177 plant (mainly cereal) impressions in pottery. There were records of impressions from 6 Neolithic and 8 early Bronze Age sites, the most important of which was the 127 identified from the Neolithic causewayed enclosure at Windmill Hill. Dennell (1976) reviewed the evidence and concluded that interpretation of trends in local agriculture based on impressions in pottery is flawed as pottery is not always made locally and is frequently traded. This is indisputable and impressions are useful mainly for identifying potential gaps in the macrofossil record. The record of impressions has been added to by Murphy (1982). The main difference between the two sets of botanical data is the presence of flax as impressions but not as macrofossils (see below).

## Flax

Ever since the identification by Helbaek (1952) of two impressions of flax seeds in pottery from the Neolithic causewayed enclosure at Windmill Hill, it has been assumed that flax was an integral part of the crop repertoire. In fact, the Windmill Hill flax seed impressions are the only ones of Neolithic date and are only added to in the early Bronze Age by an impression in a Beaker from Belle Tout, Sussex (Arthur, 1970) and an array of 15 impressions on a Beaker from Handley Down, Dorset (Helbaek, 1952). Helbaek gives measurements for the impressions and identifies them as *Linum* sp. In his discussion he concludes that those from Windmill Hill are most likely to represent *Linum usitatissimum* while those from Handley Down are smaller and may be from another species such as *Linum austriacum*. There are, to our knowledge, no examples of flax macrofossils in Southern England which are earlier than Middle Bronze Age (see below) though the evidence from the pottery impressions must confirm its existence before this. The importance of flax as a fibre and oil crop in the earlier prehistoric period is therefore not yet established in southern England. Neolithic flax macrofossils do survive from other parts of Great Britain and Ireland, such as Tankardstown in Ireland (Monk, 2000) and Balbridie in Scotland (Fairweather and Ralston, 1993).

## Oily seeds

There is little evidence for the growth of or collection of plants with oily seeds, compared with the later prehistoric period (see below). As noted above, flax would have been a useful oil source and the *Brassica rapa* (turnip, cabbage) from the palaeochannel at Anslow's Cottages (Carruthers, 1992) could have been collected for its oily seeds, but could also have grown as bankside vegetation.

## Wild fruits and nuts

Hazel nutshell is a frequent find, often in abundance, as for example at Hazleton (Straker, 1990a) and Yarnton (Robinson, 2000). It was recorded in 27 out of the 43 sites. Wild fruits are also common, found in 20 of the sites and include blackberry (*Rubus fruticosus* subgenus Glandulosus), sloe (*Prunus spinosa*), crab apple (*Malus sylvestris*) apple or pear (*Malus / Pyrus*), haw (*Crataegus* species), elder (*Sambucus nigra*), rosehip (*Rosa* sp.). The only record of acorns is from an Early Bronze Age context at Abingdon Multiplex (Pelling, unpublished). Mosely (1910, 38-9) gives examples of the use of acorns by humans noting that they can be dried, roasted and ground into flour to make a kind of coffee. He also quotes from Chaucer "wern wonte lightlie to slaken his hunger at even with akehornes of oaks" but implies that they were probably only used as a famine food by humans. Mosely (1910) and Gale and Cutler (2000) all comment that acorns are useful food for pigs but that the tannins make them indigestible for sheep and cattle. It is perhaps surprising that the Abingdon finds are the only ones recovered to date from Southern England, given that oak species were an important component of woodland.

## Exotic species

In contrast to later periods, there is little evidence for exotic species (i.e. plants which are unlikely to have been grown in the British Isles or are not regarded as native). In fact, the main cereal domesticates and flax are not native, having been domesticated in South West Asia several millennia earlier and are thus 'exotic' introductions at this early stage. These crops apart, the most notable finding is the pip of a domesticated grape from the Stepleton enclosure of Hambledon Hill in Dorset (Jones and Legge, 1987), radiocarbon dated to the mid 4th millennium BC. Despite this interesting find, the status of the grape in Neolithic Britain is not established.

## Tubers

Roots and tubers were noted in only 9 assemblages, but tuberous roots must have been an importance food source. Their presence may be under- represented, partly because they are difficult to identify and may have been overlooked in the past. The bulbils of onion couch (*Arrhenatherum elatius*) are readily recognisable and were probably uprooted with grass for use as tinder. They were found at Hazleton (Straker, 1990a), Barrow Hills, Oxfordshire (Moffett, 1999) Castle Hill, Devon (Clapham, 1999, 52) and Gravelly Guy, Oxfordshire (Moffett, 1989). The edible bulbils of pignut (*Conopodium majus*) were identified at Castle Hill and Barrow Hills.

## Problems of interpretation

The data available for the south of England poses challenges for interpretation. Plant remains are generally found in low concentrations (see above). Exceptions include Stepleton, Dorset (Jones and Legge, in press) and further north at Lismore Fields in Derbyshire (Jones, forthcoming) and Balbridie in Scotland (Fairweather and Ralston, 1993). This is despite consistent and large-scale attempts in the last 20 years to sample and extract them using flotation. The fact that wild resources such as hazel nuts are generally well-represented in these small assemblages has led various authors to suggest that that wild resources continued to be an important element of the diet (see Jones, 1981, Moffett *et al*, 1989, Robinson, 2000). Some writers also took this to infer that cereal cultivation was not carried out on a large scale. This has been challenged by Jones (2000) and Monk (2000). Jones emphasises the need to understand the taphonomic basis for interpretation of plant assemblages and the biases that may be inherent. She points out that hazel nutshell represents the waste from eating hazel nuts and the shell has little use other than as fuel. The comparison of this with accidentally burnt grain, which is the food product of a cereal crop is therefore flawed. The by-product of grain production is straw and chaff, which have many other uses and could easily be under-represented in the archaeological record. In addition, chaff and straw survives burning more poorly than the dense shell of hazelnuts. Monk points out that more attention should have been paid to the effects of taphonomy within pits, soil erosion and landscape change in the south of England which could have led to destruction of the evidence. He draws attention to the assemblage from Tankardstown in Ireland where abundant remains of emmer and other crops were recovered from the post pits and foundation trenches of two houses. A central point is that where well-preserved evidence for houses with potential for storage of crops exists, the evidence for cultivation of domesticated cereal crops does seem to indicate larger-scale arable agriculture than most of the sites in the south of England would suggest (Jones, 2000; Monk, 2000). This is certainly persuasive where Hambledon Hill, Lismore Fields, Balbridie and Tankardstown are concerned, however, the recent large-scale sampling of a Neolithic settlement with buildings at Yarnton, Oxfordshire has not provided evidence of a convincing role for cereals as a major component of local farming (Robinson, 2000).

A further perceived problem is that many of the scarce sites of Neolithic date in the south of England have a connection with ritual activity and thus are not 'domestic' contexts. This association with ritual may be exaggerated. In the case of the Hazleton assemblage, the midden deposit from which the cereal grain was recovered was in/on the old ground surface underneath the later chambered long cairn. While a theoretical ritual use such as burning crops on ground later to become the burial place of the ancestors could be postulated, it is just as likely that the area was used for domestic purposes before the long cairns were built. The radiocarbon dates do not allow a distinction to be made between the midden and burials, but there could have been a gap in use of several hundred years. It would be instructive to carry out AMS dating on some of the macrofossils in the interests of establishing whether this was the case.

While the scarcity of evidence for well-preserved settlements in the south of England cannot be disputed and may indeed have resulted in an unrepresentative record for the region, it is hard to explain why the loss of settlement sites is restricted to the Neolithic and early Bronze Age and does not include, for example, those of the Middle Bronze Age where some well-preserved sites and crop assemblages have survived. Also it is very likely that regional or even local differences in the composition and type of agriculture existed reflecting cultural preferences, suitability of soil types and local topography and climate.

## Middle Bronze Age to the late Iron Age c. 1350 cal BC to cal AD50

This period covers a number of important changes in the crop record first discussed by Martin Jones over twenty years ago (Jones, M. 1981). Two changes in the types of crop being grown were though to have occurred. Firstly the gradual replacement of emmer wheat as the main wheat crop by spelt wheat and secondly the apparent reintroduction or expansion of free-threshing wheat at the end of the Iron Age. However, with the additional data from the last 20 years this view is no longer tenable across the whole region as the picture is far from uniform. In addition it is now clear that the wave of arable intensification which was thought to begin in the late Bronze Age (Moffett *et al*, 1989, 255) actually began in the middle Bronze Age (Jones, 1988, 89). Evidence for domestic, settlement-based activity comes from a number of middle Bronze Age sites most of which provide early evidence for the use of spelt wheat. At the same time the waterlogged assemblage from Wilsford Shaft, Wilts. (Robinson, 1989) indicates that grazed chalk grassland was already established in Wessex by the middle Bronze Age. There is also good evidence for pasture on the lower parts of the Thames floodplain at Yarnton, Oxfordshire in the middle Bronze Age especially from Coleoptera but also from waterlogged plant macroscopic plant remains (Robinson, *pers comm*).

### *Coverage of the region (Figures 2 and 3)*

The number of sites dated to this period, which have been systematically sampled for charred remains, has greatly increased over recent years and there is now a substantial amount of information available. Over forty middle to late Bronze Age sites have produced charred plant remains in the region, while the number of Iron Age sites is well over fifty.

Despite this wealth of material the majority of the sites centre on one or two areas of the region. Most of the middle to late Bronze Age material has come from excavations carried out in the South West, and in the river valleys of the Thames and the Kennet. The majority of the Iron Age material, particularly that dating from the middle to late Iron Age, is derived from the Hampshire chalklands and the Thames Valley. There are a fair number of sites in Dorset, and excavations carried out along the A30 have greatly increased

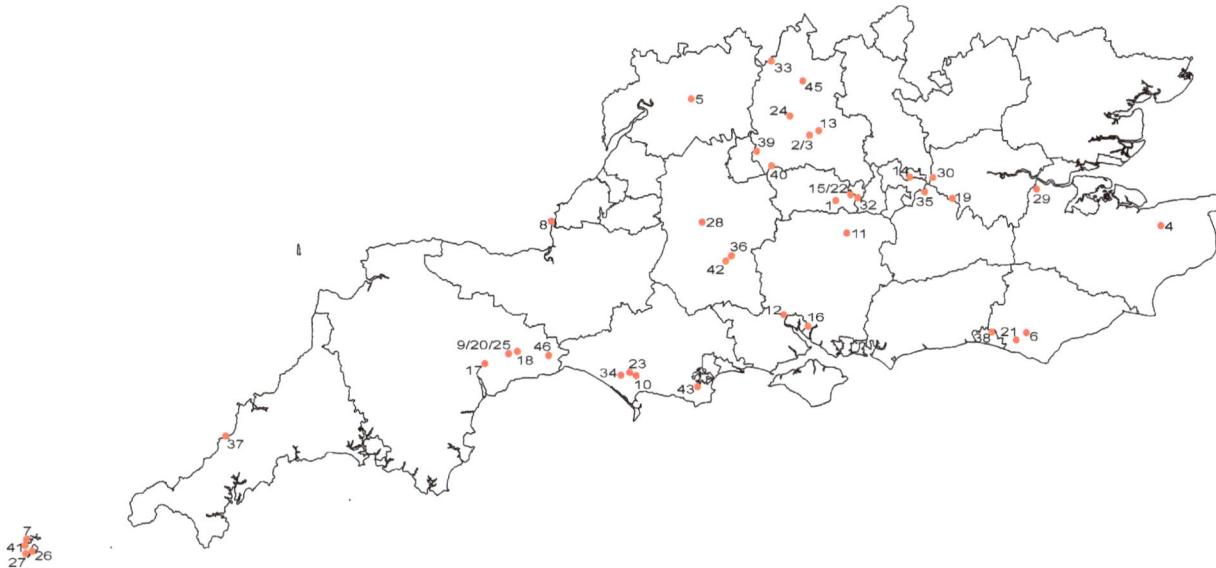

**Figure 2. Middle and late Bronze Age sites sites with archaeobotanical reports included in this study**

**No. Site**

1  Aldermaston Wharf, Berkshire
2  Ashville Trading Estate, Oxfordshire
3  Beedon Manor Farm 77 AML 3152, Berkshire
4  Bigberry 78-80, Kent
5  Birdlip By-pass. Gloucestershire (Straker, 1998)
6  Black Patch 77-9, E. Sussex
7  Bonfire Carn, Bryher, Isles of Scilly (Ratcliffe & Straker, 1996)
8  Brean Down 83-7, Somerset
9  Castle Hill, A30, Devon (Clapham, 1999)
10  Coburg Rd 88-9, Dorset
11  Cowderys Down 78-81, Hampshire
12  Dairy Lane, Nursling, Hampshire (Hinton, 1997a)
13  Eight Acre Field, Radley, Oxfordshire (Robinson, 1995)
14  Eton Wick 84-5, Berkshire
15  Field Farm 85, Berkshire
16  Grange Road, Gosport, Hampshire (Letts,1995)
17  Hayes Farm 87, Devon
18  Hayne Lane, A30, Devon (Clapham, 1999)
19  Hurst Park, East Molsey, Surrey (Hinton 1996c)
20  Langland Lane, A30, Devon, (Clapham, 1999)
21  Itford Hill 49-53, E. Sussex
22  Knights Farm 1 74-8, Berkshire

23  Maiden Castle 85-6 (a), Dorset
24  Mingies Ditch 77-8, Oxfordshire
25  Patteson's Cross, A30, Devon (Clapham, 1999)
26  Porth Cressa St Mary's, Isles of Scilly (Ratcliffe & Straker, 1996)
27  Porth Killier, St Agnes, Isles of Scilly (Ratcliffe & Straker, 1996)
28  Potterne 82-4, Wiltshire
29  Princes, Road, Dartford (Pelling, forthcoming)
30  Prospect Park, Harmondsworth (Hinton, 1996a)
31  Rams Hill 72-3, Berkshire
32  Reading Business Park 86, Berkshire
33  Rollright Stones 82-6, Oxfordshire
34  Rowden 77-84, Dorset
35  Runnymede 78, Berkshire
36  Stonehenge Environs 80-6, Wiltshire
37  Trethellan Farm, Cornwall
38  Varley Halls, Brighton, East Sussex (Hinton, 1997
39  Watchfield 83-92, Oxfordshire
40  Weathercock Hill 83, Berkshire
41  West Porth, Samson, Isles of Scilly (Ratcliffe & Straker, 1996)
42  Wilsford Shaft 60-2, Wiltshire
43  Wytch Farm 87-90, Dorset
45  Yarnton, Oxfordshire (Robinson, *pers. comn.*)
46  Yarty Floodplain, Devon

**Table 2. Middle and late Bronze Age sites with archaeobotanical reports included in this study**

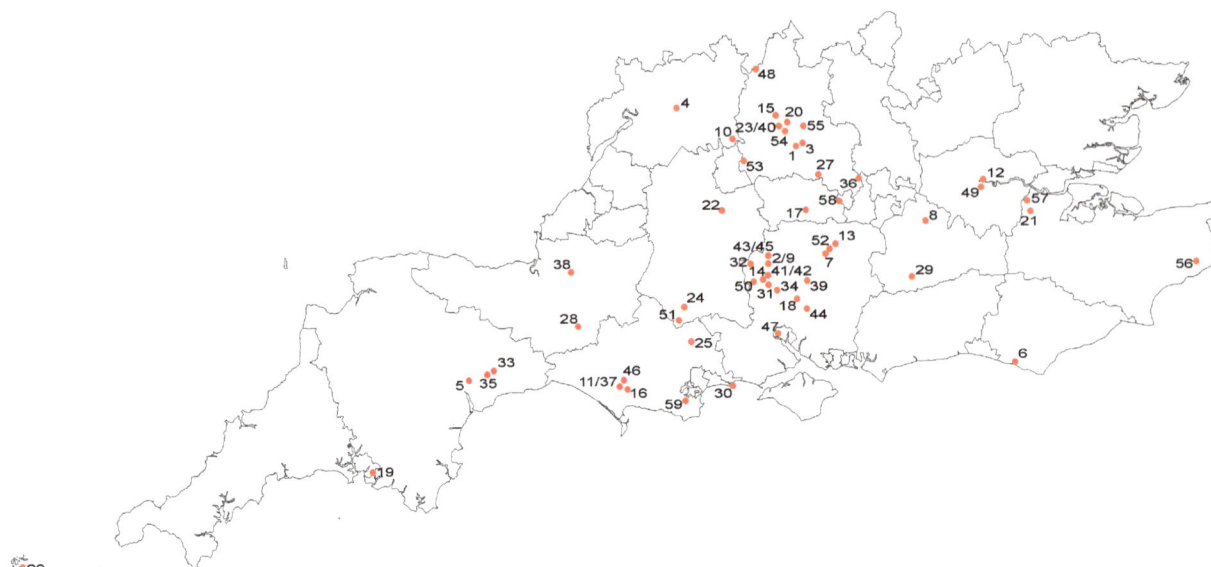

**Figure 3. Iron Age sites with archaeobotanical reports included in this study**

| No. | Site |
|-----|------|
| 1 | Ashville Trading Estate, Oxfordshire |
| 2 | Balksbury Camp 67, Hampshire |
| 3 | Barton Court Farm 72-6, Oxfordshire |
| 4 | Birdlip By-pass. Gloucestershire (Straker, 1998) |
| 5 | Blackhorse, A30, Devon (Clapham, 1999) |
| 6 | Bishopstone 72-5. E. Sussex |
| 7 | Brighton Hill South, Hampshire |
| 8 | Brooklands AML 1860, Surrey |
| 9 | Bury Hill 90, Hampshire (Campbell, 2000a) |
| 10 | Claydon Pike, Gloucestershire (Straker, unpublished( a): Jones *et al.*, unpublished) |
| 11 | Coburg Rd 88-9, Dorset |
| 12 | Copthall Ave (15-35), London |
| 13 | Cowderys Down 78-81, Hampshire |
| 14 | Danebury 78, Hampshire |
| 15 | Deer Park Rd, Witney, Oxfordshire (Robinson, 1995a) |
| 16 | Flagstones, Dorset (Straker, 1997a) |
| 17 | Dunston Park, Berkshire |
| 18 | Easton Ln, Hampshire |
| 19 | Elburton, Plymouth, Devon |
| 20 | Farmoor 74-6, Oxfordshire |
| 21 | Farningham Hill 75, Kent |
| 22 | Fifield Bavant, Wiltshire |
| 23 | Gravelly Guy AML 46/89, Oxfordshire |
| 24 | Groundwell Farm AML 4972, Wiltshire |
| 25 | Gussage All Saints 72, Dorset |
| 26 | Halangy Porth 75-6, St Mary's Isles of Scilly, |
| 27 | Halfpenny Ln 89, Oxfordshire |
| 28 | Ham Hill, Somerset |
| 29 | Hascombe 72-7, Surrey |
| 30 | Hengistbury Head, Dorset |
| 31 | Houghton Down 94, Hampshire (Campbell 2000a) |
| 32 | Lains Farm, Hampshire |
| 33 | Langland Lane, A30, Devon (Clapham, 1999) |
| 34 | Little Somborne |
| 35 | Long Range, A30, Devon (Clapham, 1999) |
| 36 | Lower Bolney 91, Oxfordshire |
| 37 | Maiden Castle 85-6 (a), Dorset |
| 38 | Meare Lake Village, Somerset |
| 39 | Micheldever Wood, Hampshire |
| 40 | Mingies Ditch 77-8, Oxfordshire |
| 41 | Nettlebank Copse 93, Hampshire (Campbell, 2000a) |
| 42 | New Buildings, Hampshire (Campbell, 2000a) |
| 43 | Old Down Farm 74-7, Hampshire |
| 44 | Owslebury 67, Hampshire |
| 45 | Portway 73-5, Hampshire |
| 46 | Poundbury 66-86, Dorset |
| 47 | Regents Park,Southampton, Hampshire |
| 48 | Rollright Stones 82-6, Oxfordshire |
| 49 | Southwark St (15-23) 80-4, London |
| 50 | Suddern Farm 91, Hampshire (Campbell, 2000a) |
| 51 | Tollard Royal, Wiltshire (Evans and Bowman, 1968) |
| 52 | Viables Farm, Hampshire |
| 53 | Watchfield 83-92, Oxfordshire |
| 54 | Watkins Farm, Oxfordshire |
| 55 | Whitehouse Rd 92, Oxford, Oxfordshire (Letts, 1993) |
| 56 | Whitfield, Kent (Campbell, unpublished) |
| 57 | Wilmington Gravel Pit AML 3611, Kent |
| 58 | Wickham's Field, Berkshire (Scaife, 1996) |
| 59 | Wytch Farm 87-90, Dorset |

**Table 3. Iron Age sites with archaeobotanical reports included in this study**

the information available for Devon (Clapham, 1999). Despite routine programmes of sampling and assessment, there is still little data for Cornwall, although recent assessment work on the Indian Queens (A30) project would suggest a greater emphasis on pasture for which the land is more suitable (Straker, unpublished a).

There is a general shortage of charred plant remains from the South Eastern part of the region, and with the exception of Black Patch, East Sussex (Hinton, 1982), all of this material consists of rich grain deposits noticed by chance, rather than material recovered as part of a flotation programme. In Kent, recent excavations carried out by the Canterbury Archaeological Trust and others are beginning to redress the balance but much still remains to be done in East Sussex, West Sussex and Surrey.

There are therefore two major gaps in our knowledge. One in the South West, where assemblages of charred plant remains are scarce, despite large sieving programmes and one in the South East where recovery of charred plant remains from sites has been poor in the past. This distribution of sites may not only reflect partly the location of long established research programmes (e.g. Iron Age sites on the Hampshire chalk,) but also the intensity of development-led archaeology in different parts of the region (e.g. gravel extraction in the Thames valley

## Charred plant remains: the nature of the evidence

This period also sees, in sharp contrast to the Neolithic and early Bronze Age period, a great increase in the quantity, in terms of actual numbers and density per litre of sediment, of charred plant remains recovered from archaeological deposits. Most of these deposits are associated with settlements and are of a domestic nature rather than a ritual one as far as can be ascertained.

Contexts associated with Bronze Age huts would appear to be especially important as a source of middle and late Bronze Age charred plant remains. At some sites the post-holes of these buildings have produced the greatest concentration of material; for example Potterne, Wilts. (Straker, 2000) and Grange Road, Gosport (Letts, 1995). Furthermore assemblages from post-holes have provided evidence that contrasts with that derived from other features. At Rowden, the post-holes provided the only evidence for the cultivation of wheat at the site (Carruthers, 1991a, 111), while at Weir Bank Stud Farm, Bray, Berkshire, post-holes associated with a round house produced large numbers of flax seeds. There was only a single seed recovered from the other features sampled at this site (Clapham, 1995). Therefore while the taphonomy of material recovered from post-holes makes interpretation difficult (see Carruthers, 1991a, 11; van Vilsteren, 1984) they provide an important source of evidence. Pits from settlements of middle Bronze Age date at Rowden, Dorset (Carruthers, 1991a) and Black Patch

(Hinton, 1982) have also produced large assemblages. However, at both these sites the pits were located inside huts.

The fills of Iron Age storage pits have proved a very rich source of material. For example, a sample from a pit at Hascombe, Surrey did not require flotation because it consisted almost of pure charred plant remains (Murphy, 1977, 82-84), producing over 9000 identifiable charred plant items per litre of soil. The large assemblages recovery from these pits in some areas may have resulted in a tendency to concentrate sampling efforts on these features, especially where funds and or time is limited. However it should be noted that large assemblages have been recovered from other Iron Age features including ovens and discreet lenses within ditch fills, for example at Nettlebank Copse, Hants (Campbell, 2000a). Also, as for the late Bronze Age, the evidence from pits maybe very different from that recovered from other Features. For example, at Tollard Royal, Wiltshire the pits produced mostly wheat, while the 'granary' post-holes contained mainly barley (Evans & Bowman, 1968).

## The crop record

Sites of this period typically give evidence for the cultivation of barley, principally the hulled form, and hulled wheat. While most settlement sites appear to be based on a mixed arable economy there are some exceptions. For example at Brean Down, Somerset, a site specialising in salt production, the paucity of crop plants and arable indicators in relation to other plant macro-fossils, particularly those indicative of grassland and marshland habitats is striking (Straker, 1990b, 216). This would seem to suggest that crops were not being grown locally. Similarly, the paucity of charred cereal remains from the late Bronze Age site at Reading Business Park (Campbell, 1992) lead to the suggestion that the site may only have been occupied during the summer months, during which flax cultivation and retting took place. However at this site, differential preservation of charred plant remains from the effects of repeated wetting and drying may have produced a rather biased picture.

### Spelt Wheat *(Triticum spelta)*

Spelt wheat has now been found at a number of middle Bronze Age sites including Black Patch, East Sussex (Hinton, 1982), Brean Down, Somerset (Straker, 1990b), Potterne, Wiltshire (Straker, 2000), and Trethellan Farm, Cornwall (Straker, 1991. There are also some very early records of spelt wheat from middle Bronze Age contexts at Yarnton, Oxfordshire (Mark Robinson, pers comm) and Princes Road, Dartford, Kent (Pelling, forthcoming) (Figure 4, Table 4) . However there is still very little evidence concerning where spelt wheat first appeared or how rapidly its cultivation spread. Some regional differences are emerging (see below) but more radiocarbon dates on spelt chaff recovered from middle Bronze Age deposits are needed to improve the chronology of these events.

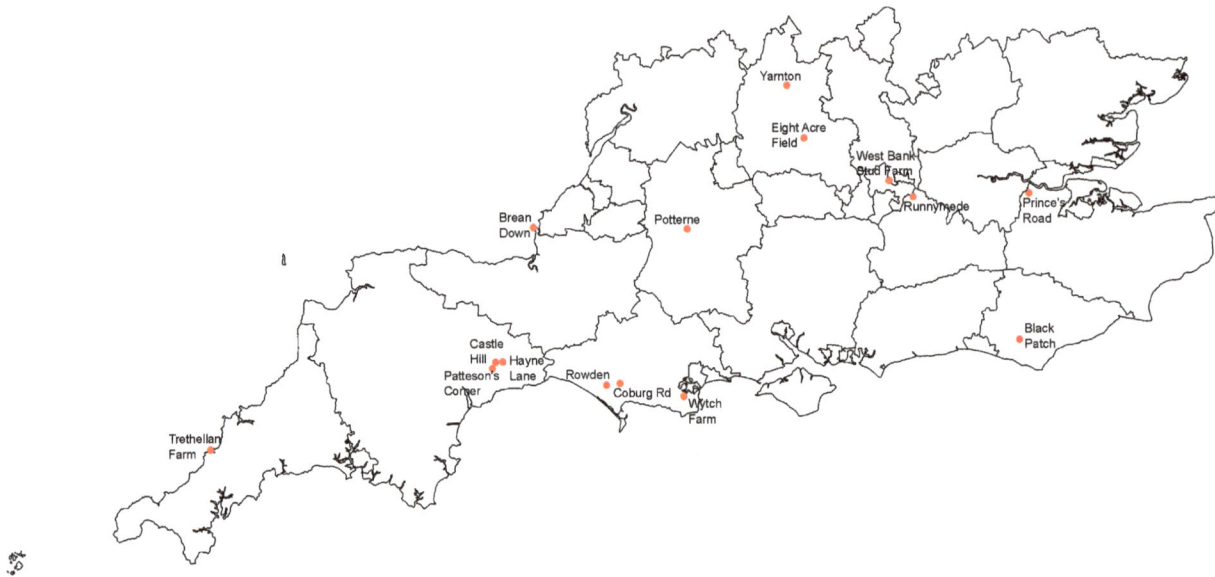

**Figure 4. Bronze Age sites with spelt wheat macrofossils**

| Site | type of material/ deposit | Uncalibrated date | Calibrated age range BC (2 sigma) | Lab code |
|------|---------------------------|-------------------|-----------------------------------|----------|
| Yarnton | spelt grain from well | 3255 ± 70BP | 1690- 1390 (95.4%) | OxA-6548 |
| Yarnton | other material from well | 3115± 70 BP | 1530 -1210 (95.4%) | OxA-6549 |
| Yarnton | ditch containing spelt glume base | 3145 ± 60BP | 1530 -1250 (95.4%) | OxA-6288 |
| Yarnton | ditch containing spelt glume base | 3045± 40BP | 1410 -1210 (90.6%)<br>1200 -1190 (1.7%)<br>1180 - 1160 (1.4%)<br>1140 - 1130 (1.7%) | OxA-6617 |
| Dartford | top of deposit producing spelt chaff | 3240±60BP | 1690 - 1400 (95.4%) | Beta-114528 |
| Dartford | bottom of deposit producing spelt chaff | 3150± 60BP | 1530 - 1250 (95.4%) | Beta-114527 |

Calibrations using OxCal v3.5 Bronk Ramsey (2000) (cub r:4 sd:2 prob usp[chron]) with atmospheric data from Stuiver et al. (1998)

**Table 4. Early records of spelt with radiocarbon dates**

## Local and regional variation: The Thames and Kennet valleys in the Middle to late Bronze Age

A number of sites dating from the middle to late Bronze Age have been excavated in the Thames and Kennet valleys in recent years (Figure 5). There is a paucity of early to middle Iron Age material from the Kennet valley (Lobb and Rose, 1996, 102) but the number of sites in the Thames valley has continued to grow. Many of these sites have produced both charred and waterlogged plant macro-remains so that there is now a substantial body of data which can be used to trace the history of crop husbandry and landscape change in this area.

Bradley has drawn attention to the lack of high status metal work in the Kennet valley as compared to the Thames and argued that the gross differences in wealth between the two areas may have been determined by their access to prestige trade (Bradley *et al*, 1980, 288, 292). Thus, while settlement in both the Kennet and the Thames valleys intensifies in the late Bronze Age, the Kennet valley remains somewhat of a 'back water' culturally in comparison to the Thames.

The evidence from plant macro-remains would lend to support this view. Crop remains from late Bronze Age sites in the Thames valley are characterised by remains of emmer and spelt wheat, six-row hulled barley, and flax. Rye and Brassica sp. are also occasional finds; recorded at Runnymede (Greig, 1991) and Weir Bank Stud Farm, Bray (Clapham, 1995, 36). Sites of the same date in the Kennet valley generally produce only emmer wheat, barley and flax. Spelt wheat has only been recovered in small amounts at one site in the Kennet valley: Reading Business Park, phase II (Campbell, forthcoming), and rye and *Brassica* sp. are absent.

By contrast, the evidence from late Bronze Age waterlogged deposits in the two river valleys, which reflect local environment rather than agricultural activity *per se*, is somewhat similar. Assemblages from Runnymede (Greig, 1991) on the Thames, and Knights Farm (Bradley et al, 1980) and Reading Business Park (Campbell, 1992) in the Kennet Valley all contained some plants indicative of grazed

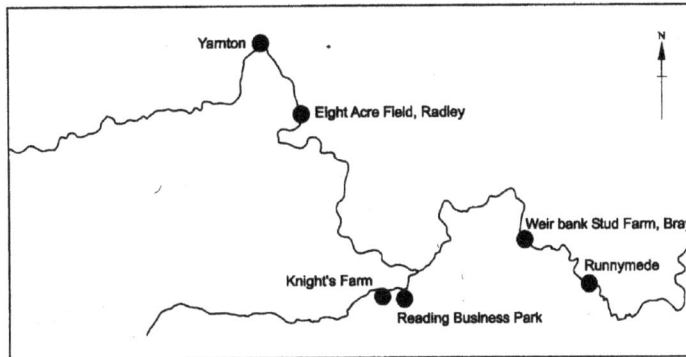

**Figure 5. Late Bronze Age sites in the Thames valley**

grassland. Species such as *Potentilla anserina* (silverweed), *Potentilla* cf. *reptans* (creeping cinquefoil), *Prunella vulgaris* (self-heal), and *Plantago major* (great plantain), and *Leontodon* sp. (hawkbit) are common finds, while assemblages from Runnymede also produced records of *Rhinanthus* (yellow-rattle) and *Sanguisorba officinalis* (great burnet). A scrub element is also present with thorny species such as *Ilex aquifolium* (holly), *Rhamnus +catharticus* (purging buckthorn), *Rubus fruticosus* agg. (bramble) *Crataegus* sp. (hawthorn), and *Cornus sanguinea* (dogwood), well represented. the general impression given is that these sites were set in areas of rough pasture with thorny scrub able to survive due to a low grazing pressure.

Overall the evidence to date would suggest that while both river valleys were experiencing a similar level of agricultural use in the late Bronze Age, the inhabitants of the Thames valley adopted the cultivation of spelt wheat earlier than those in the Kennet valley. This may reflect greater access to long distance trade in the Thames valley as compared to the Kennet.

## Free-threshing wheat

The evidence for free-threshing wheat, which is probably hexaploid (i.e. bread wheat) rather than tetraploid (i.e. rivet/ macaroni wheat) is still very unsatisfactory due to a number of related problems.

- Most of the identifications are based on grain morphology, alone which is now regarded as insufficient as a means of identification (Hillman *et al*, 1995).

- Some grain resembling free-threshing types may be badly preserved short round grains of spelt wheat. Short round grains tentatively identified as coming from spelt wheat have been identified from Iron Age sites excavated as part of the Danebury Environs project (Campbell, 2000b) and from other sites outside the region (e.g. Tiddington, Moffett, 1986).

- Some of the records of tough wheat rachis which may have been thought to represent free-threshing hexaploid wheat may in fact represent the remains of the basal portion of the wheat ear which is difficult to identify as hulled or free-threshing. The tough wheat rachis illustrated in the Barton Court Farm report (Jones, 1984,

fig 158) is clearly one such example.

- Chaff from free-threshing wheats is believed to be under represented in the archaeobotanical record both because it is removed at an early stage of crop processing and because the processing of free-threshing cereals does not require exposure to heat (Hillman, 1981). However since some sites e.g. Trethellan Farm have produced ample evidence of naked barley which is similarly likely to be under-represented (Straker, 1991) the rarity of free-threshing wheat at these sites is likely to be genuine.

While some of the records for free-threshing wheat type grain may indicate the presence of free-threshing wheat, grain has rarely been recovered in large numbers. There are two exceptions: the cremation from Ballast Hole, Berks, and the large assemblage of bread wheat from Barton Court Farm, Oxon.

The deposit of bread wheat grain (Bradley *et al*, 1980, 291) associated with a late Bronze Age/ Iron Age cremation at Hole probably represents an early misidentification since the original figure (Piggott, 1938, 52) appears to show a mixture hulled wheat and barley. Some of the material from Barton Court Farm may have been wrongly assigned. Contexts from which some free-threshing wheat grain was recovered did contain the odd sherd of early Saxon pottery (P. Booth, *pers. comm*). However, a radiocarbon date on the grain from pit 311, the sample that produced the large numbers of bread wheat grain was 2200± 70BP (400-100 cal 2 sigma BC) (Jones, 1984, fiche 9f4; Miles, 1984, 8) suggesting a late Iron Age date.

The only chaff of free-threshing wheat in this period comes from middle Iron Age deposits at Claydon Pike Gloucestershire (Straker, unpublished b), from late Iron Age contexts at Meare Lake Village East (Housley, 1987), and from in a context dated to between 400 -1 cal. BC at Blackhorse, A30, Devon (Clapham, 1999, 188). The last also produced remains of rye.

Overall the evidence suggests that free-threshing wheat if present at all was only ever a minor contaminant at most sites. It may have been a crop in its own right in the middle to late Iron Age in some areas especially the in the south west and Oxfordshire, but more data are needed to confirm this possibility.

**Figure 6. Finds of naked barley from Bronze Age sites**

## The cultivation of emmer (*Triticum dicoccum*) in the Iron Age

While the evidence from Iron Age sites on the Hampshire chalklands and the Thames valley shows that emmer is likely only to be present as a contaminant in the wheat crop from the beginning of the Iron Age, this is not the case elsewhere in the region. Grain rich deposits from late Iron Age pits in hillforts at Hascombe, Surrey, (Murphy, 1977, 82-84), and Ham Hill, Somerset (Ede, 1991, Letts, unpublished) produced substantial amounts of emmer wheat, while roughly equal proportions of emmer and spelt were recovered from a late Iron age pit at Wilmington, Kent (Hillman, 1982) and from two Iron Age sites, Blackhorse and Long Range, on the A30 (Clapham, 1999). This would suggest that emmer continued to be cultivated in some areas well into the Iron Age, either as a maslin or as a pure crop. This is likely to reflect regional variation in farming practice that currently is not evident due to the general paucity of archaeobotanical work on sites of this period away from the Hampshire chalk and Thames valley.

## A possible East-West divide

The other main cereal characteristic of this period is barley (*Hordeum vulgare)*. Most records are of hulled barley but there are also a number of records of naked barley. These records of naked barley date from the middle Bronze Age through to the Bronze Age/Iron Age transition but the most striking feature of these records is that they are confined to the South West of the region (Figure 6). The only find of naked barley in the Southeast is from the site of Aldermaston Wharf, Berkshire (Bradley *et al*, 1980, 247). The identification is not now regarded as secure and to date it has not been possible to re-examine the material.

Odd finds of naked barley have been made at Iron Age sites on the Hampshire chalklands. However these would appear to represent genetic variation within the hulled

barley population (Campbell, 2000b). The evidence for two-row barley is of a similar nature, with only the occasional rachis being identified. Once again this probably represents variation within the six-row barley population, although the genetic basis for this trait is more complex than for naked versus hulled grain (see above), involving two genes (Zohary & Hopf, 2000, 60).

To date the evidence suggests that naked barley cultivation survived in the South West far longer than in the South East and on a larger scale. This may be because it is more suited to the conditions associated with the Highland Zone. Evidence from Scotland would support this view (e.g. Milles, 1986). Why the cultivation of naked barley died out remains in question. Straker (1991, Ratcliffe & Straker, 1996, 11) has suggested that this may because hulled barley was more suited to winter sowing than naked barley. Another possibility is that the introduction of manuring of fields caused its disappearance. This is based on field experiments carried out in Northern Sweden that suggested that hulled barley is able to gain more from the extra nitrogen supplied (Joachell Regnell, *pers comm)*. However other factors may also be involved, such as the extent to which barley was used as animal fodder and for brewing.

The suggestion that oats may have been particularly suited to conditions in the South West (Straker, 1997b) is not supported by the data from sites of this period. However, any pattern may be being masked, by both, or one, of two factors. The grain of cultivated and wild oats is not distinguishable and finds of oat chaff are rare. Most of the chaff recovered from sites of this period is of the wild type. This apart, chaff from cultivated oat has been recovered from a number of Iron Age sites including Hascombe, Surrey (Murphy, 1977, 82-84) and Suddern Farm, Hampshire (Campbell, 2000c). However most of these sites date to the very end of the Iron Age.

There are only two Bronze Age records. One from a Bronze Age/ Iron Age transition deposit at Cowderys Down, Hants (Green, 1983) and one found as a pot impression from Beedon Manor Farm, Berkshire (Renfrew, 1980). The former may be intrusive from Saxon deposits while the latter may not represent local cultivation. Thus it is likely that most of the oat grain from sites of this date is probably derived from wild oat, a common arable weed, and therefore does not reflect cultivation.

## Legume crops

Records for legume crops vary greatly across the region. Generally *Vicia faba* var. *minor* (celtic bean or horse bean) is more typical of Bronze Age sites with *Pisum sativum* (pea) becoming more important in the Iron Age. Pulses are much more abundant at some sites than at others. High numbers of celtic bean were found at Bronze Age sites on the Isles of Scilly (Ratcliffe and Straker, 1996) and particularly at Rowden in Dorset (Carruthers, 1991). Large numbers of celtic beans were also recovered in late Iron Age deposits at the Meare Lake Villages (Caseldine, 1987, 223; Housley, 1987, 229; G Jones, 1981) while Bronze Age sites in Devon (Clapham, 1999) and Iron Age sites in East Kent have produced high proportions of peas (Campbell, unpublished, Ruth Pelling *pers comm*). One possible explanation could be that at these sites an intensive system of agriculture was practised (see van der Veen & O'Connor, 1998), with legume crops being used to help maintain the fertility of the arable land.

## Oil crops in the later prehistoric period

The importance of oil crops both during the Bronze Age and in the later Iron Age may well have been under estimated (Straker, 1991, 169). Flax was certainly cultivated both for its oil and for fibre and has been found both as a waterlogged macrofossil and charred at a number of sites. At Weir Bank Stud Farm remains of flax outnumbered remains of other economic plants and were closely associated with one of the middle Bronze Age roundhouses (Clapham, 1995, 43).

Opium poppy (*Papaver somniferum*) is present from at least the Middle Bronze in southern Britain. It has been found as a waterlogged macrofossil at Wilsford Shaft (Robinson, 1989, 83) and charred at Itford Hill (Helbaek, 1957, 208) and is present at many Iron Age sites. While it may only have been acting as a weed of cereals, it is equally likely that it was cultivated as an oil crop, as a spice, or for medicinal purposes. It was a recognised oil crop in central Europe from the middle Neolithic onwards (Zohary and Hopf, 2000, 137).

Another oil crop for which there is also some evidence is *Brassica* sp. or *Brassica/ Sinapis* sp (cabbage mustard, charlock etc.). The identification of *Brassica* seeds to species is difficult especially when charred. However seeds have been found at many Bronze Age sites and large assemblages recovered from some Iron Age sites. For example, at Balksbury Camp (de Moulins, 1996, Table 23), nearly 500 charred *Brassica* seeds were recovered from an Iron Age pit with very few other remains present. Another pure assemblage was found adhering to the inside

of a pot base found in an Iron Age pit at Old Down Farm (Murphy, 1977, Plate 14 & 74-5, Green, 1981). There is limited evidence for the use of brassicas in Europe from the late Neolithic, but they were well-established oil crops by the Roman period (Zohary and Hopf, 2000, 139).

*Sisymbrium officinale* (hedge mustard) may also have been used as a source of oil. Over 100 *Sisymbrium officinale* seeds were found at Trethellan Farm in a single pit fill associated with a middle Bronze Age house but only a single seed was found in the other 138 contexts sampled. This led the author to suggest that this species was being deliberately collected or cultivated since a more even distribution would be expected if it was present as an arable weed (Straker, 1991, 169). A similar interpretation has been made for large numbers of seeds of *Sisymbrium officinale* found at a Bronze Age settlement site in Yugoslavia. (Kroll, 1991, 167) and it is worth noting that Pat Hinton identified possible *Sisymbrium officinale* at Black Patch (Hinton, 1982, 383).

## Conclusions and recommendations for future work

### 1. Coverage

In the South East appropriate sieving programmes need to be carried out as part of future excavation programmes. In Devon and Cornwall analytical techniques including chemical or biomolecular studies, for example, may need to be employed or developed in order to investigate plant utilisation in the prehistoric period. We need to establish if the apparent scarcity of evidence for arable agriculture in some areas is a genuine reflection of utilisation of land predominantly for pastoralism rather than mixed agricultural economies. Not withstanding local and regional distinctiveness (see 4, below) which may also be a significant factor, the poor soils and exposed conditions would suggest that wheat and barley cultivation would have been a challenge, though spelt wheat, for example will tolerate poor conditions better than modern cultivars. The importance of pastoralism is itself not well-demonstrated in some areas as animal bones survive poorly or not at all in the predominantly acid soils. In sheltered coastal areas, where soils are often enriched with shell sand, the evidence for mixed farming can be demonstrated using both plant macrofossils and animal bones.

The varied approach to the implementation of PPG 16 with greater attention to inclusion of archaeological science in projects in some areas compared with others may play a part in the distributions. Until further syntheses such as the Regional Research Frameworks for the sub-regions are published, the importance of this is unknown.

### 2. Sampling

The data available for early prehistoric crop cultivation in southern Britain is still so inadequate that all opportunities should be taken to sample Neolithic and Early Bronze Age contexts, particularly those associated with settlement and storage. Large samples should be taken (a minimum of 40 litres / context where sufficient exists).

Contexts with waterlogged preservation are also a priority as a wider range of taxa survives than from the charred record alone. So far only three sites with waterlogged plant macrofossils (Anslow's cottages, Runnymede and Abingdon Multiplex) have been studied.

It should be appreciated that contexts which may be of Neolithic date but do not contain pottery are still worth sampling as the plant remains themselves may provide a means of absolute dating. For Bronze Age sites similar considerations apply. Contexts associated with Bronze Age hut platforms and houses should be given more attention, and where time or funds are limited these types of context should be targeted. Sampling of Iron Age sites should be more balanced seeking to recover plant remains from a range of different features including ditch fills and four-post structures, as well as pits. For all periods sampling should not be concentrated on the obviously 'rich' deposits as this minimises the chances of identifying the smaller weeds seeds and chaff typical of crop processing waste.

## 3. Radiocarbon dating

In order to trace changes in the types of crop cultivated in different areas we need to obtain radiocarbon dates. Wherever possible the plant remains, ideally diagnostic chaff in the case of wheat, should be dated directly, rather than other material from the same context. Middle Bronze Age, or earlier records of spelt, remains of free-threshing wheat of pre-Roman date and large assemblages of naked barley are of particular interest. Finds of domesticated oat from prehistoric contexts may also be worth dating.

More resources should be put into obtaining suites of radiocarbon dates on macrofossils in order to be able to separate domestic and ritual functions and allow direct comparison between sites both locally and regionally in order to identify genuine cultural similarities and differences.

## 4. Local and regional distinctiveness

For the early prehistoric period in particular, close attention should be paid to trying to identify social and cultural factors which could be reflected in developed arable agriculture or pastoral specialism in some areas and a slow change to more intensive agriculture in others. This would also consider soil type, climate and topography as other potential factors influencing local and regional differences.

From the middle Bronze Age onwards regional variation in farming practice in terms both of the types of crops grown and the speed with which change occurred is becoming increasingly apparent. There is clearly a need for projects that aim to study a particular farming system through detailed examination of different types of site at a local level. For developer-funded projects this may mean that a site that is considered typical for its period, and possibly of

limited potential, may have a considerable potential for archaeobotanical study. Plant remains from such sites provide important insights into local farming practice and in some areas of the region, especially the South East we still do not have sufficient data on the types of crop that were grown during a particular period.

## Acknowledgements

This research was funded by English Heritage. The authors would like to thank Rupert Housley, Judith Dobie and Ken Davies for their help with the illustrations. We would also like to thank many colleagues who generously provided details of their unpublished and current work.

## References

Arthur, J. R. B. (1970). Appendix I Plant remains in the pottery. In R Bradley (Ed). The excavation of a beaker settlement at Belle Tout, East Sussex, England. *Proceedings of the Prehistoric Soc*iety, **36**. 373-5.

Bradley, R., Lobb, S., Richards, J. and Robinson, M A, (1980). Two late Bronze Age Settlements on the Kennet Gravels: Excavations at Aldermaston Wharf and Knight's Farm, Burghfield, Berkshire. *Proceedings of the Prehistoric Soc*iety **46**, 217-295.

Bronk Ramsey, C. (2000). Oxcal 3.5. http://www.rlaha.ox.ac.uk/orau

Campbell, G. (1992). Bronze Age Plant Remains. In J. Moore, and D. Jennings (Eds). *Reading Business Park: a Bronze Age Landscape*, Oxford Archaeological Unit Thames Valley Landscapes: the Kennet Valley, Volume **1,** 103-110.

Campbell, G. (2000a). Charred plant remains. In B. Cunliffe, and C. Poole (Eds). *The Danebury Environs Programme The prehistory of a Wessex Landscape Volume 2 - part 5 Nettlebank Copse, Wherwell, Hants, 1993*. (English Heritage and Oxford University Committee for Archaeology Monograph 49). Oxford: Institute of Archaeology, pp. 116-27.

Campbell, G. (2000b). Plant utilisation: the evidence from charred plant remains. In B Cunliffe (Ed). *The Danebury Environs Programme The prehistory of a Wessex Landscape Volume 1: Introduction (*English Heritage and Oxford University Committee for Archaeology Monograph 48). Oxford: Institute of Archaeology, pp. 45-59.

Campbell, G. (2000c). Charred plant remains. In B. Cunliffe, and C. Poole (Eds). *The Danebury Environs Programme. The prehistory of a Wessex Landscape Volume 2 - part 3 Suddern Farm, Middle Wallop, Hants, 1991 and 1996*. (English Heritage and Oxford University Committee for Archaeology Monograph 49). Oxford: Institute of Archaeology, 193-4.

Campbell, G, forthcoming. *Charred plant remains from Reading Business Park: phase 2.*

Campbell, unpublished. *Charred plant remains from Whitfield Eastry bypass, near Whitfield* (prepared for Canterbury Archaeological Trust).

Carruthers, W. (1990). Carbonised Plant Remains. In J.Richards (Ed). *The Stonehenge Environs Project.* English Heritage Archaeological Report **16**, pp. 250-52.

Carruthers W. J. (1991). The carbonised plant remains from Rowden In P. J. Woodward (Ed). *The South Dorset Ridgeway Survey and Excavations 1977-84. Dorset Nat. Hist. Archaeol. Soc. Monograph* **8**, pp. 106-11.

Carruthers, W. J. (1992). Plant remains. In C A Butterworth and S J Lobb (Eds). Archaeological excavations at Anslow's Cottages, Burghfield. In *Excavations in the Burghfield area, Berkshire: developments in the Bronze Age and Saxon periods* (Wessex Archaeol. Rep. **1**), pp. 76-169,149-58.

Caseldine A. E. (1987). Charcoal patches from Meare Village East 1982. In J. M. Coles (Ed). *Meare Village East, the excavations of A Bulleid and H. St. George Gray 1932-56,* Somerset Levels Papers **13**, Exeter, pp. 223-6.

Clapham, A. J. (1995). Plant remains. I. Barnes, W..A. Boisnier, R.M.J. Cleal, A.P. Fitzpatrick, and M.R. Roberts (Eds). *Early Settlement in Berkshire: Mesolithic-Roman Occupation Sites in the Thames and Kennet Valleys.* Wessex Arch. Report **6**, pp. 35-45.

Clapham, A. J. (1999). Charred plant remains. In A. Fitzpatrick, C. A. Butterworth, and J. Grove (Eds). *Prehistoric sites in East Devon: the A30 Honiton to Exeter Improvements DBFO Scheme, 1996-9.* Wessex Archaeological Report **16**, pp. 51-9, 83, 112-9, 134-5, 152-5, 184-8, 196-207.

de Moulins, D. (1996). Charred Plant Remains. In G. J. Wainwright, and S. M. Davies (Eds). *Balksbury Camp, Hampshire: excavations 1973 and 1981,* pp. 87-92.

Dennell, R. W. (1976). The economic importance of plant resources represented on archaeological sites in *Journal of Archaeological Science* 3, 229-247.

Ede, J. (1991). Carbonised seeds. In G. Smith Excavations at Ham Hill, 1983, *Proceedings of the Somerset Archaeology and Natural History Society,* **134** (for 1990). 27-45, 39-43.

Evans, A. M., and Bowman, A. (1968). Appendix II: Report on carbonised grains from Tollard Royal, Berwick Down, Wilts. In G. J. Wainwright (Ed). The Excavation of a Durotrigan Farmstead near Tollard Royal in Cranbourne Chase, Southern England. *Proceedings of the Prehistoric Soc*iety, **34**, 146.

Fairbairn, A. S. (2000). On the spread of plant crops across Neolithic Britain, with special reference to southern England. In A. S. Fairbairn (Ed). *Plants in Neolithic Britain and beyond* (Neolithic Studies Group Seminar Papers **5**) Oxford: Oxbow Books, pp.107-21.

Fairweather, A. D. and Ralston, I. B. M. (1993). The Neolithic timber hall at Balbridie, Grampian Region, Scotland: the building, the date, the plant macrofossils. *Antiquity* **67**, 313-23.

Gale, R. and Cutler, D. F. (2000). *Plants and Archaeology: Identification manual of vegetative plant materials used in Europe and the Mediterranean to c. 1500.* Otely: Westbury Publishing and the Royal Botanic Gardens, Kew.

Green F. J. (1981). The botanical remains. In S. M. Davies, Excavations at Old Down Farm, Andover. Part II: Prehistoric and Roman. *Proceedings of the. Hampshire Field Club Archaeological Society,* **37**, 131-2, 140-1.

Green, F. J. (1983). The plant remains. In M Millet and S. James (Eds). Excavations at Cowdery's Down, Basingstoke, Hampshire, 1978-81. *Archaeol. J.* **140**, 151-279, 176-7 and Fiche M38.

Greig, J.R.A. (1991). The botanical remains. In S. Needham and D. Longley (Eds). *Excavation and salvage at Runnymede Bridge, Berkshire, 1978. London: British Museum,* pp.234-6.

Helbaek, H. (1952). Early crops in Southern England. *Proceedings of the Prehistoric Soc*iety, **18**, 194-233.

Helbaek, H. (1957). Carbonized cereals. In G. P. Burstow and G. A. Holleyman, Late Bronze Age Settlement on Itford Hill, Sussex *Proceedings of the Prehistoric Soc*iety, **23**, 206-209.

Hillman, G. C. (1981). Reconstructing Crop Husbandry Practices from Charred Remains of Crops. In R Mercer (Ed). *Farming Practice in British Prehistory.* Edinburgh, pp. 123-62,

Hillman, G. C. (1982). Late Iron Age glume wheats from Wilmington Gravel-pit, Kent, *Ancient Monuments Laboratory Report* **3611.**

Hillman, G. C., Mason, S., de Moulins, D. and Nesbitt, M. (1995). Identification of the archaeological remains of wheat: the 1992 London workshop. *Circaea* **12.2**, 195-210.

Hinton, P. (1982). Carbonised seeds. In P. Drewett (Ed). Later Bronze Age downland economy and excavations at Black Patch, East Sussex. *Proceedings of the Prehistoric Soc*iety, **48**, 382-90.

Hinton, P. (1996a). The Plant Remains. In A. Crockett (Ed.) Excavations at Montefiore New Halls of Residence, Swaythling, Southampton 1992. *Proceedings of the.*

*Hampshire Field Club Archaeological Society,* **51**, 5-57, 47-9 and fiche.

Hinton, P. (1996b). Plant remains. In P. Andrews (Ed). Prospect Park, Harmondsworth, London Borough of Hillingdon: Settlement and early burial from the Neolithic to the early Saxon periods, In P. Andrews and A. Crockett (Ed). *Three Excavations along the Thames and its Tributaries, 1994*, Wessex Archaeological Report **10**, 43-47.

Hinton, P. (1996c). Charred Plant Remains. In P., Andrews (Ed). Hurst Park, East Molsey, Surrey: Riverside settlement and burial from the Neolithic to the early Saxon periods. In P. Andrews and A. Crockett (Eds). *Three Excavations along the Thames and its Tributaries, 1994*, Wessex Archaeological Report **10**, 95-99.

Hinton, P. (1997a). Plant remains. In N. J. Adam, R. Seager Smith, R J. C. Smith (Eds). An early Romano-British settlement and prehistoric field boundaries at Dairy Lane, Nursling, Southampton. *Proceedings of the. Hampshire Field Club Archaeoological Society,* **52**, 1-59.

Hinton, P. (1997b). Plant remains. In I Greig (Ed). Excavation of a Bronze Age Cemetery at Varley Halls, Codean Lane, Brighton, East Sussex. *Sussex Archaeological Collections* **135**, 7-58,fiche.

Housley, R. A. (1987). The carbonised plant remains from Meare 1984. In J. M. Coles (Ed). *Meare Village East, the excavations of A Bulleid and H. St. George Gray 1932-56,* Somerset Levels Papers **13**, Exeter, 226-230.

Jessen, K. and Helbaek, H. (1944). Cereals in Great Britain and Ireland in Prehistoric and early Historic times. *Kongel. Danske Vidensk. Selsk. Biol. Skrifter* 3(2), 68pp.

Jones, G. (1981). Plant remains: the carbonised plant remains. In B.J. Orme *et al* (Eds). Meare Village West 1979. *Somerset Levels Papers* **7**, 33-5.

Jones, G. (2000). Evaluating the importance of cultivation and collecting in Neolithic Britain. In A.S. Fairbairn (Ed). *Plants in Neolithic Britain and beyond* (Neolithic Studies Group Seminar Papers **5**) Oxford: Oxbow Books, pp. 79-84.

Jones, G. forthcoming. Evidence for the importance of cereals in the Neolithic: charred plant remains from the Neolithic settlement at Lismore Fields, Buxton,. In D. Garton (Ed). *The excavation of a Mesolithic and Neolithic settlement area at Lismore Fields, Buxton, Derbyshire.*

Jones G. and Legge A. (1987). The grape (*Vitis vinifera* L.) in the Neolithic of Britain. *Antiquity* **61**, 452-5.

Jones, G. and Legge, A. J. (in press). Evaluating the role of cereal cultivation in the Neolithic: charred plant remains from Hambledon Hill, Dorset. In R. Mercer and F. Healy (Eds). *Hambledon Hill, Dorset. Excavation and Survey of*

a Neolithic Monument Complex and its Surrounding Landscape.

Jones, J. and Straker, V. (1993). Macroscopic plant remains. In P. J. Woodward, S. M. Davis, and A. H. Graham (Eds). *Excavations at the Old Methodist Chapel and Greyhound Yard, Dorchester, 1981-14. Dorset Nat. Hist. Archaeol. Soc. Monograph* **12**, 349-50.

Jones, M. (1981). The Development of crop husbandry. In M.K. Jones, and G.W. Dimbleby (Eds). *The Environment of Man; the Iron Age to the Anglo-Saxon Period* B A R **87**, Oxford, pp. 95-127.

Jones, M. (1984). The Carbonized plant remains, in Miles, 1984, *Archaeology at Barton Court Farm Abingdon, Oxon*, CBA Research Report **50**, Oxford Archaeological Unit Report **3**, Oxford.Chapter VII.

Jones, M. (1988). The arable field: a botanical battleground. In M. Jones (Ed). *Archaeology and the flora of the British Isles*, Oxford University Committee for Archaeology monograph **14**, pp. 86-92.

Jones, M. Perry, A. and Straker, V. unpublished. Charred cereals from Claydon Pike, Gloucestershire, 1979-81: The Iron Age Phases. Prepared for Oxford Archaeological Unit.

Kroll, H. (1991). Südoseuropa. In W. van Zeist, K. Wasylikowa, and K.-E. Behre (Eds). *Progress in Old World Palaeoethnobotany*, Rotterdam: Balkema 161-78.

Letts, J. B. (1993). Charred plant remains. In A. Mudd (Ed). Excavations at Whitehouse Road, Oxford, 1992. *Oxoniensia* **58**, 33-85, 74-8.

Letts, J. B.(1995). Carbonised plant remains. In M. Hall, and S. Ford (Eds). Archaeological excavations at Grange Road, Gosport. *Hampshire Field Club and Archaeological Society.* **50**, 30-31.

Letts, J. B. unpublished. Charred plant remains from Ham Hill. Somerset.

Lobb, S. J., and Rose, P, G. (1996). *Archaeological Survey of the lower Kennet Valley, Berkshire* Wessex Archaeological Report **9.**

Miles, D. (1984). *Archaeology at Barton Court Farm Abingdon, Oxon*, CBA Research Report **50**, Oxford Archaeological Unit Report **3**, Oxford.

Milles, A. (1986). Comparative analysis of charred plant remains from Ness of Grouting. In A. Whittle, *et al* (Eds). *Scourd of Brewster: An early agricultural settlement in Shetland*, Oxford University Committee for Archaeology Monograph **9**, pp. 123-4.

Moffett, L. (1986). *Crops and crop processing in a Romano-British village at Tiddington: the evidence from charred plant remains*. Ancient Monument Laboratory Report New Series **15/86**.

Moffett, L. (1988). *The Archaeobotanical Evidence for Saxon and medieval agriculture in central England c. AD 500 to AD 1500*. Unpublished M Phil Thesis, University of Birmingham.

Moffett, L. (1989). The evidence for crop processing products from the Iron age and Romano-British periods at Gravelly Guy and some earlier prehistoric plant remains. Ancient Monuments Laboratory Report (New Series) **46/89**.

Moffett, L. (1999). The Prehistoric Use of Plant Resources. In A. Barclay, and C. Halpin (Eds). *Excavations at Barrow Hills, Radley, Oxfordshire. Volume 1, The Neolithic and Bronze Age Monument Complex* (Thames Valley Landscapes Volume **11**). Oxford: Oxford Archaeological Unit/ OUCA, pp. 243-7.

Moffett, L. Robinson, M. and Straker, V. (1989). Cereals, fruit and nuts: charred plant remains from Neolithic sites in England and Wales and the Neolithic economy. In A. Milles, D. Williams, and N. Gardner (Eds). *The Beginnings of Agriculture*, BAR International Series **496**, pp. 243-61.

Monk, M. (2000). Seeds and soils of discontent: an environmental archaeological contribution to the nature of the early Neolithic. In A. Desmond, G. Johnson, M. McCarthy, J.Sheehan and E. Shee Twohig (Eds). *New agendas in Irish Prehistory: Papers in commemoration of Liz Anderson. Wordwell*, pp. 67-87.

Mosely, C. (1910). *The Oak: its natural history, antiquity, and folk-lore*, London: Elliot Stock.

Murphy, P.A. (1977). *Early agriculture and environment on the Hampshire chalklands: c. 800BC-400AD*, unpublished M. Phil Thesis: University of Southampton.

Murphy, P. (1982). Plant impressions on local Neolithic and Bronze Age pottery and daub in the Dept. Antiquities, Ashmolean Museum. In H. J. Case, and A. W. R Whittle (Eds). *Settlement patterns in the Oxford region: excavation at the Abingdon Causeway enclosure*. CBA Research Report **44** and Dept. Antiquities, Ashmolean Museum. 152 XX.

Pelling, R. forthcoming. The charred plant remains. In P. Hutchings, Ritual and riverside settlement. Excavation of a multiperiod site at Princes Rd, Dartford 1997-9. *Archaeologia Cantiana*, **123**.

Pelling, R. unpublished. *ABMULT 97: Evaluation of Charred and Waterlogged Plant Remains* (Abingdon Multiplex Cinema for Oxford Archaeology).

Piggott, C. M. (1938). The Iron Age Pottery from Theale. *Trans. Newbury and District Field Club* **8**, 52-60.

Ratcliffe, J. and Straker, V. (1996). *The early Environment of Scilly: palaeoenvironmental assessment of cliff-face and intertidal deposits, 1989-1993*, Cornwall County Council.

Renfrew, J. (1980). *Beedon Manor Farm 1977 the seed impressions*. Ancient Monuments Laboratory Report (old series) **3152**.

Robinson, M. A. (1989). Seeds and other plant macrofossils. In P. Ashbee, M. Bell and E. Proudfoot (Eds). *Wilsford Shaft: excavations 1960-2*. English Heritage Archaeological Report, **11**. London, pp. 78-90.

Robinson, M. A (1995a). The macroscopic plant remains. In T. G. Walker (Ed). A Middle Iron Age Settlement at Deer Park Farm, Witney: Excavations in 1992. *Oxoniensia* **60**, pp. 67-92, 86-88.

Robinson, M. A. (1995b). Plant and Invertebrate remains. In A. Mudd *et al* (Eds). The Excavation of A Late Bronze Age/ Early Iron Age site at Eight Acre Field, Radley. *Oxoniensia* **60**, pp. 21-66, 41-50.

Robinson, M. A. (2000). Further considerations of Neolithic charred cereals, fruits and nuts. In A.S. Fairbairn (Ed.) *Plants in Neolithic Britain and beyond* (Neolithic Studies Group Seminar Papers **5**) Oxford: Oxbow Books, pp. 85-90.

Scaife, R (1981). *An Early Bronze Age record of* Vicia faba *L. (Horsebean) from Newbarn Down, Isle of Wight* Ancient Monuments Laboratory Report (Old Series) **3501**.

Scaife, R. (1996). Charred and Waterlogged plant remains. In A. Crockett, Iron Age to Saxon settlement at Wickham's Field, near Reading, Berkshire, Excavations on the site of the M4 motorway service area. In P. Andrews and A. Crockett (Eds). *Three Excavations along the Thames and its Tributaries, 1994*, Wessex Archaeological Report **10**, pp. 157-64.

Straker V. (1990a). Plant and molluscan remains. In A. Saville A. (Ed). *Hazleton North 1979-82: the excavation of a Neolithic long cairn of the Cotswold-Severn group* (English Heritage Archaeological Report **13**) pp. 215-9.

Straker, V. (1990b). Charred plant macrofossils. In M. Bell (Ed). *Brean Down Excavations 1983-1987*, English Heritage Monograph **15**, pp. 211-9.

Straker, V, (1991). Charred plant macrofossils. In J. A Nowakowski, Trethellan Farm, Newquay: the excavation of a lowland Bronze Age settlement and Iron Age cemetery. *Cornish Archaeology*. **30**, 161-79.

Straker, V. (1997a). Charred plant remains. In R. J. C. Smith, F. Healy, M. J. Allen, E. L. Morris, I. Barnes and P. J. Woodward (Eds). *Excavations Along the Route of the Dorchester By-pass, Dorset, 1986-8*. Wessex Archaeological Report **11**, 184-90.

Straker, V, (1997b). The Ecofactual Assemblage In R. Harry, and C.D. Morris (Eds). Excavations on the Lower Terrace, Site C, Tintagel Island 1990-4. *The Antiquaries Journal* **77**, 82-108.

Straker, V. (1998). Charred plant macrofossils. In C. Parry (Ed). Excavations near Birdlip, Cowley, Gloucestershire, 1987-8. *Transactions of the Bristol and Gloucestershire Archaeological Society*, **116**, 76-80; 86-87.

Straker, V. (2000). Charred plant remains. In A.J. Lawson (Ed). *Potterne 1982-5: Animal Husbandry in late Prehistoric Wiltshire*. Wessex Archaeological Report **17**, 84-91.

Straker, V. unpublished a. Indian Queens assessment reports. Prepared for Cornwall Archaeological Unit.

Straker, V. unpublished b. Claydon Pike, Gloucestershire: Carbonised cereals from the late Iron Age to Roman Periods. Prepared for Oxford Archaeological Unit.

Stuiver M., Reimer, P.J., Bard, E., Beck, J.W., Burr, G.S. Hughen, K.A. Kromer, B., McCormac, G. van der Plicht, J. and Spurk, M. (1998). INTCAL98 Radiocarbon Age Calibration, 24000-0 cal BP. *Radiocarbon* **40** (3) 1041-1083.

van der Veen, M. and O'Connor, T. (1998). The expansion of agricultural production in the late Iron Age and Roman Britain. In J. Bayley (Ed). *Science in Archaeology an agenda for the future* 127-44. English Heritage.

van Vilsteren, V.T. (1984). The medieval village of Dommelen: A case study for the interpretation of charred plant remains from post-holes. In W. van Zeist and W.A. Casparie (Eds). *Plants and Ancient Man*. Rotterdam: Balkema, pp. 227-236.

Whittle, A., Davies, J. J., Dennis, I., Fairbairn, A.S. and Hamilton, M. A. (2000). Neolithic activity and occupation outside Windmill Hill causewayed enclosure, Wiltshire: survey and excavation 1992-93. *Wiltshire Archaeology and Natural History Magazine* **93.**

Zohary, D. and Hopf, M. (2000). *Domestication of Plants in the Old World*. Oxford: Oxford University Press, 3rd edition.

# The recognition, interpretation and management of archaeological sites and landscapes using GPS survey and three-dimensional computer modelling

Henry Chapman

Centre for Wetland Archaeology, University of Hull, Hull HU6 7RX.

## Introduction

Techniques of archaeological survey have developed greatly over the last few decades, but the motivations for conducting surveys of sites and landscapes have remained largely unchanged. Firstly, plans resulting from survey can assist in the interpretation of a site by highlighting the spatial relationships between anthropogenic and natural features. Secondly, a plan can form the basis of the management of an archaeological site or landscape, both to mitigate against future damage by locating features before development, and also to understand the present state of the archaeological resource. However, traditional methods of survey and representation have been restricted in their usefulness. The results from plans may not display the relationships between archaeological and natural features clearly, and also the results are not interactive and therefore do not lend themselves well for comparison with other sources of data. Within this paper a different outline will be suggested that follows a digital approach to site and landscape survey and data processing. This procedure provides an interactive model of the area that can assist in the recognition of sites and landscapes, their interpretation and their management.

## Methods

In order to provide comparative results the two sites were selected from contrasting contexts. These sites were chosen on the basis of their both having been previously surveyed. This enabled a comparison of the results from the different period surveys and provided an opportunity for measuring site preservation and degradation through time.

### Survey methods
The survey of each of the two sites was undertaken using a *Geotronics © System 2000 L1 - RTK* differential Global Positioning System (GPS) (Figure 1). This equipment receives radio signals transmitted from a constellation of 24 satellites controlled by the U. S. Air Force at Colorado. These signals provide data relating to time, taken from the atomic clocks aboard the satellites, and velocity. Each satellite can be tracked over time and thus its orbit can be calculated from predictions of its position at a given time. When data are collected from several satellites at the same time, the intersections of these orbits can be calculated to provide a position on the Earth' s surface.

Inaccuracies within the system stem from a number of sources including 'multi-path' and 'selective availability', the latter added by the USAF to provide security. An allowance can be made for these by combining two receivers that record data from the same group of satellites at the same time, known as differential GPS. By keeping a base station stationary throughout the survey, data from the roving receiver can be calibrated to provide centimetre accuracy relative to it. Absolute co-ordinates (relative to National Grid) can be obtained through a transformation of the GPS grid (which is recorded in the spherical WGS-84 co-ordinate system) and by locating points on the ground of known position such as benchmarks.

**Figure 1. GPS survey in progress.**

The accuracy of the GPS was investigated in order to understand the potential for error and to provide tolerances. Two pegs were surveyed (A and B) during five separate surveys and the position of A was corrected and the variation in B was recorded. During this experiment the position of point B showed a maximum range of 0.054m for the x-co-ordinate, 0.056m for the y-co-ordinate and 0.029m for the z-co-ordinate. The differences in standard deviation between these points do not hold equal accuracy weighting - calculating a mean of these values is therefore not appropriate to check the overall standard deviation of the equipment in practice. Rather, the most accurate values are likely to be those with the lowest standard deviation recorded in the original point calculation. For the landscape scale of the current research a potential error range of between 0.029m and 0.056m was considered acceptable.

### Data-processing methods
The GPS survey data were recorded in a coded format that was corrected to National Grid values and converted to a CSV (comma separated value) file, consisting of x-co-ordinates, y-co-ordinates and z-co-ordinates, using software developed by Richard Middleton (University of Hull). These data were processed to generate a digital elevation model (DEM) within *ARC/INFO© version 7.2.1* Geographical Information System (GIS) software run through a UNIX platform.

The variably spaced point data were converted to form a triangulated irregular surface (TIN) using the CREATETIN command. The accuracy of surfaces interpolated as a TIN model is dependent upon the function of the triangulation process. ARC/INFO employs a process known as Delaunay Triangulation, which dictates the size and shape of the triangles formed in the generalised surface (Goucher 1997). The criterion of this process is that a circle drawn through the vertexes of each triangle will contain no other co-ordinate points. There are three advantages of this system. Firstly, the triangles remain more equiangular, which provides better geometry than triangles with acute angles and therefore generates more accurate surfaces. Secondly, it reduces the distances from every interpolated point to a known point, or triangle vertex. Thirdly, each survey point is given equal priority in the generation of the surface.

A cell-based surface was created from the TIN using the TINLATTICE command. This process has been used elsewhere in the generation of DEMs representing archaeological landscapes (e.g. Goucher 1997). Once the TIN has been created using the CREATETIN function, it is converted to a cell-based surface, or lattice, by using the TINLATTICE function. This is a vector/raster conversion that interpolates a continuous grid using the TIN as a reference. The function places a grid of cells at a pre-determined density across the area covered by the TIN that are referenced in terms of x- and y- co-ordinates. A height attribute for each cell is then interpolated from the TIN. ARC/INFO allows for a number of different ways to convert a TIN to a lattice using this function. Linear interpolation treats the TIN's arcs between nodes as straight lines that are reflected directly in the heights of the cells across it. The areas enclosed by the TIN's triangles are then treated as flat plates. Surfaces constructed using linear interpolation often look faceted and unnatural, though the potential for interpolation inaccuracies is reduced. Quintic interpolation applies smoothing to the areas inside of the TIN triangles. This method appreciates that the surface being represented is without the harsh breaks in slope represented through linear interpolation. Instead a continuous surface is created that runs through the nodes and forms a smooth interpolation through the areas between. The resulting surface is not only more realistic and aesthetically pleasing, but is potentially also more accurate. The present study used the latter process so that the generation of the surface is an objective and repeatable process and, ultimately, this makes the surface potentially more accurate.

## Site 1- the Yorkshire Wolds

### Background
The first site consists of the southern terminus of a ploughed out cursus feature (cursus A -the Woldgate cursus - Figure 2) on the Yorkshire Wolds. It forms part of a complex of at least four cursuses that converge around the village of Rudston. The area is surrounded by many other broadly contemporary features including at least three long barrows (Kilham long barrow (Greenwell 1877: 553-556, Manby 1976), Rudston long barrow (Greenwell 1877: 497) and the Denby long barrow); two great barrows (Southside Mount and Willie Howe), Maiden's Grave henge (McInnes 1964);

several mortuary enclosures and many early Bronze Age ring ditches. Central to the cluster of cursuses is a large monolith, together suggesting the high ceremonial importance of this area during the Neolithic and early Bronze Age periods.

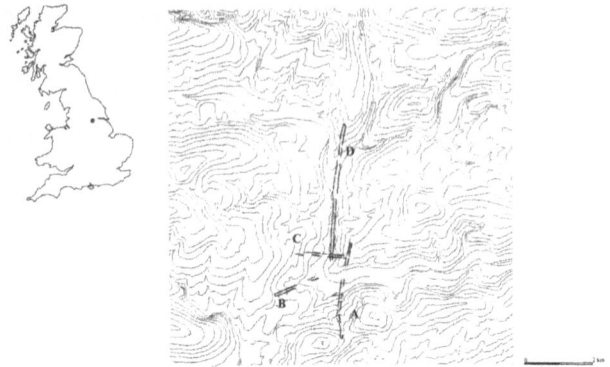

**Figure 2. Location map for Site 1 - the Yorkshire Wolds**.

Evidence from a number of sites within the area has demonstrated that the current intensive agricultural regime has persisted within the area for nearly two millennia. Aerial photography has revealed extensive field systems relating to Roman period settlements and perhaps earlier (Stoertz 1997). Similarly excavations across the ditches a third of the way along cursus 'A' revealed buried furrows containing Medieval pottery, indicating that the site was under ridge and furrow cultivation at that time (Abramson 1997).

The cursuses were identified from aerial photography over a number of years (Dymond 1966, Riley 1988, Stoertz 1997). In the 19th century, prior to the classification of cursuses, the southern terminus of the Woldgate cursus (cursus A) was excavated by Greenwell (1877: 253-257). At this time the feature had already been damaged by agriculture. Greenwell identified the terminus as the remains of three conjoining long barrows, mentioning that the biggest was aligned east-west and was 137' (41.7m) long and 40' (12.2m) wide. At its eastern end it survived to 5.5' (1.7m) high and at its eastern end it was 4.5' (1.4m) high, though lower between. In the late 1950s the site was partially excavated and a topographic survey was conducted in 1964, published as a contour plot with intervals set at three inches (Dymond 1966). Despite ploughing, the overall shape of the cursus terminus was still discernible with the higher southeastern, and southwestern corners. Comparisons with the earlier measurements for bank height could not be made accurately because of the natural slope of the topography. However, the overall maximum height at the southern end shown on the 1964 survey suggested that the bank survived to a maximum of approximately 5' (1.5 m), indicating that at least 6" (0.15m) of vertical erosion had occurred on the site between the 1860s and the 1960s.

The continued ploughing of the site since 1964 suggests that the potential for further damage is very high. This is a significant problem since the site is under protection through scheduling (Scheduled Ancient Monument No. Humberside 105). The site continues to be ploughed and consequently a recent contour survey was considered useful to measure the possibilities of erosion. An area slightly larger than that surveyed in 1964 was chosen and surveyed using the method outlined above at a constant surface resolution of between 3m and 5m intervals aligned on ranging rods. A total of 772 points were recorded over an area of approximately 11,378 $m^2$ providing a mean density of 0.07 points per $m^2$ (678 points per hectare). From this survey a DEM was generated with an interpolated surface resolution of 1 m.

## Site 1 Results

The results from the DEM were represented using contour banding on a linear scale of 0.25 m per shading band and are shown in Figure 3. The shape of the model shows the same overall pattern as the 1964 contour plot, with the distinct U-shaped plan of the terminus clearly visible, along with the shape of the natural slope falling away to the north.

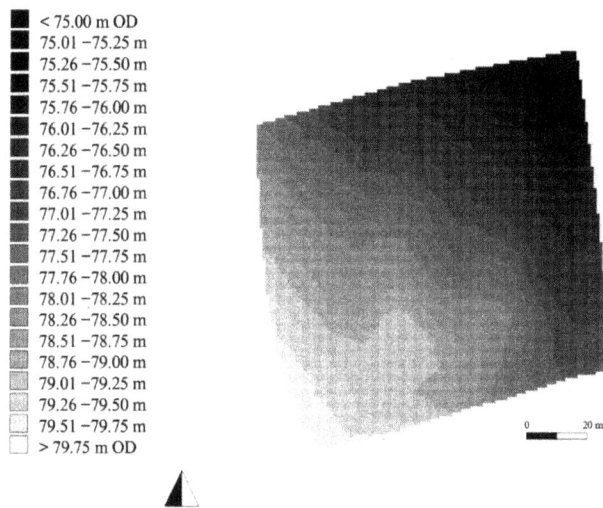

Figure 3. The basic DEM surface of cursus A.

To make the results from the two surveys more directly comparable it was advantageous to reproduce them within the same analytical environment – the GIS. The published contours from the earlier survey were digitised and labelled so that they could be used to interpolate a continuous surface. Unfortunately these were not produced with a height datum and so any direct comparison on the basis of erosion and scale was not possible. Therefore a visual, qualitative approach was used to assess erosive damage. A common visual platform was chosen in the form of the GIS and so each of the surfaces resulting from the two surveys was generalised into comparable contour diagrams with vertical intervals of 0.1m (Figure 4). The results from this comparison demonstrate how the overall shape has remained the same although detail has been lost. The shape of the terminus has become 'generalised' and less distinct, though this is hard to quantify. It is possible however to display the area of full contours as shown on the earlier survey from the highest point and compare the area covered by the change in height.

To provide a more quantifiable measurement of erosion between the two contour plots a visual comparison of scale was accented by displaying the ratio between vertical height and horizontal area. If erosion has occurred in the time

between the two surveys then the horizontal area covered for a given drop in height will be greater. While it must be noted that the relationship between the two is not a linear one due to the influences of irregular topography, natural slope and colluviation, it may be assumed that erosion will be reflected in an increase in horizontal area.

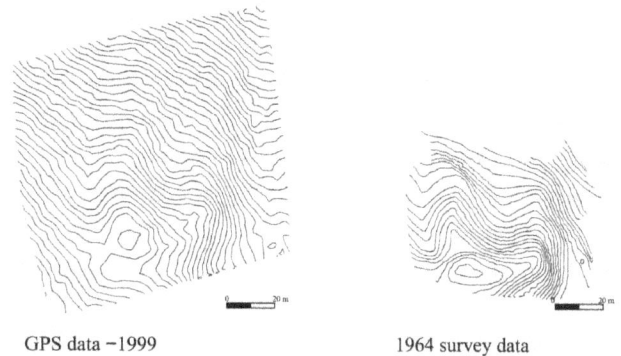

GPS data –1999                    1964 survey data

**Figure 4. Comparative contour models (0.1.m intervals).**

By highlighting the contours representing this drop in height, the expanded area can be seen, demonstrating erosive action. Further, if a horizontal measurement is taken from the highest contour to the highest point between the cursus banks 2m below for each of the surveys an indication of scale can be given. The results from this show a distance of 35.1m in 1964 compared with a distance of 38.7m in 1999; a difference of 3.6m. Although there are many variables that influence these measurements, the differences between the two indicate that a considerable amount of erosion has occurred, which would seem to confirm the visual assessment.

## Site 2 -Sutton Common

### Background
The second site of Sutton Common lies within the wetlands of the Humberhead Levels in South Yorkshire (Figure 5). This site consists of a pair of earthwork enclosures dating from the early Iron Age, lying on opposing sides of the relict palaeochannel of the Hampole Beck. These enclosures occupy islands within the late Devensian Lake Humber deposits that have been reworked predominantly by later aeolian and fluvial action (Lillie 1997). They were depicted on Ordnance Survey maps dating to 1845 made shortly after the area was enclosed, though it was not until the 1930s that recorded excavations took place, when a more detailed survey of the earthworks was undertaken and published (Whiting 1936). This and more recent archaeological work at the site has demonstrated that it consists of two main phases; the first characterised by an oak palisade surrounding the area of the larger enclosure, and the second characterised by the replacing of these features by complex earthworks following a phase of abandonment. During the second phase it is also believed that earthworks were erected around the smaller island to form the smaller enclosure (cf. Parker Pearson and Sydes 1997; Van de Noort and Chapman 1999).

Increasingly intensive ploughing has taken place in the surrounding area since the 1970s. Despite being scheduled in 1937, the area of the larger enclosure on the eastern side of the palaeochannel was bulldozed in 1979 and the area put under arable cultivation. Consequently the upstanding earthworks were comprehensively destroyed and the ditches infilled. A second phase of bulldozing was initiated at the southern end of the smaller enclosure but this was halted at an early stage. From this time onwards the site was regularly ploughed such that the perimeter of the larger enclosure could only be seen as a soil mark on aerial photographs. In 1997 the site was purchased by the Carstairs Countryside Trust with grant support from English Heritage and the Heritage Lottery Fund to ensure its continued protection and has not been farmed since 1997.

**Figure 5. Location map for Site 2 - Sutton Common.**

The damage to the upstanding remains on the site has meant that the main problem with trying to understand the site on the ground is the lack of upstanding earthworks representing the large enclosure and the incomplete earthworks of the smaller enclosure. This has repercussions for both the interpretation of the site and for its management.

## Site 2 Results

A total of 5,290 points were recorded over an area of 286,754m$^2$, providing an overall resolution of 0.02 points per m$^2$ (184 points per hectare). The survey was again conducted in transects aligned on ranging rods at a surface resolution typically between 3m and 8m, increasing over areas of high topographic variability such as the earthworks of the smaller of the two enclosures. The surface was recreated digitally within the GIS using the methods outlined above at intervals of 1m. Any lower resolution would have resulted in 'quantizing errors' whereby there would have been more survey points than interpolated area, leading to under-interpolation, which would have been visible as excessive stepping across the site. The basic DEM demonstrated the topographic position of the site with the area of the palaeochannel of the Hampole Beck and the various re-worked islands (Figure 6). A raised area possibly representing a causeway is also visible on this model.

By applying a virtual light-source and an exaggerated vertical scale more features become visible. Figure 7 shows the site exaggerated vertically ten times with a light source positioned to the northwest, at an azimuth of 45° relative to the centre of the model. Here it is possible to see the outline of the larger enclosure despite the seventeen years of ploughing. It is also possible to see a depression along the western edge of the site indicating the position of a ditch, perhaps defined through differential shrinkage of its peaty fill.

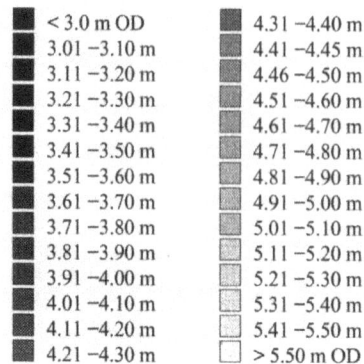

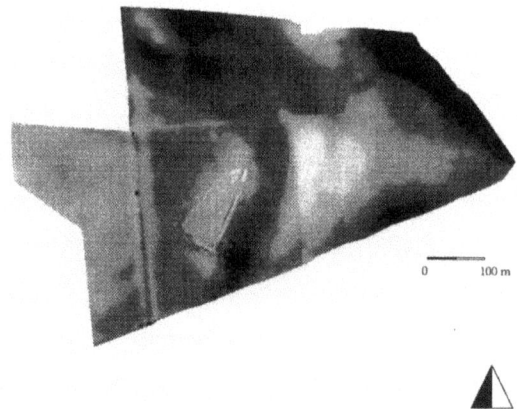

**Figure 6. The basic DEM surface of Sutton Common.**

To understand how closely these features compared to the outlines from the earlier surveys, the positions of the banks were digitised to form an overlay (Figure 8). Correlations can be seen between the two surveys verifying what had been seen on the recent model. It also seems that a number of features were missed when the earlier survey was conducted.

**Figure 7. Perspective light-shaded model of Sutton Common (x10 vertical exaggeration).**

For example, on the western side of the smaller enclosure the earlier plan showed a number of breaks along its length, but this is not reflected by the DEM which shows a continuous bank running along this length. Perhaps the "long grass and rough vegetation of the common" (Whiting 1936: 66) hindered their visibility at the time of the earlier survey, but that the later survey method was able to overcome this.

**Figure 8. Light-shaded model of Sutton Common showing the positions of the banks from the 1930s survey. The position of the larger enclosure is depicted by outlines. The positions of the banks of the smaller enclosure as understood at this time are shown in black.**

## Conclusions

Through the examination of these two sites I hope to have demonstrated the potential of a combined technique of differential GPS survey and data modelling using GIS. In the introduction the two main functions of archaeological survey were defined as assisting interpretation and cultural resource management. In terms of interpretation, the possibilities of seeing a site in plan continue but the digital framework creates much more potential. Firstly, with each of the sites it was possible to see buried archaeological features through the application of GIS tools, particularly at the second site. Secondly, it is valuable to be able to see both archaeological and natural features together in order to understand their interaction with one another and thereby to understand features of architecture. This is further enhanced through the differential state of preservation displayed by the earthworks. By using this method it has been possible to see and understand upstanding earthworks, levelled earthworks and the natural topography simultaneously enabling a more holistic understanding of form and relationships between them. In terms of cultural resource management, contemporary site condition can be assessed qualitatively and quantitatively. Current surface conditions can be recorded and investigated visually and may be compared to past and future conditions in a more complete and impartial way than is possible using more conventional surveys.

## References

Abramson, P. (1997). *Excavation at Pits Plantation, Rudston: archaeological excavation for Perenco UK Ltd.* NAA report 97/51.

Dymond, D.P. (1966). Ritual monuments at Rudston, East Yorkshire, England. *Proceedings of the Prehistoric Society* **32**, 86-95.

Goucher, K. (1997). Hill of Tara topographical survey and mapping. In C. Newman (Ed) *Tara: an archaeological survey,* pp. 245-252. Dublin: Discovery Programme Monograph 2.

Greenwell, Canon W. (1877). *British barrows.* Oxford: Clarendon Press.

Lillie, M. (1997). The palaeoenvironmental survey of the Rivers Aire, Went, former Turnbridge Dike (Don north branch), and the Hampole Beck. In R. Van de Noort and S. Ellis (Eds.) *Wetland Heritage of the Humberhead Levels: an archaeological survey,* pp. 47-78. Hull: Humber Wetlands Project, University of Hull.

Manby, T.G. (1976). Excavation of the Kilham long barrow, East Riding of Yorkshire. *Proceedings of the Prehistoric Society,* **42**, 111-159.

McInnes, I.J. (1964). A class II henge in the East Riding of Yorkshire. *Antiquity,* **38**: 218-219.

Parker Pearson, M. and Sydes, R.E. (1997). The Iron Age enclosures and prehistoric landscape of Sutton Common, South Yorkshire. *Proceedings of the Prehistoric Society,* **63**, 221-259.

Riley, D.N. (1988). Air survey of Neolithic sites on the Yorkshire Wolds. In T.G. Manby (Ed.) *Archaeology in eastern Yorkshire, essays in honour of T.C.M Brewster,* pp. 89-93. Sheffield: Department of Archaeology and Prehistory, University of Sheffield.

Stoertz, C. (1997). *Ancient landscapes of the Yorkshire Wolds: aerial photographic transcription and analysis.* Swindon: RCHME.

Van de Noort, R. and Chapman, H. (1999). *An archaeological assessment in preparation of a management plan at Sutton Common, Sutton, South Yorkshire.* Unpublished CWA Report CWA/RES/EH-Sutton/99-1.

Whiting, C.E. (1936). Excavations on Sutton Common, 1933, 1934 and 1935. *Yorkshire Archaeological Journal* **33**, 57-80.

# Chaos and patterns: reconstructing past environments using modern data. The molluscan experience

Paul Davies

Quaternary Research Unit, School of Science and the Environment, Bath Spa University College, Newton Park, Bath BA2 9BN.

## Abstract

A general problem in using modern analogue data in sub-fossil molluscan studies is the very specific nature of the data available, particularly when molluscan communities have non-linear characteristics. However, working from the general to the particular, patterns will emerge. Such patterns in the modern record can be compared to those in the fossil record. When matching occurs either between modern-modern, modern-fossil or fossil-fossil, interpretation is enhanced. Consideration of data from modern flood-pastures and from Holocene overbank alluvium demonstrates the importance of deliberately looking for patterns, first general, then specific.

Keywords: Mollusca, chaos, palaeoecology, overbank alluvium

## Introduction – the general nature of the problem

One of the major problems with using modern data analogously as a basis for environmental reconstruction is the specificity of the modern data available to be used. For example, Robinson's (1988) study of floodplain pasture of the River Thames found only the amphibious *Lymnaea truncatula* and *Anisus leucostoma*, whilst Davies, Gale and Lees (1996) found such pastures in the Wylye and Test valleys to be characterised by *Vallonia pulchella*, *Trichia hispida* and *Cochlicopa*, with only a subsidiary amphibious component. If one wishes, therefore, to use such modern data analogously, which should we consider *right* and *applicable*. The answer, of course, is twofold and seemingly contradictory. Both are right, in that they evidently describe flood-pasture faunas. Equally, however, neither is right in *fully* describing the variety of faunas that *may* be or *might once have been* found in flood-pastures. Notwithstanding the problems of a uniformitarianist approach to either species or

environment (Evans 1991; Harris and Thomas 1991), there is also a problem of *complexity*. In particular, "the complexity of organisation increases through time and space considered" (Gell-Mann 1994, p20). As far as we are concerned here, this means that we can view grasslands at different levels, from the general to the particular (Figure 1). The major problem becomes one of position. Modern sampling tends to sample the particular (or the complex), but environmental reconstruction has largely dealt with the general (or the simple). We are trying to marry data from either end of a bifurcation diagram (Figure 2).

There is a further general complication. Floras and faunas are not established merely as a genetic response. The molluscan fauna of any specific grassland is not merely the sum of all species that *can* be there, it is also subject to random processes and stochastic events. Historical accidents, modifications, biogeography, storms, extinctions *etc.* all have a part to play. We can only reckon with the modern when we have reckoned with its past (Dennett 1995). The problem for palaeoecology is that we also need to consider the processes and events that influenced and shaped the communities whose remnants we are recovering as fossil assemblages. These, obviously, differed from those affecting any modern fauna we choose to study. Where does this leave us? If each situation is 'unique', how can we proceed with interpreting palaeoecological material on the basis of neoecological data? At best the problems are difficult (Harris and Thomas 1991).

The problem is one of non-linearity. As Gell-Mann (1994, p25) states "The outcome of a dynamical process is so sensitive to initial conditions that a minuscule change in the situation at the beginning of the process results in a large difference at the end". For Mollusca this converts to saying that communities (established through the dynamic process of colonisation, and the subsequent dynamic processes of landscape change and modification) will vary from place to place (and from time to time) even though the habitats they

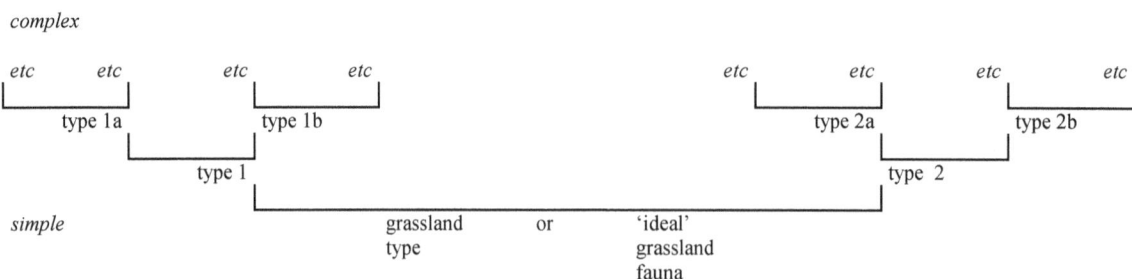

**Figure 1 – Building from the simple to the complex for either grassland types _or_ 'ideal grassland molluscan faunas.**

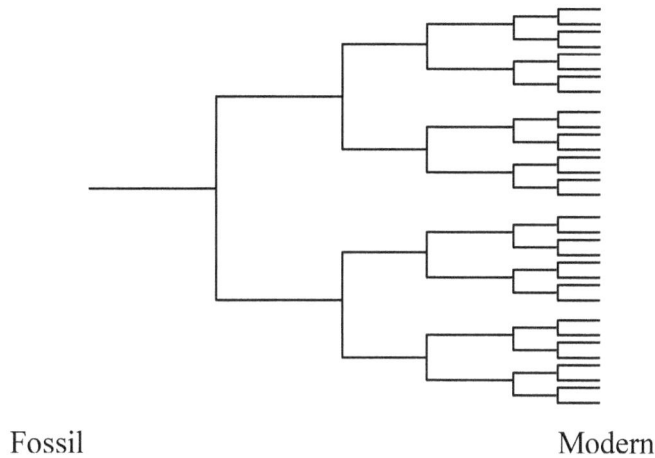

Fossil                                                    Modern

**Figure 2 – Classic bifurcation diagram. Modern samples tend to be recovered and assessed from the complex side, sub-fossil material from the simple.**

occupy (as we generally class them) may appear identical. In short, molluscan communities show every sign of being *chaotic*.

Chaos is defined as the unpredictability of complex non-linear systems. In interpreting fossil snails using modern analogues, this seems to leave us with a fundamental problem. A deeper consideration is, however, more encouraging, since there is another important aspect of chaotic systems, that is that complex numbers of possibilities arise from underlying simplicities. Review Figure 1 and substitute start for simple, end for complex. The role of modern analogue studies becomes one in which the underlying simplicities should be sought, not the complex end points, which mask them. Consequently the species data we collect in modern studies might be useless (in terms of applicability to the past) as specific species data, but will be highly useful in revealing underlying patterns. If we return now to where we began, the studies of Robinson (1988) and Davies *et al.* (1996) are paradoxically both useless and useful to fossil studies. They are useless if we consider named species, useful if we recognise the underlying pattern:

*simple unstructured environments → few molluscan species*

This can then become:

*few molluscan species → simple, unstructured environments*

when considering the sub-fossil record. Simple unstructured environments, as far as Mollusca are concerned, are those with little vegetative structure, such as short-sward, grazed grassland. Complex structured environments are fens, woodland, abandoned grassland etc. It should be noted that it is also possible that few species could result from differential preservation, although usually this would be obvious since in poor preservation situations all molluscan species tend to be affected to a noticeable degree.

Eventually, given more and more data, other regularities will emerge (Figure 3).

The final 'states' should not be viewed as fixed species compositions, but as varied states with underlying

*commonalities*. This applies to sub-fossil material too (see Evans 1991; Evans, Davies, Mount and Williams. 1992; Davies 1996 for examples).

## More specific problems of non-linear systems

There are, of course, other fundamental problems to consider. The above tended to consider 'end-points', that is communities in equilibrium, whether modern or fossil. What happens if we are considering transient habitats and/or dynamic communities of snails? Even simple situations will tend to make interpretation difficult.

Consider, for example, a newly created habitat. Further consider that only 6 species of snail *can* live in that habitat and that none were there before. Furthermore, allow that they all *can actually get to* the newly emerged habitat. Given that they will not arrive *en masse* (different species will have different migration rates) we have complex possibilities emerging. With just six species there are 720 arrival combinations, and before saturation (i.e. all have arrived) there are 60 possible 'snapshot' standing crops.

*simple*

| | |
|---|---|
| No species | |
| Species A | A |
| Species B | A+B, A or B |
| Species C | A+B+C, A+B, A+C, B+C, A or B or C |
| Species D | *etc.* |
| Species E | *etc.* |
| Species F | *etc.* |

*complex*

Let us now consider that we are dealing here with a grassland. When, on the basis of the molluscan data alone can we recognise a grassland fauna (and therefore grassland in the fossil record)? At time zero when there are no snails? Certainly not. After all have arrived? Certainly. But what about all the states in-between?

As interpreters of the fossil record two things come to our

37

**a)** from sub-fossil and modern data

|  | *similarity* → |  |
|---|---|---|
| *difference* ↓ | few species<br>many species | simple vegetation structure<br>complex vegetation structure |

**b)** from sub-fossil and modern data

|  | *similarity* → |  |
|---|---|---|
| *difference* ↓ | 'open' sp.<br>'shade' species | simple structure<br>complex structure |

**c)** from modern data

|  | *similarity* → |  |  |
|---|---|---|---|
| *difference* ↓ | fen<br>abandoned pasture | carr<br>meadow | marsh<br>open marsh |

**d)** from modern data

|  | *similarity* → |  |
|---|---|---|
| *difference* ↓ | carr<br>fen<br>pasture | rough grassland |

**Figure 3 – Similarity-Difference matrices of wetland molluscan characteristics. a), b), and c) after Davies (1992). d) after Davies *et al.* (1996). All following Hodder ((1986, p126).**

aid. The first, of course is time-averaging. Through time the discrepancy in information between organism and environment will reduce (as long as the environment remains constant). Generally, as palaeoecologists we are dealing with assemblages. Our samples will therefore tend toward endpoints than beginnings. Furthermore, it has been appreciated since Darwin's time that snails are very good colonisers (Darwin 1872). Interpretation of time-averaged fossil data works because, crucially, equilibrium communities (as far as such things exist) *are* often a component of the recovered assemblages. There is a case, perhaps, for considering that modern studies move away from the 'snapshot' approach, and consider total recovered assemblages, that is the living and dead components. With few exceptions it would seem to make little sense to compare the characteristics of sub-fossil assemblages with those of modern standing crops. Likewise, where the fossil record tends toward preservation of a death assemblage (for example on the surfaces of buried soils), modern total assemblages (that is both the living and dead component recovered) would seem to be better for comparative purposes (Davies 1999).

The second aid is related to rate of establishment of equilibrium communities, or the speed of ecological saturation. The example of the six species given above is of course not an adequate model of the real world. If we now consider a grassland becoming established within a generally wooded habitat (through clearing perhaps), some of the species that will end up as components of the grassland fauna were already components of the woodland fauna, albeit perhaps very minor ones. The grassland equilibrium fauna that will be, is already partly established as soon as clearance occurs. Generalist species are not without their uses. What becomes problematical now is not so much how we recognise woodland to grassland clearance events, but whether there was a *phase* of clearance, or a *single* clearance event. Both will leave the same imprint. In the fossil record the pattern might be:

*many species (woodland)* → *many species (grassland but woodland snails still predominant in assemblage therefore not recognised)* → *few species (grassland)*

Short term isolated clearances may not necessarily be recognisable, even if the clearance is spatially extensive:

*many species (woodland)* → *many species (grassy clearing but woodland snails still predominant in assemblage)* → *many species (woodland)*

Let us take this further with another example, this time the establishment of a woodland in an otherwise generally open landscape. If the gap between new woodland and any potential source area for Mollusca that like such shaded habitat is great, dispersal and establishment of an equilibrium woodland fauna in the new wood is likely to be slow, depending as it does purely on chance events. If, on the other hand the new woodland is becoming established from other woody components in the landscape, for example a hedge, much of the woodland fauna to be are, in effect, 'ready and waiting'. Again, a 'near-equilibrium' fauna will rapidly become established. Returning to our patterns, we will see the rapid change from:

*few species (grassland)* → *more species (woodland)*

It is worth noting that until recent (largely upland) plantation practices emerged, 'new' woodlands generally were not established as total isolates, but were regenerated from other woody stock, whether with a helping hand or without. We might expect, therefore, such open to wooded transitions to appear quite rapidly in the sub-fossil record. Again the modern data are lacking. There are some applicable modern data demonstrating the influence of isolation on Mollusca (Cameron, Down and Pannett 1980). More are in preparation (Davies and Wolski 2001).

## Punctualism *v.* gradualism

Before we return to consideration of the relationship between neo- and palaeoecology, it is worth exploring the nature of molluscan community change, both in the fossil and modern record.

The two examples given above serve to illustrate that though snail colonisation is a dynamic process, each species responding separately and the process at face value therefore seeming to be gradualistic, the net result is actually punctualistic. In our example of the new grassland above, the fossil record of such an event would tend to show a 'flip' from one static state (a woodland fauna) to another (a grassland fauna). In the other example the 'flip' would be in the opposite direction. The transient communities would not be recognised. Indeed, in the examples above they may hardly have ever existed. Transient phases at the general level (the habitat) are not necessarily similarly reflected at the more specific level (the Mollusca).

## Patterns in the modern and sub-fossil record – examples

Theories, conjectures and models are all very well, but observational data is necessary. As already outlined above it is most useful to work from the simple to the complex, building up sets of similarity or difference at a general level and then working on from there. To return to flood-pastures much of the general level is apparent (see Figure 3), but how do we move to the particular while maintaining possibilities of finding (deeper) patterns? One recent approach has been to look at definable intra-habitat variations, principally the drains and carriers of relict water-meadow systems within the Wylye valley, Wiltshire (Davies and Grimes 1999). As well as the published data from the Wylye there are as yet unpublished data available from similar intra-habitat features from the nearby Test valley, Hampshire (Davies, unpublished). The comparative process works at two levels. At the intra-site level one can compare the ridges and furrows at a single location, looking for changes in molluscan species composition over small distances related to hydrology and associated slight vegetation structural changes (see Davies and Grimes (1999) for a detailed discussion of the intra-site variability at Wylye). At the inter-site level one can look for similarities or differences at larger spatial scales and with relation to other known variants between sites (Table 1).

Starting from the simplest level we can state that:

*pasture* → *few species*

This is a good first step since it confirms the observational data from elsewhere (see above). If we now take the Wylye carriers and drains we can state:

*carriers* → *few species*
*drains* → *more species*

we already know (see above) that in relative terms:

*more species* → *more structured (complex) habitat*

and we can again confirm this using observational or other data (Davies and Grimes 1999).

These general conclusions are confirmed by an identical pattern from another location, namely at Bossington on the River Test (Table 1).

To explore the complexity of the data further we can compare carrier with carrier and drain with drain. At this stage we seem to hit the problem of non-linearity, all four situations differ. There seems to be no direct comparisons between the actual faunal compositions of carrier against carrier, drain against drain *or* carrier against drain. Here we need to consider the second level (inter-site comparisons) of analysis again. Data is available from elsewhere, the sub-fossil record. We can now note that Evans *et al.* (1992) and Davies (1996) found the following taxocenes (recurrent species associations) in assemblages recovered from Holocene overbank alluvium in river valleys of the same region (including The Wylye):

*Taxocene 1* – *Vallonia pulchella, Trichia, Cochlicopa*
*Taxocene 2* – *As Taxocene 1 but also with Lymnaea truncatula, Carychium*
*Taxocene 6* – *As Taxocene 1 but with Pupilla*

39

|  | **Bossington** | **Wylye** |
|---|---|---|
| **Carrier** | *Pupilla/Trichia* | *Trichia/Vallonia pulchella/Cochlicopa* |
| **Drain** | *Pupilla, Trichia, Vallonia, Cochlicopa* | as carrier but also *Carychium, Lymnaea truncatula* |

**Table 1 – Modern faunas of relic carriers and drains from two floodplain locations in central southern England.**

Now we can state that:

*Wylye carrier* →     *Taxocene 1*
*Wylye drain* →      *Taxocene 2*
*Bossington drain* →    *Taxocene 6*

This transforms into:

*Taxocene 1* →    *indicative of environmental conditions akin to Wylye carrier*
*Taxocene 2* →    *indicative of environmental conditions akin to Wylye drain*
*Taxocene 6* →    *indicative of environmental conditions akin to Bossington drain*

We can now interpret sub-fossil sequences with reference to modern analogue material. Note that we have not stated habitat equivalence through time, only common environmental characteristics.

We are left with the 'unique' *Pupilla/Trichia* fauna of the Bossington carriers. This can, however, also be considered, starting first in general terms:

*Bossington* →    *Pupilla always present*
*Wylye* →        *no Pupilla*

This is a clear general difference between the two locations, we now need to find others. One obvious one is:

*Bossington* →    *presently cattle-grazed*
*Wylye* →        *presently sheep-grazed*

We can now think of the possibility that:

*Cattle-grazed flood-pasture* →    *Pupilla*
*Sheep-grazed flood-pasture* →    *no Pupilla*

From here we can consider the possibility that in the sub-fossil record from Holocene overbank alluvium:

*Taxocene 6* →    *indicates cattle-grazed flood-pasture*

Obviously there are going to be other differences between the Wylye and Bossington locations, and I am not arguing here that *Pupilla* actually is indicative of cattle-grazing. The ecological status of *Pupilla* within overbank alluvium has been debated with reference to other factors (Davies 1996). The important thing is that some basic modern survey work has led us to another possibility, and one that has the prospect of discerning between sheep-grazed and cattle-grazed flood-pasture in the fossil record. Such precision

would be an advance on current sub-fossil interpretation, and of obvious archaeological interest.

## Conclusion and potential

Although faunas have unique qualities through space and time, there are underlying patterns. As general patterns are found and confirmed, such as few species indicates simple unstructured environment, deeper patterns can then be sought. These lead us away from the general (characteristics of the entire fauna), to the particular (characteristics of individual species), as outlined above. Patterns will be evident in both modern and sub-fossil material, particularly in the latter when data are obtained from autochthonous contexts (see Evans 1991). Seeking similarities between present and past strengthens the prospect of past patterns being 'real', and will help enormously in refining sub-fossil interpretation. The fact that advances in sub-fossil analysis will be facilitated by concentrating on modern faunal studies has been stated for some time (Thomas 1985; Davies *et al.* 1996; Evans and O'Connor 1999). The present study demonstrates that patterns, from simple to complex, will only be revealed through common approaches, in other words 'groups' of data must relate to one another. To return once more to where we began, we can note that Robinson (1988) collected his Mollusca by pitfall trap, a method not particularly well suited to that taxonomic group. Other studies (including Davies *et al.* 1996) have tended to use turves. Replicate sampling through space (and time) is important, standardisation is necessary. Without it deeper patterns will not emerge. Along the way, other problems will be addressed too. This paper, for example, has considered the ability of the fossil record to preserve transient molluscan communities and transient habitat change. There really are still adventures.

## Acknowledgements

The influence of Murray Gell-Mann's *The Quark and the Jaguar: adventures in the simple and the complex* will be obvious to those who have read that book. To those who have not, it is highly recommended. Discussions with various colleagues at Bath Spa University College have helped clarify certain points – all are thanked.

## References

Cameron, R.A.D., Down, K. and Pannett, D.J. (1980). Historical and environmental influences on hedgerow snail faunas. *Biological Journal of the Linnean Society* **13**, 75-87.

Darwin, C. (1872). (6ᵗʰ edition). *The Origin of Species.*

London: John Murray.

Davies, P. (1992). *Sub-fossil Mollusca from Holocene overbank alluvium and other wet-ground contexts in Wessex.* Unpublished PhD thesis. Department of Archaeology, University of Wales, College of Cardiff.

Davies, P. (1996.) The ecological status of *Pupilla muscorum* (Linné) in Holocene overbank alluvium at Kingsmead Bridge, Wiltshire. *Journal of Conchology* **35**, 467-471.

Davies, P. (1998). Numerical analysis of subfossil wet-ground molluscan taxocenes from overbank alluvium at Kingsmead Bridge, Wiltshire. *Journal of Archaeological Science* **25**, 39-52.

Davies, P. (1999). Molluscan total assemblages across a woodland-grassland boundary and their palaeoenvironmental relevance. *Environmental Archaeology* **4**, 57-66.

Davies, P. and Grimes, C.J. (1999). Small scale spatial variation of pasture molluscan faunas within a relic watermeadow system at Wylye, Wiltshire, UK. *Journal of Biogeography* **26**, 1057-1063.

Davies, P. and Wolski, C. (2001, in press). Later Neolithic woodland regeneration in the long barrow ditch fills of the Avebury area: the molluscan evidence. *Oxford Journal of Archaeology* **20 (4).**

Davies, P. Gale, C.H. and Lees, M. (1996). Quantitative studies of modern wet-ground molluscan faunas from Bossington, Hampshire. *Journal of Biogeography* **23**, 371-377.

Dennett, D. (1995). *Darwin's dangerous idea.* London: Penguin Books Ltd.

Evans, J.G. (1991). An approach to the interpretation of dry-ground and wet-ground molluscan taxocenes from central-southern England. In D.R. Harris and K.D. Thomas (Eds) *Modelling Ecological Change*, pp.75-89. London: Institute of Archaeology, UCL.

Evans, J.G. and O'Connor, T. (1999).. *Environmental Archaeology: principles and methods.* Stroud: Sutton.

Evans, J.G., Davies, P., Mount, R. and Williams, D. (1992.) Molluscan taxocenes from Holocene overbank alluvium in central southern England. In S. Needham and M.G. Macklin (Eds) *Alluvial Archaeology in Britain*, pp. 65-74. Oxford: Oxbow Monograph No. 27.

Gell-Mann, M. (1994) *The Quark and the Jaguar: Adventures in the simple and the complex.* London: Abacus.

Harris, D.H. and Thomas, K.D. (1991) Modelling ecological change in environmental archaeology. In D.R. Harris and K.D. Thomas (Eds) *Modelling ecological change*, pp.91-102. London: Institute of Archaeology, UCL.

Hodder, I. 1986. *Reading the past.* Cambridge: Cambridge University Press.

Robinson, M. (1988) Molluscan evidence for pasture and meadowland on the floodplain of the upper Thames basin. In P. Murphy and C. French (Eds) *The exploitation of wetlands*, pp. 101-112. Oxford: British Archaeological Reports, British Series 186.

Thomas, K.D. (1985.) Land snail analysis in archaeology: theory and practice. In N.R.J. Fieller, D.D. Gilbertson and N.G.A. Ralph (Eds) *Palaeobiological Investigations: Research design, methods and data analysis,* pp. 131-156. Oxford: British Archaeological Reports, International Series 266.

# A new method for estimating gestational age from skeletal long bone length

Rebecca L. Gowland and Andrew T. Chamberlain

Department of Archaeology and Prehistory, University of Sheffield, Northgate House, West Street, Sheffield, S1 4ET, UK.

## Introduction

The ability to reliably estimate age at death of skeletal remains is one of the most fundamental requirements of osteoarchaeology and biological anthropology. Age estimation involves establishing the physiological development of the skeleton and correlating this with chronological age (Saunders, 2000). The skeletal growth and maturation of infants and children has been characterised by numerous measurable parameters including: dental development and eruption, long bone growth and epiphyseal fusion. These skeletal markers vary in the accuracy with which they reflect chronological age, and dental development is generally considered to be the most accurate because it is least affected by environmental factors (Ubelaker, 1989a, b; Saunders, 2000). However, the small size of the tooth buds at birth means that they are only infrequently recovered from archaeological sites and are, therefore, of limited value in establishing the age at death of archaeological foetal and perinatal skeletons.

The estimation of age at death from long bone growth is considered to be less accurate than dental development because the environment exerts a powerful influence on skeletal growth. This results in a high degree of variability in linear growth between both individuals and populations. Nutrition and infection, or the synergistic interaction of both, are the most influential environmental components impacting on growth (King and Ulijaszek, 1999; Humphrey, 2000). Factors that influence foetal growth, however, differ from the postnatal period in that they have very little to do with the genetic make-up of the foetus itself. Intrauterine growth is primarily influenced by the maternal environment and genotype (Roberts, 1986). The intrauterine environment acts as a buffer, protecting the foetus to an extent, from any physical onslaught endured by the mother. Social and environmental stresses experienced by the mother while not exerting a strong influence on foetal growth will, however, increase the risk of perinatal mortality, leading to increased numbers of pre-term births and stillbirths (Mutale et al, 1991). This maternal buffering against environmental onslaught, together with the rapidity of growth during the pre- and perinatal period of skeletal development, results in large differences in bone size between age categories. Thus long bone length is one of the most important methods of estimating gestational age, both in clinical science and in osteoarchaeology.

The long bones begin to ossify in utero, between the 8th and 12th gestational weeks, linear diaphyseal growth is most rapid around the 4th and 5th lunar months and a uniform, linear level of longitudinal growth then occurs at a reduced rate between the 6th to 9th lunar months (Tanner, 1974; Fazekas and Kosa, 1978; Mendez, 1985). After approximately the 36th gestational week there is another period of reduced growth rate up until term, although this rate increases to the pre-36 week rate during the immediate postnatal period (Tanner, 1974; Mendez, 1985). The ratio between different long bones lengths also changes throughout the period of foetal growth. The humerus is initially longer, (or as long as) the femur, at the 6th lunar month the humerus is still longer than the tibia and the ulna is also similar in length to the tibia during the fifth lunar month (Fazekas and Kosa, 1978). The rate of growth of the lower limbs increases during gestation in comparison to the upper limbs, thus decreasing the upper to lower limb ratio (Jeanty et al., 1982). With respect to postnatal growth, velocities are highest for the first year after birth, with a velocity of approximately 30 cm/year in the first two months (Mendez, 1985), but declining dramatically after 12 months (Johnston, 1986).

### Long Bone Age Estimation Methods

Numerous techniques have been used to characterise foetal and perinatal long bone growth. Ultrasonic studies recognised a close correlatation between femur length and gestational age (e.g. O'Brien et al, 1981; O'Brien and Queenan, 1981; Jeanty et al., 1981, 1982, 1984; Yeh et al 1982; Hadlock et al 1982)and the femur is now measured routinely along with the biparietal diameter in clinical estimations of gestational age (Hohler, 1984; Jeanty et al., 1981). Further ultrasound studies of foetal growth have modelled the relationship between the other major long bones and gestational age (Jeanty et al., 1982, 1984). Prior to the development of ultrasonic techniques, known gestational age data was obtained through radiographs or the measurement of dry bone specimens of pre-term and term stillbirths (e.g. Fazekas and Kosa, 1978). The method of Scheuer et al. (1980) was based on radiographic examinations of live premature infants of various gestational ages. This latter study is the most widely used method for estimating the age at death of perinatal skeletons from archaeological contexts.

All of the above studies have modelled the relationship between long bone length and gestational age through the use of linear or curvilinear regression equations. These regression equations are then used to predict the gestational age of foetal and perinatal remains of unknown age from long bone length measurements. Each of these methods of age estimation, based upon known age patterns of skeletal growth, are grounded in the uniformitarian assumption proposed by Howell (1982); that the relationship between age and long bone length will remain constant across samples (i.e. archaeological populations). Under this assumption, the ages of the perinatal infants may be estimated from their long bone lengths, with any methodological inaccuracies being subsumed under the error term of the equation (Chamberlain, 2001).

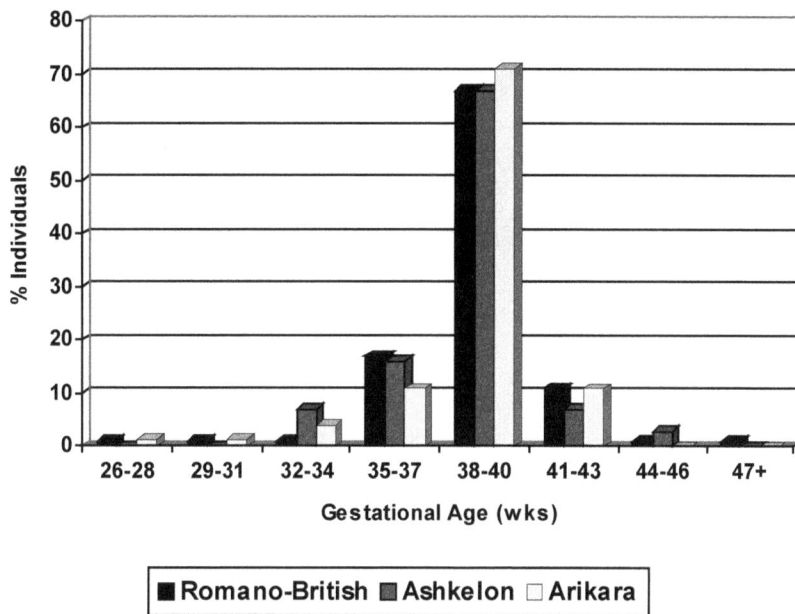

**Figure 1. Age distributions of perinatal archaeological samples from Romano-British sites (Mays, 1993), Late Roman Ashkelon, Israel (Smith and Kahila, 1992) and the native American Arikara population (Owsley and Jantz, 1985). In each case the ages were estimated using the Scheuer *et al.* (1980) method.**

## Regression Problems

A number of statistical problems have been identified in the application of regression methods to skeletal ageing. Bocquet-Appel and Masset (1982) demonstrated that regression equations can introduce a systematic statistical bias in the estimation of age from the skeleton. When chronological age is estimated from the state of a skeletal indicator, the distribution of estimated ages in the 'target' population (the archaeological population of unknown age) is, to an extent, dependent on the age distribution of the reference sample (the skeletal population of known aged individuals upon which the ageing method was devised). This "mimicry" of the reference sample age structure becomes more marked when the correlation between skeletal indicator and chronological age is low. Bocquet-Appel and Masset (1982) state that this effect can "lead one to superimpose on the mortality structure of cemetery populations the structure

of other populations entirely alien to them" (*ibid*: 321). The effect of this bias may account for the surprisingly close similarity between the age distributions of perinatal archaeological samples where gestational age was determined using the Scheuer *et al.* (1980) method. For example, three geographically diverse sites shown in Figure 1 all have a pronounced neonatal peak, with 65% to 70% of the perinatal skeletons having estimated ages between 38 and 40 gestational weeks. This pattern may simply be replicating the neonatal peak observed in the reference sample used by Scheuer *et al.* (1980) (Figure 2). The remarkable similarity between the age at death distributions of the different archaeological populations, coupled with the fact that they appear to mimic the age distribution of the Scheuer *et al.* (1980) reference sample, suggests that the Scheuer *et al.* (1980) method may be generating artificially narrow age at death distributions when applied to archaeological samples.

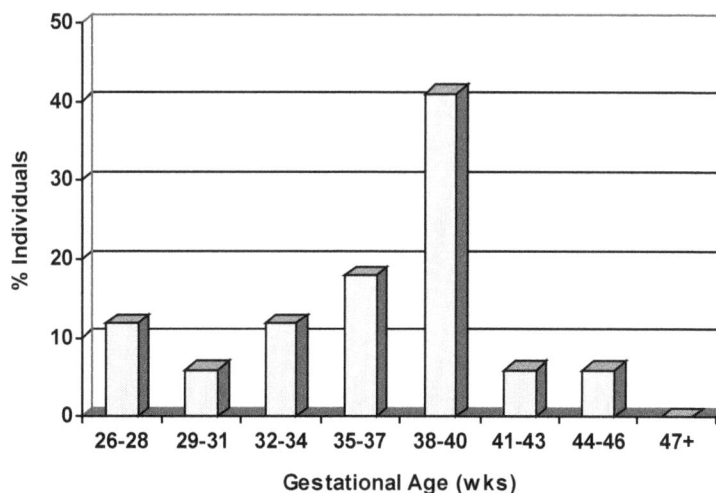

**Figure 2. Age distribution of the Scheuer *et al.* (1980) reference sample.**

Since Bouquet-Appel and Masset's (1982) paper, several studies have addressed the problems of applying regression analysis in the estimation of age from the skeleton (e.g. Bocquet-Appel and Masset, 1985, 1996; Konigsberg and Frankenberg, 1992, 1994; Konigsberg *et al.*, 1997; Lucy *et al.*, 1996; Aykroyd *et al.*, 1997, 1999). Konigsberg and Frankenberg (1994) and Aykroyd *et al.* (1997, 1999) demonstrated that regressing age on a particular skeletal indicator (as per the above methods) is to identify age as the *dependent* variable and the skeletal indicator as the *independent* variable; essentially the reverse of the actual biological relationship. Such a regression model will assume that all errors are in the *y* direction (the known age) which is clearly not the case (Lucy, 1997). Aykroyd *et al.* (1997) state that the poorer the correlation of the skeletal indicator with age, the more that estimates of unknown quantities will reflect the age distribution of the reference sample. Because long bone length may have a relatively poor correlation with age due to individual variability in size, the reference sample age structure exerts a profound effect on the age distribution of the target populations. This study produces a method of estimating the gestational age of foetal and perinatal individuals from long bone length that does not replicate this statistical bias.

**Bayesian Solutions**
Recent publications on skeletal age estimation have explored the use of Bayesian and Maximum Likelihood methods (e.g. Konigsberg and Frankenberg, 1992; Lucy, 1997; Hoppa and Vaupel, 2002). Bayesian data analysis allows us to make inferences from data using probability models for observable quantities and for quantities that are unknown, but we wish to learn about (Gelman *et al*, 1995). Bayes' theorem provides a formal framework whereby we may quantify and state our scientific preconceptions (Grayson, 1998). The application of Bayesian statistics in archaeology has focused mainly on dating techniques (e.g. radiocarbon) (Buck *et al.*, 1996). However, Bayesian approaches are increasingly being applied to human skeletal ageing. This work has culminated in the 'Rostock manifesto' which arose from a workshop entitled 'Mathematical Modelling for Palaeodemography: Coming to Consensus' held in Rostock, Germany in June 1999 (Hoppa and Vaupel, 2002: 2). Essentially this 'manifesto' establishes a theoretical framework which states that the future of human skeletal ageing will rest upon the collection and publication of 'raw' known age skeletal indicator data in a way that allows for their probabilistic manipulation using Bayesian statistical techniques. Bayesian methods have had an extremely important impact on skeletal age estimation (e.g. Konigsberg and Frankenberg, 1992; Bocquet-Appel and Masset, 1996; Chamberlain, 2000; Gowland and Chamberlain, 2002; Hoppa and Vaupel, 2002). However, the use of Bayesian statistics within palaeodemography has so far been primarily restricted to adult skeletal remains (exceptions include Konigsberg and Holman 1999, Gowland and Chamberlain 2002, Millard and Gowland in press). This study explores the importance of Bayes' theorem for ageing perinatal skeletal remains from long bone length measurements and outlines a Bayesian technique for age estimation. When approaching

archaeological samples from a demographic perspective, the ultimate goal is to determine the spread of ages responsible for the spread of skeletal indicator states in the entire sample, rather than to make accurate estimates of each skeleton's age at death. This method, therefore, focuses on ascertaining the distribution of gestational ages for an entire population sample.

**Method**

It was first necessary to collate long bone length data from infants of known gestational ages. Infants may be born at the same gestational age but be different sizes, just as babies of the same size may be different gestational ages. In order to take into account this variation, a complete distribution of the known ages and long bone lengths for each major long bone is required. These data may be summarised in the form of contingency tables that show the spread of long bone lengths for various gestational ages. Table 1 below shows the clinical data obtained for the diaphyseal lengths of the femur. Bone lengths were aggregated into categories separated by 5mm, and gestational ages were aggregated into intervals of two weeks.

The data for each table were obtained from the known age and long bone length data provided by Maresh and Deming (1939), Maresh (1955), Fazekas and Kosa (1978), Jeanty *et al.* (1981, 1982) and Scheuer *et al.* (1980) (NB only the BCH data were available from Scheuer *et al*'s study). This known age data was obtained using different techniques (e.g. radiography, ultrasound), and on a mixture of living foetuses, live births, still-births and perinatal deaths. Despite this, a close correspondence existed between the results of different studies. Any error that may be incurred through the use of data derived from different methods, it is argued, will be largely subsumed within the chosen long bone length categories of 5mm. It was necessary to use known age data from several studies because no single method had a representative number of individuals for each age category, and only the Maresh and Deming (1939) and Maresh (1955) data provided long bone measurements for infants in the immediately postnatal period. It should be noted that ultrasound femur lengths were not included in the contingency table for this particular long bone as the measurement differed anatomically from that of the other techniques. Furthermore, the Scheuer *et al.* (1980) data were not included in the tables for the tibia or ulna, as the known ages for these long bones were not published in their study.

The contingency tables of gestational ages and long bone lengths in known age individuals provide sufficient information to calculate the probability of age given length, which may in turn be used to estimate gestational age in the archaeological samples. From Table 1, however, it can be seen that there are not equal numbers of individuals in each age category, which will influence the calculation of probabilities of age given long bone length. We address this problem by applying Bayes' theorem, using a non-parametric approach. A strict implementation of Bayesian

**Long Bone Length (mm)**

| Gest.Age (wks) | 15- | 20- | 25- | 30- | 35- | 40- | 45- | 50- | 55- | 60- | 65- | 70- | 75- | 80- | 85- | 90- | 95- | Total |
|---|---|---|---|---|---|---|---|---|---|---|---|---|---|---|---|---|---|---|
| 16 | 3 | 6 | | | | | | | | | | | | | | | | 9 |
| 18 | | 3 | 10 | 2 | | | | | | | | | | | | | | 15 |
| 20 | | | 1 | 10 | 2 | | | | | | | | | | | | | 13 |
| 22 | | | | 4 | 7 | | | | | | | | | | | | | 11 |
| 24 | | | | | 7 | 5 | 1 | | | | | | | | | | | 13 |
| 26 | | | | | 2 | 6 | 5 | 1 | | | | | | | | | | 14 |
| 28 | | | | | | 2 | 10 | | | | | | | | | | | 12 |
| 30 | | | | | | | 8 | 4 | 1 | | | | | | | | | 13 |
| 32 | | | | | | | | 2 | 6 | | 1 | | | | | | | 9 |
| 34 | | | | | | | | | 3 | 4 | 1 | | | | | | | 8 |
| 36 | | | | | | | | | | 4 | 2 | 2 | | | | | | 8 |
| 38 | | | | | | | | | | 1 | 2 | 6 | 2 | 2 | | | | 13 |
| 40 | | | | | | | | | | | 2 | 9 | 25 | 6 | | | | 42 |
| 42 | | | | | | | | | | | 2 | 7 | 18 | 14 | | | | 41 |
| 44 | | | | | | | | | | | | 3 | 14 | 18 | 5 | | | 40 |
| 46 | | | | | | | | | | | | | 4 | 20 | 35 | 14 | | 78 |
| 48 | | | | | | | | | | | | | | 1 | 7 | 10 | 15 | 33 |

**Table 1: Femur diaphyseal lengths of known age individuals. The cells in the table contain the number of individuals in the reference population with a given age and long bone length**

methods for continuous data requires advanced techniques of numerical analysis (Buck *et al.*, 1996), but for data in discrete categories the application of Bayes' theorem is simple and straightforward (Chamberlain, 2000, 2001). Bayes' theorem provides a formal inferential framework for updating prior beliefs in light of new evidence. The theorem states that one's *posterior belief* in an eventuality is equal to the *standardised likelihood* of *data* predicted by that eventuality multiplied by one's *prior belief* in the eventuality:

$$p(\theta|x) = \frac{p(x|\theta) \times p(\theta)}{p(x)}$$

Where $p(\theta|x)$ is the probability of eventuality $\theta$ given an item of data $x$, and $p(x|\theta)$ is the probability of data $x$ given eventuality $\theta$, and $p(x)$ = the sum of $[p(x|\theta) \times p(\theta)]$ across all values of $\theta$.

The problem of inferring age, given knowledge of the state of a skeletal indicator can be stated in terms of prior and posterior probabilities, as follows:

Equation (1):  $p(A_i|L_j) = \frac{p(L_j|A_i) \times p(A_i)}{p(L_j)}$

Where A = age and L = skeletal indicator (long bone length).

In the above equation, $p(A_i|L_j)$, represents the probability of being in age category $i$ given the particular indicator state $j$ and is referred to as the *posterior probability*, as it represents opinion that is revised in reference to the datum, after observing the indicator state represented by $L_j$. The probability of possessing a particular indicator state given age, shown in the equation as $p(L_j|A_i)$, is referred to as the *likelihood*, as it is the conditional probability of possessing indicator state $j$ given a particular age category $i$. The overall probability of possessing a particular indicator state is

represented by $p(L_j)$, calculated as the sum of $[p(L_j|A_i) \times p(A_i)]$ over all categories of A. The term $p(A_i)$ is referred to as the *prior probability* because it represents an opinion of the probability of being in $A_i$ before any data has been observed (Phillips, 1973).

There are several alternative prior probabilities of age that we may assume. We may use the reference sample as our choice of prior probability, as Aykroyd *et al.* (1999) did in their study of age estimation from dental observations. We have, however, already stated the problems encountered when using the reference sample as a source of prior probabilities of age when there are not equal numbers of individuals in each age category, so this choice may be eliminated. In the absence of any prior information concerning the age structure of our archaeological population, we may assume a uniform prior probability of age at death. By doing so we are assuming that there is an equal probability of death across all age categories (this is analogous, for example, to the assumption that on rolling an unbiased die all numbers are equally probable). Equation (1) then becomes:

$$p(A_i|L_j) = \frac{p(L_j|A_i)}{\sum p(L_j|A_i)}$$

Where the denominator $\sum p(L_j|A_i)$ represents the sum of the probabilities of a particular length given age across all age categories.

Table 2 represents the posterior probability distribution for the femur when a uniform prior probability of death has been assumed[*]. By using a uniform prior probability distribution it is possible to obtain an age distribution which is independent of the age structure of the reference series. This probability distribution of age given long bone length

---

[*] Posterior probability distributions based on uniform priors for all other long bones are presented in the appendix.

**Long bone length (mm)**

| Gest.Age (wks) | 15- | 20- | 25- | 30- | 35- | 40- | 45- | 50- | 55- | 60- | 65- | 70- | 75- | 80- | 85- | 90- | 95- |
|---|---|---|---|---|---|---|---|---|---|---|---|---|---|---|---|---|---|
| 16 | 1.00 | 0.77 | | | | | | | | | | | | | | | |
| 18 | | 0.23 | 0.90 | 0.11 | | | | | | | | | | | | | |
| 20 | | | 0.10 | 0.61 | 0.10 | | | | | | | | | | | | |
| 22 | | | | 0.29 | 0.43 | | | | | | | | | | | | |
| 24 | | | | | 0.37 | 0.39 | | | | | | | | | | | |
| 26 | | | | | 0.10 | 0.44 | 0.19 | 0.12 | | | | | | | | | |
| 28 | | | | | | 0.17 | 0.44 | 0.00 | | | | | | | | | |
| 30 | | | | | | | 0.33 | 0.51 | 0.07 | | | | | | | | |
| 32 | | | | | | | | 0.37 | 0.60 | | 0.15 | | | | | | |
| 34 | | | | | | | | | 0.34 | 0.46 | 0.17 | 0.00 | | | | | |
| 36 | | | | | | | | | 0.00 | 0.46 | 0.34 | 0.21 | | | | | |
| 38 | | | | | | | | | | 0.07 | 0.21 | 0.39 | 0.09 | 0.10 | | | |
| 40 | | | | | | | | | | | 0.06 | 0.18 | 0.37 | 0.09 | | | |
| 42 | | | | | | | | | | | 0.07 | 0.15 | 0.27 | 0.22 | | | |
| 44 | | | | | | | | | | | | 0.06 | 0.22 | 0.29 | 0.14 | | |
| 46 | | | | | | | | | | | | | 0.03 | 0.17 | 0.53 | 0.30 | |
| 48 | | | | | | | | | | | | | 0.02 | 0.13 | 0.33 | 0.70 | 1.00 |

**Table 2: Posterior probabilities of age given femur length, assuming uniform prior probabilities of age.**

may then be used to obtain the age distribution of the perinatal sample from the archaeological sites by matrix mulitplying the distribution of long bone lengths by the probability distribution.

**Model Prior Probabilities**

In reality, natural populations rarely have a constant probability of death across age categories, and this is particularly true of the perinatal period. Assuming uniform prior probabilities across all age groups, although necessary when no prior knowledge concerning the data is available, may not, therefore, always be the most appropriate procedure. Another way of obtaining a prior age distribution

that is independent of the age structure of the reference sample, is to use model prior probabilities (Chamberlain, 2001). These incorporate prior knowledge concerning the differential risks of mortality with each gestational age from an appropriate model life table based on natural patterns of mortality. For the purposes of this study, the natural mortality distribution of perinatal infants was obtained from a life table produced from the 1958 British perinatal mortality survey (Butler and Alberman, 1969). This study was chosen because it presents gestational age at death data for almost 17 000 births in a format appropriate for this study. These data (Figure 3) were then used to generate model prior probabilities for each gestational age category.

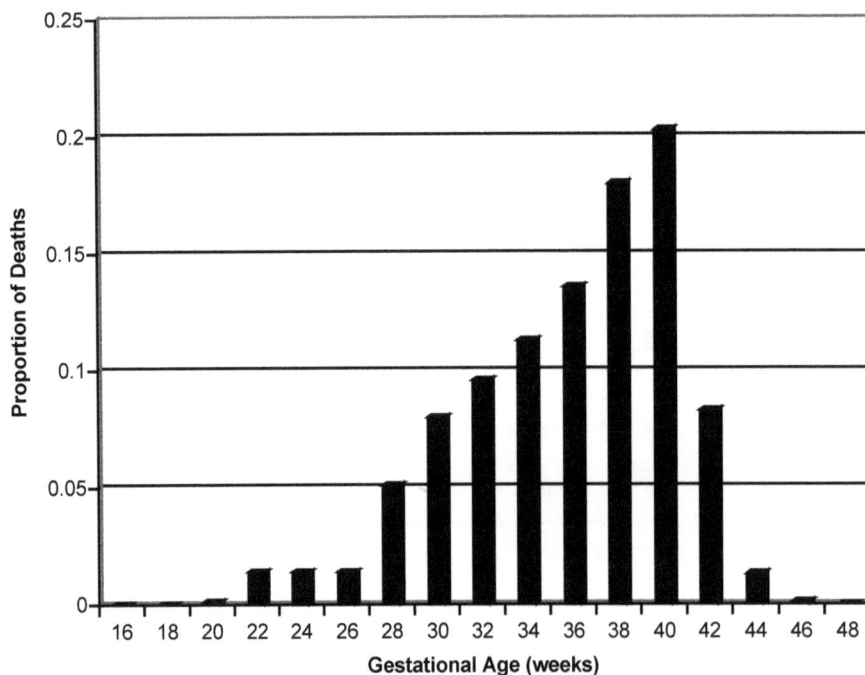

**Figure 3: The proportions of perinatal deaths at each gestational age, based on survival records from the 1958 British perinatal mortality survey (Butler and Alberman, 1969).**

**Long bone length (mm)**

| Gest. Age (wks) | 15- | 20- | 25- | 30- | 35- | 40- | 45- | 50- | 55- | 60- | 65- | 70- | 75- | 80- | 85- | 90- |
|---|---|---|---|---|---|---|---|---|---|---|---|---|---|---|---|---|
| 16 | 1 | 0.69 | | | | | | | | | | | | | | |
| 18 | | 0.31 | 0.84 | 0.01 | | | | | | | | | | | | |
| 20 | | | 0.16 | 0.1 | 0.01 | | | | | | | | | | | |
| 22 | | | | 0.89 | 0.48 | | | | | | | | | | | |
| 24 | | | | | 0.41 | 0.27 | 0.01 | | | | | | | | | |
| 26 | | | | | 0.11 | 0.3 | 0.05 | 0.02 | | | | | | | | |
| 28 | | | | | | 0.42 | 0.43 | | | | | | | | | |
| 30 | | | | | | | 0.5 | 0.53 | 0.05 | | | | | | | |
| 32 | | | | | | | | 0.45 | 0.57 | | 0.11 | | | | | |
| 34 | | | | | | | | | 0.38 | 0.41 | 0.14 | | | | | |
| 36 | | | | | | | | | | 0.49 | 0.34 | 0.19 | | | | |
| 38 | | | | | | | | | | 0.1 | 0.28 | 0.47 | 0.15 | 0.3 | | |
| 40 | | | | | | | | | | | 0.1 | 0.25 | 0.64 | 0.31 | | |
| 42 | | | | | | | | | | | 0.04 | 0.08 | 0.19 | 0.31 | | |
| 44 | | | | | | | | | | | | 0.01 | 0.03 | 0.07 | 0.62 | |
| 46 | | | | | | | | | | | | | | 0.01 | 0.32 | 0.55 |
| 48 | | | | | | | | | | | | | | | 0.07 | 0.45 |

**Table 3: Posterior probability of age given femur length assuming model prior probabilities of age.**

It could be argued that perinatal mortality in a modern western population is likely to differ substantially from that experienced by an ancient population. However, a comparative study of perinatal mortality in socially advantaged and disadvantaged groups in the USA has shown that while the overall mortality rates were much higher in the disadvantaged group, the *distribution* of mortality in relation to gestational age was similar in the two groups (Allen *et al.*, 2000). The model prior probabilities in this study are based on the relative age distribution of mortality, not the absolute level of mortality, and we therefore feel justified in deriving these data from a modern population. Once the model prior probabilities have been obtained, the probability of age given long bone length can then be determined using the following equation:

$$p(A_i|L_j) \quad = \quad \frac{p(L_j|A_i) \times p^*(A_i)}{\sum [p(L_j|A_i) \times p^*(A_i)]}$$

Where $p^*(A_i)$ refers to the prior probability obtained from the model life table for that particular age category. Application of the model prior probabilities to our clinical data, using the Bayesian equation shown earlier allows us to obtain a table of posterior probabilities (Table 3) which may then be used to age an archaeological sample without those biases discussed previously*.

**Application to an Archaeological Sample**

Both the uniform and model probability distributions were applied to an archaeological sample of perinates excavated from Romano-British cemetery and settlement sites (Figure 4). The age distribution generated using the uniform prior probability table is a broader distribution with a greater number of individuals in the older gestational age groups. This illustrates the effect that inclusion of known age data from the immediately post-natal period has on the age

distribution obtained. Neither the uniform nor the model prior probabilities show such a strong central tendency at full term that is evident with the Scheuer *et al.* (1980) method. This is particularly striking in view of the fact that the model prior actually incorporated a higher probability of death at full term, in accordance with the perinatal mortality survey data. The age distributions generated by the different methods were compared using the Kolmogorov-Smirnoff statistical test. This showed that there is a statistically significant difference between the age distributions obtained from the model priors and the Scheuer *et al.* (1980) method (Dmax$_{obs}$=0.367, Dmax$_{0.05}$=0.114) and between the uniform priors and the Scheuer *et al.* (1980) method (Dmax$_{obs}$=0.432, Dmax$_{0.05}$=0.114).

It can be seen that when the influence of the age distribution of the reference sample is removed through the use of uniform probabilities, a much flatter distribution is obtained, showing no distinct peak at full term and a greater degree of dispersion. There is also a significant increase in the number of individuals within the older gestational age categories (those of 42 weeks and above). When model prior probabilities are assumed, despite the probability of mortality being significantly higher between weeks 36-40, the central tendency is still less than that observed using the Scheuer *et al.* (1980) method. The mode of the distribution obtained using the model prior probabilities has also shifted to the right by one age category (2 weeks) in comparison to that obtained from the Scheuer *et al.* (1980) method.

## Conclusion

We have demonstrated that the use of the regression methods for estimating perinatal gestational age generates an artificially narrow age distribution. This study has shown that through the use of a large sample of known age individuals and the assumption of realistic prior probabilities, this bias

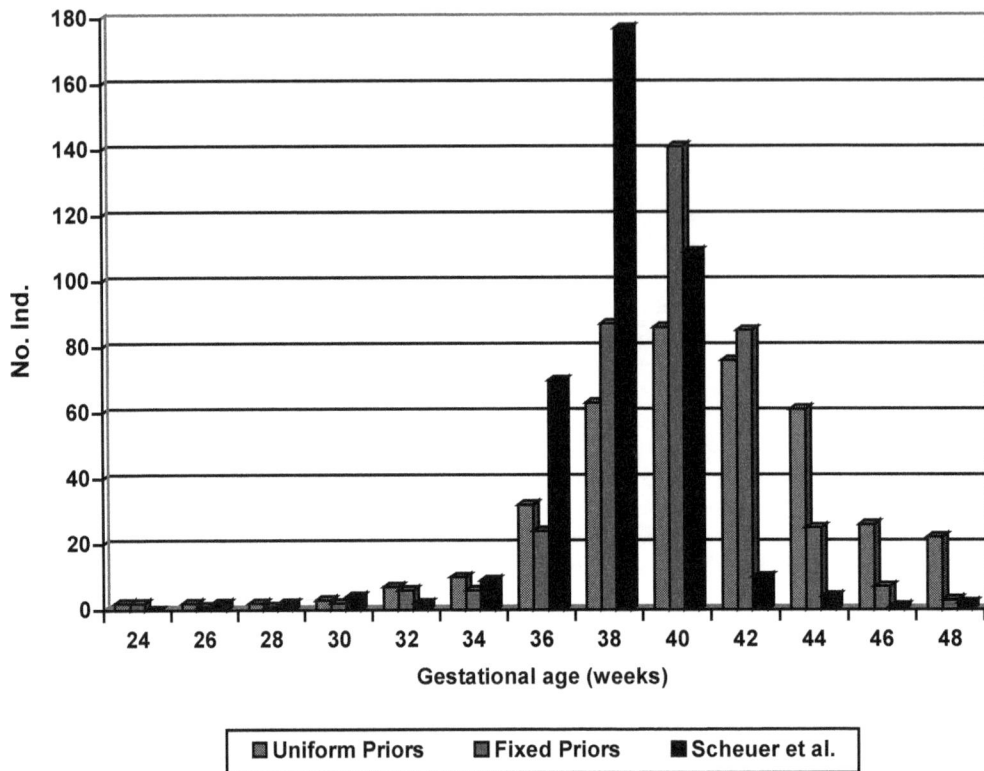

**Figure 4. Application of the uniform and model priors to an archaeological sample of perinatal skeletons from Romano-British cemetery and settlement sites.**

may be removed and a more reliable representation of the age distribution of the archaeological sample obtained. We have previously shown that traditional methods of estimating age at death in adult skeletons are affected by reference population bias, and that this bias can be removed through adopting Bayesian estimation methods (Chamberlain, 2000). This study has implications not only for the estimation of age at death of archaeological skeletal remains, but also for obstetrical studies of foetal growth. The application of Bayesian statistics to the field of obstetrical ultrasound has yet to be conducted and yet this method could present an important breakthough both in the identification of foetal growth anomalies and in the more reliable estimation of birth dates. It is evident that anthropological methods for estimating sub adult age at death are potentially susceptible to reference population bias, leading, in some instances, to incorrect interpretations of mortality patterns in past populations.

## Acknowledgments

We are grateful to many museum workers and archaeologists for facilitating access to skeletal material and for providing information about sites. We also thank Dr Andrew Millard for useful comments on an earlier draft of this paper. Rebecca Gowland acknowledges the support of the Natural Environment Research Council and the Arts and Humanities Research Board.

## References

Allen, M.C., Alexander, G.R., Tompkins, M.E., and Hulsey, T.C. 2000. Racial differences in temporal changes in newborn vitality and survival by gestational age. *Paediatric and Perinatal Epidemiology* **14**, 152-158.

Aykroyd, R. G., Lucy, D., Pollard, A. M., and Solheim, T. (1997). Technical note: Regression analysis in adult age estimation. *American Journal of Physical Anthropology* **104**, 259-265.

Aykroyd, R. G., Lucy, D., Pollard, A. M., and Roberts, C. A. (1999). Nasty, brutish, but not necessarily short: a reconsideration of the statistical methods used to calculate age at death from adult human skeletal and dental age indicators. *American Antiquity* **64**, 55-70.

Bocquet-Appel, J-P., and Masset, C. (1982). Farewell to palaeodemography. *Journal of Human Evolution* **11**, 321-333.

Bocquet-Appel, J. P., and Masset, C. (1985). Palaeodemography: resurrection or ghost? *Journal of Human Evolution* **14**, 107-111.

Bocquet-Appel, J. P., and Masset, C. (1996). Palaeodemography: expectancy and false hope. *American Journal of Physical Anthropology*, **99**, 571-584.

Buck, C. E., Cavanagh, W. G., and Litton, C. D. (1996). *Bayesian Approach to Interpreting Archaeological Data*. Chichester: John Wiley and Sons.

Butler, N. R., and Alberman, E. D. 1969. *Perinatal Problems*. Edinburgh: Livingstone.

Chamberlain, A. T. 2000. Problems and prospects in palaeodemography. In (M. Cox and S. Mays, Eds). *Human Osteology in Archaeology and Forensic Science*. London: Greenwich Medical Media, pp. 101-115.

Chamberlain, A. T. 2001. Palaeodemography. In (D. R. Brothwell and A. M. Pollard, Eds). *Handbook of Archaeological Sciences*. Chichester: Wiley, pp. 259-268.

Fazekas, I. Gy. and Kosa, F. 1978. *Forensic Fetal Osteology*. Budapest: Akademiai Kiado.

Gelman, A., Carlin, J. B., Stern, H. S., and Rubin, D. B. (1995). *Bayesian Data Analysis*. London: Chapman and Hall.

Gowland, R. L. and Chamberlain, A. T. 2002. A Bayesian approach to ageing perinatal skeletal material from archaeological sites: implications for the evidence for infanticide in Roman Britain. *Journal of Archaeological Science*, **29**, 677-685.

Grayson, D. A. (1998). The frequentist façade and the flight from evidential inference. *British Journal of Psychology*, **89**, 325-345.

Hadlock, F. P., Harrist, R. B., and Deter, R. L. (1982). Fetal femur length as a predictor of menstrual age: sonographically measured. *American Journal of Radiology*, **138**, 875-878.

Hohler, C. W. (1984). Ultrasound estimation of gestational age. *Clinical Obstetrics and Gynaecology*, **141**, 759-762.

Hoppa, R. D. and Vaupel, J. W. 2002. The Rockstock Manifesto for paleodemography: the way from age to stage. In Hoppa, R. D. and Vaupel, J. W. (eds), *Paleodemography: Age Distributions from Skeletal Samples*. Cambridge: Cambridge University Press, pp. 1-8.

Howell, N. (1982). Village composition implied by a palaeodemographic life table: the Libben site. *American Journal of Physical Anthropology*, **59**, 263-269.

Humphrey, L. T. (2000). Growth studies of past populations: an overview and an example. In Cox, M. and Mays, S. (eds.) *Human Osteology in Archaeology and Forensic Science*. London: Greenwich Medical Media, pp. 23-38.

Jeanty, P. Dramaix-Wilmet, M., van Kerkem, J., and Schwers, J. (1982). Ultrasonic evaluation of fetal limb growth. Part I. *Radiology* **143**, 751-754.

Jeanty, P., Kirkpatrick, C., Dramaix-Wilmet, D., and Struyven, J. (1981). Ultrasonic evaluation of fetal limb growth. Part II. *Radiology* **140**, 165-168.

Jeanty, P., and Romero, R. (1984). *Obstetrical Ultrasound*. London: McGraw Hill.

Johnston, F. E. (1986). Somatic growth of the infant and preschool child. In Falkner, F. and Tanner, J. M. (eds.), *Human Growth*, Vol 2. New York: Plenum Press, pp. 3-24.

King, S. E. and Ulijaszek, S. J. (1999). Invisible insults during growth and development. In Hoppa, R. D. and Fitzgerald, C. M. (eds.), *Human Growth in the Past*. Cambridge: Cambridge University Press, pp. 161-182.

Konigsberg, L. W., and Frankenberg, S. R. (1992). Estimation of age structure in anthropological demography. *American Journal of Physical Anthropology* **89**, 235-256.

Konigsberg, L. W., and Frankenberg, S. R. (1994). Palaeodemography: "Not quite dead". *Evolutionary Anthropology* **3**, 92-105.

Konigsberg, L. W., Frankenberg, S. R., and Walker, R. B. (1997). Regress what on what?: Palaeodemographic age estimation as a calibration problem. In (R. R. Paine, Ed) *Integrating Archaeological Demography: Multidisciplinary Approaches to Prehistoric Populations*. Center for Archaeological Investigations, Southern Illinois University, Carbondale: Occasional Paper No. 24., pp. 64-88.

Konigsberg, L. W. and Holman, D. 1999. Estimation of age at death from dental emergence and implications for studies of prehistoric somatic growth. In R. D. Hoppa and C. M. Fitzgerald, (eds) *Human Growth in the Past*. Cambridge: Cambridge University Press, pp. 264-289.

Lucy, D. (1997). *Human Age Estimation from Skeletal and Dental Evidence*. Ph.D. Thesis, University of Bradford.

Lucy, D., Aykroyd, R. G., Pollard, A. M., and Solheim, T. (1996). A Bayesian approach to adult human age estimation from dental observations by Johanson's age changes. *Journal of Forensic Sciences* **41**, 189-194.

Maresh, M. M. (1955). Linear growth from long bones of extremities from infancy through adolescence. *American Journal of Diseases in Childhood*, **89**, 725-742.

Maresh, M. M. and Deming, J. (1939). The growth of long bones in 80 infants. *Child Development* **10**, 91-100.

Mays, S. A. (1993). Infanticide in Roman Britain. *Antiquity* **67**, 883-888.

Mendez, H. (1985). Introduction to the study of pre- and postnatal growth in humans: A review. *American Journal of Medical Genetics*, **20**, 63-85.

Mutale, T. Creed, F., Maresh, M. and Hunt, L. (1991). Life events and low birthweight- analysis by infants preterm and small for gestational age. *British Journal Of Obstetrics and Gynaecology*, **98**, 166-172.

O'Brien, G. D. and Queenan, J. T. (1981). Growth of the ultrasound fetal femur length during normal pregnancy. Part 1. *American Journal of Obstetrics and Gynecology*, **141**, 833-837.

O'Brien, G. D., Queenan, J. T. and Campbell, S. (1981). Assessment of gestational age in the second trimester by real-time ultrasound measurement of femur length. *American Journal of Obstetrics and Gynecology*, **139**, 540-545.

Owsley, D. W., and Jantz, R. L. (1985). Long bone lengths and gestational age distributions of post-contact Arikara Indian perinatal infant skeletons. *American Journal of Physical Anthropology* **68**, 321-328.

Phillips, L. D. (1973). *Bayesian Statistics for Social Scientists*. London: Nelson.

Roberts, D. F. (1986). The genetics of human fetal growth. In Falkner, F. and Tanner, J. M. (eds.), *Human Growth. Vol. 3*. New York: Plenum Press, pp. 113-143.

Saunders, S. R. (2000). Subadult skeletons and growth-related studies. In (M.A. Katzenberg and S.R. Saunders, Eds) *Biological Anthropology of the Human Skeleton*. New York: Wiley-Liss, pp. 135-161.

Scheuer, J. L., Musgrave, J. H., and Evans, S. P. (1980). The estimation of late fetal and perinatal age from limb bone length by linear and logarithmic regression. *Annals of Human Biology* **7**, 257-265.

Smith, P. and Kahila, G. (1992). Identification of infanticide in archaeological sites: a case study from the late Roman-early Byzantine periods at Ashkelon, Israel. *Journal of Archaeological Science*, **19**, 667-675.

Tanner, J. M. (1974). Variation in growth and maturity of newborns. In Lewis, M. and Rosenblum, L. A. (eds.), *The Effect of the Infant on its Caregiver*. New York; London: Wiley-Interscience, pp. 77-103.

Ubelaker, D. H. (1989)a. *Human Skeletal Remains*, 2nd edition. Washington, D. C.: Taraxacum.

Ubelaker, D. H. (1989)b. The estimation of age at death from immature human bone. In (M. Y. Iscan, Ed). *Age Markers in the Human Skeleton*. Springfield, Illinois: C. C. Thomas, pp.55-70.

Yeh, M-N., Bracero, L., Reilly, K. B., Murtha, L., Aboulafia, M. and Barron, B. A. (1982). Ultrasonic measurement of the femur length as an index of fetal gestational age. *American Journal of Obstetric Gynecology*, **144**, 519-522.

# Appendix: Posterior Probability Tables

## Long bone length (mm)

| GEST. AGE (WKS) | 15- | 20- | 25- | 30- | 35- | 40- | 45- | 50- | 55- | 60- | 65- | 70- | 75- | 80- |
|---|---|---|---|---|---|---|---|---|---|---|---|---|---|---|
| 16 | 0.89 | 0.21 | | 0.05 | | | | | | | | | | |
| 18 | 0.11 | 0.64 | 0.24 | | | | | | | | | | | |
| 20 | | 0.15 | 0.57 | 0.19 | | | | | | | | | | |
| 22 | | | 0.19 | 0.43 | 0.21 | | | | | | | | | |
| 24 | | | | 0.29 | 0.32 | 0.16 | | | | | | | | |
| 26 | | | | | 0.37 | 0.2 | 0.13 | 0.05 | | | | | | |
| 28 | | | 0.03 | | 0.1 | 0.36 | 0.11 | 0.07 | | | | | | |
| 30 | | | | | | 0.24 | 0.25 | 0.15 | 0.06 | | | | | |
| 32 | | | | | | 0.04 | 0.38 | 0.2 | 0.09 | 0.03 | | | | |
| 34 | | | | | | | 0.05 | 0.25 | 0.28 | 0.06 | | | | |
| 36 | | | | | | | 0.08 | 0.19 | 0.24 | 0.13 | | | | |
| 38 | | | | | | | | 0.08 | 0.19 | 0.21 | 0.11 | | | |
| 40 | | | | | | | | | 0.03 | 0.31 | 0.17 | | | |
| 42 | | | | | | | | | 0.11 | 0.15 | 0.25 | 0.06 | | |
| 44 | | | | | | | | | | 0.07 | 0.2 | 0.23 | 0.31 | |
| 46 | | | | | | | | | | 0.03 | 0.11 | 0.37 | 0.3 | 0.31 |
| 48 | | | | | | | | | | | 0.16 | 0.34 | 0.4 | 0.69 |

**Table A1: Posterior probabilities of age given tibia length, assuming uniform prior probabilities of age.**

## Long bone length (mm)

| GEST AGE (WKS) | 15- | 20- | 25- | 30- | 35- | 40- | 45- | 50- | 55- | 60- | 65- | 70- | 75- | 80- |
|---|---|---|---|---|---|---|---|---|---|---|---|---|---|---|
| 16 | 0.76 | 0.7 | | | | | | | | | | | | |
| 18 | 0.24 | 0.25 | 0.52 | 0.04 | | | | | | | | | | |
| 20 | | 0.05 | 0.48 | 0.25 | 0.07 | 0.07 | | | | | | | | |
| 22 | | | | 0.7 | 0.23 | 0.07 | | | | | | | | |
| 24 | | | | | 0.5 | 0.2 | 0.07 | | | | | | | |
| 26 | | | | | 0.17 | 0.28 | 0.17 | 0.08 | 0.03 | | | | | |
| 28 | | | | | | 0.25 | 0.35 | 0.11 | | | | | | |
| 30 | | | | | 0.03 | 0.14 | 0.27 | 0.18 | 0.06 | | | | | |
| 32 | | | | | | | 0.1 | 0.26 | 0.17 | 0.05 | | | | |
| 34 | | | | | | | | 0.26 | 0.17 | 0.09 | 0.02 | | | |
| 36 | | | | | | | 0.04 | 0.11 | 0.24 | 0.17 | | | | |
| 38 | | | | | | | | | 0.28 | 0.26 | | | | |
| 40 | | | | | | | | | 0.02 | 0.25 | 0.25 | 0.01 | | |
| 42 | | | | | | | | | 0.03 | 0.11 | 0.32 | 0.09 | 0.02 | |
| 44 | | | | | | | | | | 0.03 | 0.24 | 0.27 | 0.14 | |
| 46 | | | | | | | | | | 0.02 | 0.1 | 0.36 | 0.31 | |
| 48 | | | | | | | | | | 0.02 | 0.07 | 0.26 | 0.53 | 1 |

**Table A2: Posterior probabilities of age given humerus length, assuming uniform prior probabilities of age.**

**Long bone length (mm)**

| GEST. AGE (WKS) | 15- | 20- | 25- | 30- | 35- | 40- | 45- | 50- | 55- | 60- | 65- |
|---|---|---|---|---|---|---|---|---|---|---|---|
| 16 | 0.95 | 0.15 | | | | | | | | | |
| 18 | 0.05 | 0.85 | 0.05 | | | | | | | | |
| 20 | | | 0.49 | 0.03 | | | | | | | |
| 22 | | | 0.37 | 0.17 | | | | | | | |
| 24 | | | 0.09 | 0.34 | 0.11 | | | | | | |
| 26 | | | | 0.36 | 0.2 | | | | | | |
| 28 | | | | 0.07 | 0.39 | 0.06 | | | | | |
| 30 | | | | | 0.24 | 0.23 | 0.04 | 0.01 | | | |
| 32 | | | | | 0.06 | 0.25 | 0.09 | 0.06 | | 0.06 | |
| 34 | | | | | | 0.33 | 0.17 | | | | |
| 36 | | | | | | 0.07 | 0.3 | 0.08 | 0.04 | | |
| 38 | | | | | | | 0.24 | 0.15 | 0.06 | | |
| 40 | | | | | | | 0.07 | 0.25 | 0.07 | | |
| 42 | | | | | | | 0.05 | 0.19 | 0.16 | | |
| 44 | | | | | | | | 0.16 | 0.21 | 0.08 | |
| 46 | | | | | | | | 0.05 | 0.27 | 0.31 | 1 |
| 48 | | | | | | | | | 0.2 | 0.52 | |

**Table A3: Posterior probabilities of age given radius length, assuming uniform prior probabilities of age.**

## Long bone length (mm)

| GEST AGE (WKS) | 15- | 20- | 25- | 30- | 35- | 40- | 45- | 50- | 55- | 60- | 65- | 70- |
|---|---|---|---|---|---|---|---|---|---|---|---|---|
| 14 | 0.47 | | | | | | | | | | | |
| 16 | 0.3 | 0.2 | 0.05 | | | | | | | | | |
| 18 | 0.23 | 0.26 | 0.05 | 0.02 | | 0.03 | | | | | | |
| 20 | | 0.41 | 0.27 | | | | | | | | | |
| 22 | | 0.13 | 0.39 | 0.11 | | | | | | | | |
| 24 | | | 0.24 | 0.3 | 0.08 | | | | | | | |
| 26 | | | | 0.38 | 0.2 | 0.04 | | | | | | |
| 28 | | | | 0.16 | 0.31 | 0.15 | | | | | | |
| 30 | | | | | 0.25 | 0.22 | 0.13 | | | | | |
| 32 | | | | | 0.07 | 0.32 | 0.18 | 0.03 | | | | |
| 34 | | | | | 0.09 | 0.14 | 0.3 | 0.08 | | | | |
| 36 | | | | | | 0.09 | 0.22 | 0.26 | 0.12 | | | |
| 38 | | | | | | | 0.14 | 0.45 | 0.15 | | | |
| 40 | | | | | | | 0.04 | 0.13 | 0.25 | 0.23 | | |
| 42 | | | | | | | | 0.05 | 0.29 | 0.19 | 0.14 | |
| 44 | | | | | | | | | 0.19 | 0.28 | 0.15 | |
| 46 | | | | | | | | | 0.01 | 0.2 | 0.36 | 0.19 |
| 48 | | | | | | | | | | 0.1 | 0.35 | 0.81 |

**Table A4: Posterior probabilities of age given ulna length, assuming uniform prior probabilities of age.**

## Long bone length (mm)

| GEST AGE (WKS)) | 15- | 20- | 25- | 30- | 35- | 40- | 45- | 50- | 55- | 60- | 65- | 70- | 75- | 80- |
|---|---|---|---|---|---|---|---|---|---|---|---|---|---|---|
| 16 | 0.89 | 0.21 | | | | | | | | | | | | |
| 18 | 0.11 | 0.64 | | | | | | | | | | | | |
| 20 | | 0.15 | 0.01 | | | | | | | | | | | |
| 22 | | | 0.99 | 0.58 | 0.21 | | | | | | | | | |
| 24 | | | | 0.38 | 0.33 | 0.15 | | | | | | | | |
| 26 | | | | | 0.37 | 0.19 | 0.09 | 0.03 | | | | | | |
| 28 | | | | 0.04 | 0.09 | 0.31 | 0.07 | 0.04 | | 0.006 | | | | |
| 30 | | | | | | 0.29 | 0.21 | 0.11 | 0.03 | | | | | |
| 32 | | | | | | 0.06 | 0.47 | 0.21 | 0.06 | 0.017 | | | | |
| 34 | | | | | | | 0.05 | 0.19 | 0.15 | 0.024 | | | | |
| 36 | | | | | | | 0.11 | 0.24 | 0.22 | 0.087 | | | | |
| 38 | | | | | | | | 0.19 | 0.34 | 0.272 | 0.21 | | | |
| 40 | | | | | | | | | 0.06 | 0.442 | 0.37 | 0.34 | | |
| 42 | | | | | | | | | 0.14 | 0.135 | 0.34 | 0.28 | | |
| 44 | | | | | | | | | | 0.017 | 0.07 | 0.3 | 0.86 | |
| 46 | | | | | | | | | | | | 0.06 | 0.1 | 0.57 |
| 48 | | | | | | | | | | | | 0.02 | 0.04 | 0.43 |

**Table A5: Probability of age given tibia length, assuming a model prior probability of age.**

**Long bone length (mm)**

| GEST AGE (WKS) | 15- | 20- | 25- | 30- | 35- | 40- | 45- | 50- | 55- | 60- | 65- | 70- | 75- |
|---|---|---|---|---|---|---|---|---|---|---|---|---|---|
| 16 | 0.76 | 0.7 | | | | | | | | | | | |
| 18 | 0.24 | 0.25 | 0.52 | | | | | | | | | | |
| 20 | | 0.05 | 0.48 | | | | | | | | | | |
| 22 | | | | 1 | 0.25 | 0.07 | | | | | | | |
| 24 | | | | | 0.53 | 0.21 | 0.06 | | | | | | |
| 26 | | | | | 0.18 | 0.29 | 0.15 | 0.05 | 0.01 | | | | |
| 28 | | | | | | 0.25 | 0.28 | 0.07 | | | | | |
| 30 | | | | | 0.04 | 0.18 | 0.29 | 0.15 | 0.03 | | | | |
| 32 | | | | | | | 0.15 | 0.33 | 0.12 | 0.03 | | | |
| 34 | | | | | | | | 0.24 | 0.09 | 0.04 | 0.01 | | |
| 36 | | | | | | | 0.07 | 0.16 | 0.2 | 0.12 | | | |
| 38 | | | | | | | | | 0.47 | 0.34 | | | |
| 40 | | | | | | | | | 0.05 | 0.37 | 0.51 | 0.118 | |
| 42 | | | | | | | | | 0.03 | 0.1 | 0.4 | 0.457 | 0.31 |
| 44 | | | | | | | | | | 0.01 | 0.08 | 0.353 | 0.48 |
| 46 | | | | | | | | | | | | 0.058 | 0.13 |
| 48 | | | | | | | | | | | | 0.014 | 0.08 |

**Table A6: Probability of age given humerus length, assuming a model prior probability of age.**

**Long bone length (mm)**

| GEST AGE (WKS) | 15- | 20- | 25- | 30- | 35- | 40- | 45- | 50- | 55- | 60- | 65- |
|---|---|---|---|---|---|---|---|---|---|---|---|
| 16 | 0.95 | 0.15 | | | | | | | | | |
| 18 | 0.05 | 0.85 | | | | | | | | | |
| 20 | | | | | | | | | | | |
| 22 | | | 0.79 | 0.18 | | | | | | | |
| 24 | | | 0.2 | 0.37 | 0.1 | 0.01 | | | | | |
| 26 | | | | 0.38 | 0.18 | 0.02 | | | | | |
| 28 | | | | 0.07 | 0.34 | 0.04 | 0.02 | | | | |
| 30 | | | | | 0.28 | 0.2 | 0.02 | 0.01 | | | |
| 32 | | | | | 0.1 | 0.31 | 0.06 | 0.04 | | 0.38 | |
| 34 | | | | | | 0.31 | 0.09 | | | | |
| 36 | | | | | | 0.11 | 0.25 | 0.06 | 0.06 | | |
| 38 | | | | | | | 0.39 | 0.23 | 0.18 | | |
| 40 | | | | | | | 0.13 | 0.43 | 0.25 | | |
| 42 | | | | | | | 0.05 | 0.19 | 0.36 | 0.26 | |
| 44 | | | | | | | | 0.04 | 0.13 | 0.21 | |
| 46 | | | | | | | | | 0.02 | 0.1 | 1 |
| 48 | | | | | | | | | | 0.05 | |

**Table A7: Probability of age given radius length, assuming a model prior probability of age.**

**Long bone length (mm)**

| GEST AGE (WKS) | 15- | 20- | 25- | 30- | 35- | 40- | 45- | 50- | 55- | 60- | 65- | 70- |
|---|---|---|---|---|---|---|---|---|---|---|---|---|
| 16 | 0.56 | | | | | | | | | | | |
| 18 | 0.44 | | | | | | | | | | | |
| 20 | | 0.01 | | | | | | | | | | |
| 22 | | 0.98 | 0.62 | 0.11 | | | | | | | | |
| 24 | | | 0.38 | 0.31 | 0.07 | | | | | | | |
| 26 | | | | 0.39 | 0.17 | 0.03 | | | | | | |
| 28 | | | | 0.16 | 0.26 | 0.1 | | | | | | |
| 30 | | | | 0.03 | 0.28 | 0.19 | 0.07 | | | | | |
| 32 | | | | | 0.12 | 0.41 | 0.15 | 0.02 | | 0.02 | | |
| 34 | | | | | 0.11 | 0.13 | 0.19 | 0.03 | | | | |
| 36 | | | | | | 0.14 | 0.22 | 0.16 | 0.08 | | | |
| 38 | | | | | | 0 | 0.27 | 0.56 | 0.2 | | | |
| 40 | | | | | | | 0.09 | 0.18 | 0.39 | 0.57 | | |
| 42 | | | | | | | | 0.04 | 0.28 | 0.29 | 0.72 | |
| 44 | | | | | | | | | 0.05 | 0.11 | 0.2 | |
| 46 | | | | | | | | | | 0.01 | 0.06 | 0.42 |
| 48 | | | | | | | | | | | 0.02 | 0.58 |

**Table A8: Probability of age given ulna length, assuming a model prior probability of age.**

# Phosphate redistribution within the fabric of 5 prehistoric pottery sherds from north Wales

David A. Jenkins and Andy Owen

School of Agricultural & Forest Sciences , University of Wales, Bangor, Deiniol Road , Bangor , Gwynedd , LL57 2UW.

## Abstract

Funerary and domestic sherds from Bronze to Iron Age sites in north Wales have been found to contain isotropic brown void infillings (cutans) reminiscent of phosphate-rich cutans in sediments underlying strata rich in bones. Thin-sections of 5 sherds were prepared for SEM/EDXRA studies and their cutans analysed for P, Fe, Al, Mn, Si, Ca and K. Phosphorus was found to be sporadically enriched in the Fe/Al/Mn-dominated cutans up to 500-fold above its crustal average, and up to 50% of the theoretical limit. This is interpreted as mobilisation of phosphate anions from bone material or food debris, and its translocation and adsorption by positively charged Fe/Al hydrous oxides within the sherd microfabric. The use of such analytical data for interpretation of pottery usage is considered.

## Introduction

Phosphorus is an element which is strongly concentrated within the biosphere and which is also subsequently immobilised within the environment. It is concentrated in biological systems through its crucial role in energy storage and distribution and because of its subsequent disposal in certain organisms as a waste product in the form of skeletal bone. It is immobilised because of the low solubility of various $Al/Fe^{3+}$ and Ca phosphates in low and high $pH$ environments respectively. This behaviour is discussed in the accompanying paper (Owen and Jenkins 2001) in the general context of its spatial distribution in acidic archaeological soils in which bone had been buried. Here the more specific instance is considered of the localised redistribution of phosphorus from bone material within the microfabric of funerary pottery from two Bronze Age sites in Anglesey and domestic pottery from an Iron Age settlement in Gwynedd.

This investigation derived from a study of phosphate-rich deposits underlying bone beds in a sedimentary sequence in the Palaeolithic hominid cave site of Pontnewydd, north east Wales (Green 1984). As part of a general environmental investigation of this important site, a micromorphological study of thin-sections from these deposits using polarised light microscopy identified the source of the phosphate as Ca/Fe/P-rich orange-brown isotropic cutans coating void surfaces (Jenkins 1994, 1997). However, it was noted that these cutans bore similarities to features that had been observed during an unrelated routine petrographic study of funerary and domestic pottery in North Wales to assess the provenance of component materials and to assist in their classification (Williams and Jenkins 1999). Whilst petrographic analysis is adequate for the identification of most minerals, for isotropic materials it needs to be supplemented by chemical analysis. It was therefore decided to test the hypothesis that the features observed in these sherd fabrics were similarly enriched in phosphorus, and establish whether this could provide another source of useful information in the study of archaeological pottery and the interpretation of its usage. Following a description of the ceramic materials investigated and the analytical methods employed, the results of microchemical analysis for P and associated elements in a number of cutanic features are presented and discussed.

### Sample choice and analytical methods

Notes on thin-sections prepared from over 100 sherds from archaeological sites ranging from the Neolithic to the Iron Age in north Wales were investigated for the occurrence of orange brown cutans and the relevant sections re-examined. In 45 instances where original material was still available,

| | PP1 | CM4 | CM5 | CM11 | BF2 |
|---|---|---|---|---|---|
| **Site** | Plas Penrhyn | Cae Mickney | Cae Mickney | Cae Mickney | Bush Farm |
| **Location** | Anglesey | Anglesey | Anglesey | Anglesey | Gwynedd |
| **Age** | Bronze Age | Bronze Age | Bronze Age | Bronze Age | Iron Age |
| **Pot type** | Funerary urn | Funerary urn | Funerary urn | Funerary urn | Domestic pot |
| Reference | 1 | 1 | 1 | 1 | 2 |
| **Total p (%)** | 0.53 | 0.13 | 0.46 | (no data) | (no data) |
| matrix % | 38.8 | 46.5 | 58.0 | 44.8 | 41.2 |
| grains % | 4.5 | 14.0 | 3.1 | 2.5 | 16.0 |
| grog % | <0.2 | <0.2 | 0.2 | 5.4 | <0.3 |
| clasts % | 50.7 | 33.1 | 34.7 | 29.8 | 29.1 |
| **voids %** | 5.7 | 6.2 | 3.7 | 17.1 | 13.7 |

Refs.1 -Williams and Jenkins (1999); 2- Jenkins and Williams in Longley and Johnstone(1998)
**Table 1: Some details of the sherds analysed**

59

| | Pot sherd cutan Analyses (n=89) Mean Range | | | Natural Fe/Al/Mn Deposits[1] (n=12) Range | | Average Crustal Abundance[2] |
|---|---|---|---|---|---|---|
| **P** | 3.1 | 0.1 - | 10.4 | 0.003[3] - | 0.01 | 0.1 |
| **Fe** | 23.9 | 0.1 - | 60.3 | 3.6 - | 63.6 | 5.4 |
| **Al** | 13.9 | 2.7 - | 26.5 | 4.6 - | 8.1 | 8.1 |
| **Mn** | 5.8 | <0.1 - | 14.5 | <0.1 - | 25.6 | 0.1 |
| **Si** | 9.3 | 2.8 - | 21.0 | <0.1 - | 6.7 | 28.2 |
| **K** | 2.0 | <0.1 - | 6.5 | <0.1 - | 0.6 | 2.1 |
| **Ca** | 2.1 | 0.5 - | 9.7 | <0.1 - | 3.0 | 4.1 |

N.B.[1] deposits comprised 3 iron pans from stagnopodzols (Hiraethog series) and 9 hydroelectric tunnel deposits (Waite, 1998)
N.B.[2] from Krauskopf and Bird 1995
N.B.[3] values for P obtained by colorimetric/FIA analysis
**Table 2: Overall composition (%) of cutanic material in sherds**

small portions of the sherds were also taken for total phosphorus analysis using the FIA procedure described by Owen *et al.* (1999). The values obtained ranged from 640-6140µg g[-1] with a mean value of 2520 µg/g, compared to a crustal average for phosphorus of 1100µg/g (Krauskopf and Bird 1995). On the basis of observed cutans and the phosphorus values, 5 samples were selected for the preparation of new thin-sections from the resin-impregnated sherds. From the data in Table 1, all the sherds can be seen to be "heavily tempered" (i.e. ≥30%: Kidder and Shepard 1936) with clasts and, in the case of CM5 and 11, minor grog, and with porosities varying from relatively low for such sherd fabrics (c.f. Williams and Jenkins 1999: <5% in CM5) to high (>15% in CM 1). Of the funerary urns, only one (PP1) is recorded as having contained bone material during excavation, specific details for the Cae Mickney urns not being recorded (Lynch 1991). Full details of the site, and of the pottery typology and petrography are given Williams and Jenkins (1999; Cae Mickney and Plas Penrhyn, Anglesey) and Longley and Johnstone (1998; Bush Farm in Gwynedd).

Standard procedures were used in thin-section preparation apart from the blocks and thin-sections being polished successively with 6, 3 and 1 µm diamond pastes and covered temporarily with glass slips using immersion oil. Areas with suitable cutanic features were located and recorded photographically at various scales (x1-x400) to facilitate subsequent location of features on the SEM. The selected areas were trimmed to 1cm squares which were cleaned, attached to SEM stubs and coated with 50nm of carbon in a Jeol Coating Unit in preparation for microchemical analysis. Two analytical procedures were employed. All samples were analysed using a Hitachi S520 SEM, fitted with a Link QX2000-2LZ4 detector in the Electron Microscope Unit, University of Wales, Bangor. This system was calibrated empirically for the elements primarily involved (Al, Si, P, Ca, Mn, Fe and at a later stage K) using appropriate sets of standards prepared from $FePO_4.2H_2O$, $Fe_2O_3$, $Al_2O_3$, $CaCO_3$, $Mn_3O_4$ and muscovite ($KAl_2AlSi_3O_{10}(OH)_2$). The results obtained for the standards and a sample of CM4 were subsequently checked using the Camebax twin-spectrometer microprobe fitted with a Link AN10000 (10/85s) analytical system and using Link ZAF4 FLS data correction software at the Electron Probe Facility, University of Manchester. The difference between the SEM/EDXRA and Camebax results ranged up to 30% but with significant (P=0.05) $r^2$ values obtained for all elements except Si. For the purpose of this exploratory and comparative exercise, this validated the SEM/EDXRA results obtained in Bangor.

A series of 4 to 7 analyses of 2 to 4 individual cutanic features in each of the 5 sherds was obtained. A static

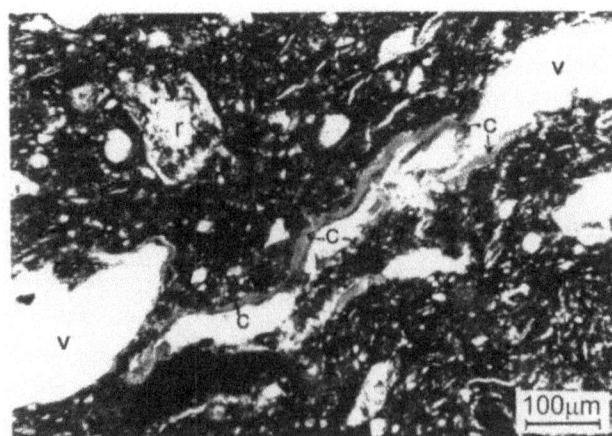

**Figure 1a. Typical isotropic cutans (c) lining voids (v) in a cinerary sherd (CM5) (r-rock clast; m-sherd matrix)**

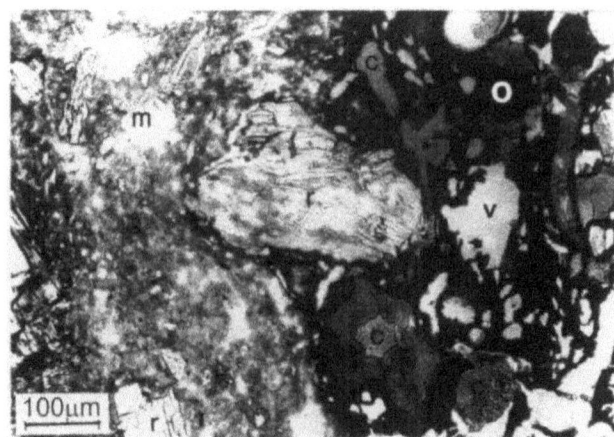

**Figure 1b. Isotropic cutans (c) filling voids (v) in dark organic debris (o) in domestic pot sherd BF2 (r-rock clast; m-sherd matrix)**

| | PP1 N=36, 4 sites | | CM4 N=13, 2 sites | | CM5 N=13, 3 sites | | CM11 N=10, 2 sites | | BF2 N=17, 3 sites | |
|---|---|---|---|---|---|---|---|---|---|---|
| | **Mean** (SD) *Range* (%) | | | | | | | | | |
| P | **2.2** | (0.4) | **5.5** | (1.0) | **0.3** | (0.5) | **5.0** | (2.1) | **2.2** | (0.8) |
| | 0.4 - | 3.3 | 3.6 - | 8.6 | <0.1 - | 2.4 | 2.6 - | 10.4 | <0.1 - | 4.1 |
| Fe | **17.1** | (7.8) | **12.9** | (5.7) | **20.7** | (6.1) | **11.2** | (6.7) | **51.2** | (12.9) |
| | 7.2 - | 27.3 | <0.1 - | 21.4 | 13.6 - | 28.7 | 1.3 - | 20.3 | 46.9 - | 55.6 |
| Al | **14.1** | (4.3) | **18.1** | (3.0) | **14.8** | (2.5) | **17.0** | (3.7) | **7.5** | (2.9) |
| | 8.3 - | 18.4 | 12.7 - | 26.5 | 13.2 - | 16.7 | 11.9 - | 22.7 | 4.5 - | 13.5 |
| Mn | **6.9** | (3.3) | **7.3** | (3.0) | **8.3** | (3.4) | **3.3** | (4.1) | **3.3** | (1.5) |
| | 0.1 - | 13.1 | <0.1 - | 11.0 | 5.4 - | 11.1 | <0.1 - | 10.5 | <0.1 - | 4.6 |
| Si | **10.7** | (2.6) | **10.6** | (2.3) | **9.5** | (3.0) | **14.0** | (4.4) | **3.5** | (0.7) |
| | 5.8 - | 15.5 | 7.9 - | 17.6 | 4.8 - | 15.4 | 9.4 - | 21.0 | 2.8 - | 6.0 |
| K | **1.2** | (1.1) | **3.7** | (1.3) | **2.4** | (1.8) | **3.7** | (1.2) | **0.9** | (0.6) |
| | <0.1 - | 4.1 | 2.0 - | 6.5 | <0.1 - | 4.8 | 1.7 - | 5.4 | 0.1 - | 2.4 |
| Ca | **1.6** | (0.4) | **2.8** | (0.6) | **1.1** | (0.2) | **4.3** | (2.3) | **1.6** | (2.4) |
| | 0.9 - | 2.4 | 1.7 - | 3.6 | 0.8 - | 1.5 | 2.5 - | 9.7 | 0.5 - | 9.5 |

N = number of analyses, sites = cutan features within sherd analysed. **PP** = Plas Penrhyn and **CM** = Cae Mickney, both BA sites on Anglesey, N. Wales, with Funerary urns (Williams and Jenkins 1999); **BF** = Bush Farm, Gwynedd, N. Wales, an IA site with domestic ware (Jenkins and Williams 1998)

**Table 3: Composition (5) of cutanic material in individual sherds**

## Results and discussion

focus (ca. 2μm$^2$) beam was used and, where the visible homogeneity of the feature permitted, a scanned raster ca. 30-40μm square. A typical example from PP1 is illustrated in Figure 2.

The cutanic material was seen to infill sporadically portions of linear voids in the sherd fabric from 20-200μm wide and up to several mm long (Figure 1a). The material ranges in colour from pale yellow-brown to dark red-brown and may occasionally vary even within one void. It is generally isotropic, showing no interference colours when viewed between crossed polars. However, a patchy, streaky, birefringence is occasionally visible (e.g. CM11) which is length-slow (relative to the void), with first order grey/whites masked by the colour of the cutan; this is interpreted as arising from thin seams of oriented clay mineral particles included within the cutan. In the case of the domestic sherd

(BF2), the cutanic material is accompanied by opaque degraded cellular debris (Figure 1b) which was found to have a similar composition in relation to P/Fe/Al, but is not included in this discussion.

The microchemical analyses indicated that the cutans comprised Fe>Al>Mn-rich materials in which phosphorus levels were sometimes considerably enhanced (up to 100x) relative to both average crustal abundance and some comparable natural Al/Fe/Mn deposits (Table 2). Such enhancement indicates a source of phosphate anions, which is lacking in podzolic soils and hydroelectric tunnel deposits, but is provided by bone material in the funerary urns and by food debris in the domestic pottery. More importantly, it is to be expected given the nature of colloidal Fe(OH)$_3$, precipitated from Fe$^{2+}_{aq}$ in solution with rising redox potential (Eh) and $p$H, or of Al(OH)$_3$ precipitated with rising $p$H. Both these precipitates bear positive charges at $p$H values below their "pzc" (point of zero charge) at $p$H 8 and so attract and adsorb anions such as H$_2$PO$_4^-$. Such adsorption

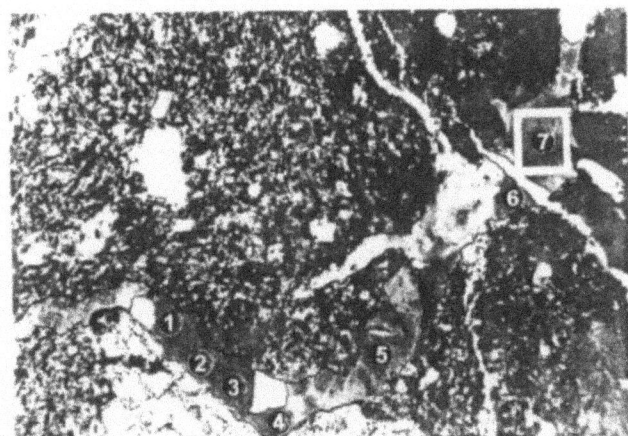

### 7 analyses of cutan 26, sherd PP1

| Site No. | P | Fe (%) | Al | Mn |
|---|---|---|---|---|
| 26.1*s* | 4.38 | 37.5 | 25.4 | 15.7 |
| 26.2*s* | 4.00 | 32.6 | 29.2 | 14.3 |
| 26.3*s* | 3.76 | 45.7 | 14.8 | 21.8 |
| 26.4*s* | 0.89 | 51.9 | 14.5 | 20.7 |
| 26.5*s* | 4.90 | 38.2 | 26.5 | 14.2 |
| 20.6*s* | 4.11 | 31.1 | 25.3 | 15.2 |
| 26.7*R* | 5.38 | 17.5 | 35.4 | 8.5 |

(*s* – spot analysis; *R* – raster analysis)

**Figure 2: Typical SEM/EDXRA analysis of a cutanic feature in sherd PP1**

may lead ultimately to the development of $FePO_4.2H_2O$ (strengite - barrandites - variscite) - $AlPO_4.2H_2O$, (Lindsay *et al.* 1989; Nriagu 1994) setting upper limits of 17.0% and 20.1% respectively to the P contents. As can be seen from the values for P in Table 2, some cutanic material is already effectively 50% "saturated" at a 10% P content.

By contrast, colloidal $MnO_2.nH_2O$, similarly precipitated from $Mn^{2+}_{aq}$ with rising Eh and *p*H, bears a negative charge at low *p*H values (pzc at *p*H 2) and consequently adsorbs cations, and not phosphate, whilst clay minerals exhibit limited anion adsorption being close to their pzc values at *p*H 5, conditions typical of many Welsh soils. The presence of small amounts (<0.05-10%) of clay minerals such as hydrous mica is suggested by the positive correlation between values of K, Si and Al evident in the general correlation matrix (Figure 3) confirming the optical microscopic evidence. The low Ca values (2%) relative to those obtained at Pontnewydd (15%; Jenkins 1994) indicate that these sherd cutans, although similar in appearance to those in the hominid limestone cave, are not Fe/Ca/P compounds. From Figure 3 it is also evident that phosphorus shows no overall significant correlation with the other elements recorded, other than a predictably weak negative correlation with Mn.

|    | P | Fe | Mn | Al | Si | K |
|----|---|----|----|----|----|----|
| Fe | ● |    |    |    |    |    |
| Mn | – | ●  |    |    |    |    |
| Al | ● | =  | ●  |    |    |    |
| Si | ● | =  | ●  | ★  |    |    |
| K  | ● | –  | –  | +  | +  |    |
| Ca | ● | –  | ●  | ●  | ●  | ★  |

★ strong +ve correlation (P = 0.01)
\+ moderate +ve correlation (P = 0.1)
= strong -ve correlation (P = 0.01)
– moderate -ve correlation (P= 0.1)

**Figure 3. Correlation matrix for 89 elemental analyses of 5 sherds**

Considered in relation to individual sherds the analytical results (Table 3) are more revealing. The patterns of concentration levels and heterogeneity appear to be specific to each sherd as might be expected with differing original uses and environmental histories of the five pots. The cutans in BF2 and CM5 have Fe>Al whilst the opposite is true for CM4 and CM11, presumably reflecting locally different soil environments of pot burial. In CM5 phosphorus is only slightly enhanced (3x), but with a large Coefficient of Variation (CV = 170%) as compared to CM4 and CM11 where the opposite is true (large enhancement - x50; little variation - CV = 20-40%). Phosphorus again shows little significant correlation with other elements except weakly with Fe in CM5 and Al in PP1 (P=0.5) and, more strikingly, with Ca in CM11 (P = 0.01); contents of Ca are generally low, but reach almost 10% in CM11, perhaps reflecting a common origin of Ca and P in bone material. In all but CM11, where they are relatively low, the levels of Fe and Mn show high, to very high, positive correlations (P = 0.1-0.01) which is explicable in terms of their similar redox chemistry.

However, in BF2, Ca and K levels in the cutans, although again relatively low, are highly positively correlated (P = 0.01), the explanation for which is not immediately obvious. Values for %K also vary between samples, being consistently higher in CM4 and 11 (up to *ca.* 30%): this suggests that clay mineral colloids (most likely hydrous mica in the soils concerned) have also been mobilised and redeposited with Fe/Al to a greater extent in these two sherds. This would dilute the potential enhancement of P in their Fe/Al fractions accordingly.

## Conclusions

The results indicate that phosphate can be highly concentrated in Fe/Al colloidal deposits within sherd fabrics. Two conditions would be required for this – mobilised/redeposited Fe/Al and a source of phosphorus. Weathering of bone material (19% P), intact, crushed or incinerated, would provide the latter in the funerary urns, whilst food debris might do the same in domestic pottery. An alternative source that should also be considered is the addition of phosphate fertilisers in the post-war period, but the sherds from both Bronze Age sites were recovered over 70 years ago (Cae Mickney 1882 and Plas Penrhyn 1926; Lynch 1991), whilst the Bush Farm site itself was uncultivated. The source of Fe/Al in the cutans is presumably pedogenic, these two elements being mobilised under conditions of acid leaching or gleying, often in the form of soluble organic matter complexes or "chelates". These materials are subsequently redeposited at depth in soils as thin iron-pans ("placic Bf" horizons) characteristic of podzol and stagnopodzol profiles, and these deposits have similar colours and isotropic properties and modes of occurrence to the material infilling voids or coating surfaces (cutans) in the sherds. Porous pottery sherds provide suitable sites for such deposition, and this archaeological evidence could incidentally enable a limiting date to be put on the start of such processes which would be useful in interpreting the developmental history of the soils.

A feature of the enhanced phosphate levels in sherds is their sporadic distribution. This spatial heterogeneity is to be expected given the geometry of the system. Leaching would concentrate phosphate towards the bottom of the pot and also selectively in the more permeable portions. Around 70% of the Bronze Age urns recovered from the site of Capel Eithin on Anglesey (White and Smith 2000) were in an inverted position, such that phosphate deposition would occur in the rim of the urn, whilst in the other 30% deposition would occur in the base of the urn. Rim and base sherds are less likely to be released for petrographic analysis and the chances generally of a sherd some 5 cm square corresponding to a relevant, more permeable portion of the pot are probably low, and this would explain the very variable phosphate enhancement. It is therefore the occurrence of high individual phosphate values in a sherd, rather than high average values, that is significant.

These sherd studies illustrate another detail of the selective mobilisation and concentration of phosphorus in the environment of relevance in archaeology. They suggest that phosphate analysis could have a potential role in the interpretation of pottery usage. In sherds of uncertain utilitarian context enhanced phosphate levels could indicate a funerary role or, as one sherd has shown, a domestic role. More analyses of domestic sherds are clearly needed to ascertain whether this chemical approach could provide further criteria for distinguishing different sources of enhanced phosphate and perhaps linkage with trace organic analysis of the sherds could be particularly useful. This study has proven the hypothesis that brown isotropic cutanic features in 5 samples of pots can contain enhanced levels of phosphorus. It has established that such void features should be noted during routine petrographic analysis of sherds as they can indicate a possible means of detecting enrichment of phosphorus, although confirmation by SEM/EDXRA is a costly and lengthy procedure.

## Acknowledgements:

We would wish to acknowledge with gratitude constructive comments on the text by our colleagues Ian Kelso and John Williams (UW Bangor) and the assistance of David Plant in analysis at the NERC Electron Microprobe Unit at the University of Manchester.

## References:

R.P. Evershed, S.N. Dudd, S. Charters, H. Mot tram, A.W. Stott, A. Raven, P.F. van Bergen and H. A. Bland (1999). Lipids as carriers of anthropogenic signals from Prehistory. *Philosophical Transactions of the Royal Society* **354**,19-31.

Green, H.S. (1984). *Pontnewydd cave. A Lower Palaeolithic Hominid site in Wales. The first report.* Cardiff: The National Museum of Wales.

Jenkins, D.A. (1994). Interpretation of Interglacial cave sediments from a hominid site in North Wales: translocation of Ca-Fe phosphates. In A.J. Ringrose- Voase and G.S. Humphreys (Eds) *Soil Micromorphology: studies in management and genesis.* pp. 293-306, Developments in Soil Science **22**, London: Elsevier.

Jenkins, D.A. (1997). Phosphorus redistribution in cave sediments from the Lower Palaeolithic site of Pontnewydd. In A. Sinclair, E. Slater and J. Gowlett (Eds). *Archaeological Sciences 1995*, pp.282-286. Oxford: Oxbow Monograph 64.

Jenkins, D.A. and Williams, J.LI.W (1998). Petrographic analysis of six potsherds from Bush Farm, In D. Longley and N. Johnstone (Eds). *Excavations at two farms of the Romano-British period at Bryn Eryr and Bush Farm, Gwynedd*, p.206. Britannia XXIX, 185-246.

Kidder, A.V. and Shepard, A.O. (1936). The pottery of Pecos 2. *Papers Phillips Academy, Southwestern Expedition* **7**, 389-587.

Krauskopf, K.B. and Bird, D.K. (1995). *Introduction to Geochemistry* (3rd edn.) London: McGraw-Hill.

Lindsay, W.L., Vlek, P.L.G. and Chien, S.H. (1989). Phosphate Minerals. In J.B. Dixon and S.B. Weed (Eds). *Minerals in Soil Environments* (2nd edn) pp.639-672. Soil Science Society of America, Madison.

Longley, D. and Johnstone, N. (1998). *Excavations at two farms of the Romano-British period at Bryn Eryr and Bush Farm, Gwynedd.* Britannia XXIX, 185-246 .

Lynch, F. (1991). *Prehistoric Anglesey*, 2nd edn. Anglesey: Anglesey Antiquarian Society, Llangefni.

Nriagu, J.O. (1994). Phosphate minerals: their properties and general mode of occurrence. In J.O. Nriagu and P.B. Moore (Eds) *Phosphate Minerals*, pp.400-424. Berlin: Springer Verlag.

Owen, A.G. and Jenkins, D.A. (2002) Sampling for phosphate over a grave site: theory and practice. In Robson Brown (Ed) *Archaeological Sciences 1999*

Waite. C. (1998) *Manganese-rich deposits formed within a hydro-electric tunnel system.* Unpublished MSc thesis, University of Wales.

White, S.I. and Smith, G.H. (2000). Excavations of Neolithic, Bronze Age, Roman and Early Christian features at Capel Eithin, Gaerwen, Anglesey, 1980 and 1981. *Transactions of Anglesey Antiquarian Society.*

Williams, J.LI.W. and Jenkins, D.A. (1999). A petrographic investigation of a corpus of Bronze Age Funerary urns from the Isle of Anglesey. *Proceedings of the Prehistoric Society* **65**, 191-232.

# Assessing and modelling faunalturbation

Stephen Lancaster and Ian A. Simpson

Department of Environmental Sciences, University of Stirling, Stirling, FK9 4LA, UK.

## Introduction

Understanding the stratigraphy of a site is fundamental to archaeology. Not only is the information derived from stratigraphic analysis essential in its own right for the reconstruction of the history of a site, it is the foundation of all further analyses, be they of artefacts, biological material, dateable material or chemical markers.

It is generally accepted that to understand the stratigraphy of a site it is necessary to understand the processes by which it has formed (Barker 1977, Schiffer 1983). This includes both the processes of deposition and processes of post-depositional modifications. There have been a number of reviews of post-depositional processes (e.g. Rolfsen 1980, Schiffer 1983) as a whole, and a few investigations of the effects of particular processes e.g. the 'churning' effect found in expanding clay rich vertisols (Duffield 1970), or the impact of trampling on lithic distributions in sandy soils and sediments (Villa & Courtin 1983). However many of the processes that have the potential to affect the stratigraphy of a site have not been investigated. Where a given process has been investigated, the study is usually more concerned with the movement of artefacts, rather than alteration of the stratigraphic units themselves.

One of the most significant classes of post-depositional is faunalturbation. Faunalturbation is the reworking and mixing of soils and sediments by animals. This paper will examine what is, in temperate Europe, the most ubiquitous set of faunalturbation processes: those of the invertebrates.

It has long been appreciated that earthworms may be responsible for the burial and movement of small objects, including archaeological artefacts (Darwin 1881). More recently the movement of biological remains which are used in palaeoenvironmental research has also been noted (Armour-Chelu & Andrews 1994, Carter 1990). There has been relatively little appreciation of the possible effects of the movement and mixing of archaeological sediments at the particulate level by invertebrates or research on the subject. The exact results of faunalturbation of stratigraphy depends on the particular groups of organisms involved, the nature of the archaeological strata and the duration of faunalturbation. The broad effect of faunalturbation can, however, be summarised as tending partially or completely to homogenise some or all of the originally discrete deposits on a site through the intermixing of the component particles. At one extreme is the complete 'loss' of discrete units. This loss of data may conceivably create an apparent hiatus in the stratigraphic sequence of a site. Towards the other end of the scale are more subtle effects, such as the small-scale introduction of material from one part of the archaeological profile to another. Such small scale movement of material could include the movement of very small biological remains or chemical markers into contexts where they would not otherwise have been present, thus giving false results to analyses looking at these types of evidence.

Given the potential problems associated with the faunalturbation of archaeological sites, it is essential to be able to identify the evidence of faunalturbation and the organisms responsible and to be able to assess the impact invertebrate faunalturbation has had upon a stratigraphic sequence. To this end a multi-technique research project has been executed at the University of Stirling, including soil micromorphology and $^{137}Cs$ profiling. The aim of this paper is to demonstrate one aspect of this project; the application of field recording techniques and thin-section micromorphology to the identification and assessment of invertebrate faunalturbation.

## Methodology

### Site selection and sampling

The sites selected are all situated on the island of Sanday in the Orkney Islands (see Figure 1). The University of Stirling has a long running, ongoing research programme in the North Atlantic region and the selection of locality reflects this. The sites all belong to a class of monument called farm mounds. This class of settlement site was selected, as it is a significant type in the North Atlantic region (Bertelsen & Lamb 1995). A site of this type comprised a mound up to 3m high of midden material, formed of a variety of materials probably including ash, animal manure and turf (Davidson et al. 1986). The depth of this type of site was a further factor in the selection of this class of monument, as it was hoped that this would allow some assessment to be made of the depth to which invertebrate faunalturbation may occur. Individual sites were selected on the basis of suitability with regard to the different techniques being used in the project, and to try to provide a range of sites within the class under consideration.

On each site an archaeological profile was exposed. From this profile undisturbed samples were collected in Kubiena tins for the manufacture of thin section slides. The samples were taken as a series of overlapping samples from the top 40cm of the profile to correspond with the sampling patterns of the other techniques used. Further samples for thin section slide production were collected from the boundaries of the different stratigraphic/pedological units and to assist in the characterisation of these units where the sampling of the top 40cm did not cover these units (see Figures 2-4).

### Field recording

The exposed profiles were described using methods derived both from standard field archaeological practice and soil

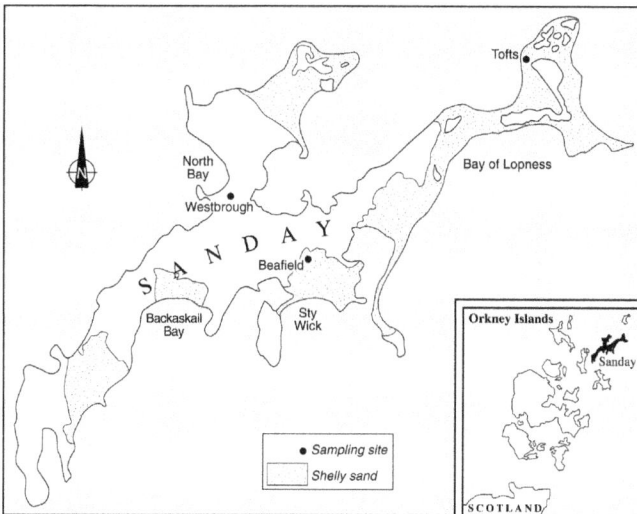

**Figure 1. The locations of the sites**

surveying (Hodgson 1974). The combined approach was adopted, as neither set of protocols by itself was capable of fully describing the profiles. Particular attention was given to possible indicators of invertebrate activity, such as stone lines or regions of finer material underlying stones or at the boundaries of stratigraphic units.

**Thin section micromorphology**
Thin sections were prepared at the Micromorphology Laboratory, University of Stirling, based on the procedures of Murphy (1986). All water was removed from the samples by specific gravity measurement. The samples were impregnated using polyester crystic resin 'type 17449' and the catalyst 'Q17447' (methyl ethyl ketone peroxide, 50% solution in phthalate). The mixture was thinned with acetone and a standard composition of 180 ml resin, 1.8 ml catalyst and 25 ml acetone used for each Kubiena tin. No accelerant was used but the sample was impregnated under vacuum to ensure outgassing of the soil. The blocks were sliced, bonded to a glass slide and precision lapped to 30 um. Coverslipping completed manufacture of the section. Thin sections were examined using a Zeiss polarising microscope.

Basic description was carried out using the international system for soil thin section description, with the slides being divided into zones on the basis of different fabric types (Bullock *et al* 1985). All Tables are presented in the Appendix. A range of magnifications (x10 - x400 and light sources (plane polarised, cross polarised and oblique incident) were used. Identification and interpretation of faunalturbation and the groups of organisms responsible were based on Bullock *et al*. (1985), Courty *et al* (1989) and Fitzpatrick (1993). A number of different pedofeatures were selected as traces for faunalturbation (see Table 1). To quantify the effects of faunalturbation, each of the slides was divided up in a 1cm$^2$ grid. Half of these 1cm$^2$ squares were then visually assessed to give the percentage area coverage, to the nearest 5%, of the square by each of the selected pedofeatures. Where less than 5% coverage was noted the occurrence of the pedofeature has been classified as 'trace', and is marked with an 'X' on Tables 8-10.

For the purposes of interpretation and presentation each the coverage results of all the traces of faunalturbation from each 1 cm$^2$ within each 1 cm band of depth on a slide have been averaged (see Tables 8-10) and totalled (see Figures 2-4).

## Results and Discussion

### Field descriptions
The basic descriptions are given in Tables 2-4. The spatial relationships of the different units can be seen in Figures 2-4. The soils and sediment units of the three sites can be classified into two broad groups. The first group includes the modern 'A' horizons that have developed on the sites and the other units which closely resemble them. They are characterised by a texture that is loamy, a crumb/incipient crumb structure and a fairly homogenous appearance. They also appear to contravene the rules of archaeological stratigraphy by completely surrounding other units, and thus, as Harris (1989) has noted, require further explanation in terms of their formation processes. All the current 'A' horizons and one of the other units of this group contain stone lines, a feature generated by earthworm activity in biologically active soils which are not undergoing any other significant process of pedoturbation (Edwards & Bohlen 1996).

The other group of units tends to be predominantly or totally composed of grey and/or orange mottles and often much black flecking. No consistent type of texture is associated with this group, in contrast to the 'A' horizon type of deposit. Where such deposits are substantial (e.g. Westbrough) a laminated structure is apparent. The uppermost of this type of deposit on each site often appears to have been penetrated with material from the 'A' horizon above. Such deposits would probably be interpreted as ash deposits by a field archaeologist.

### Soil thin sections
The basic descriptions of the thin section slides are presented in Tables 5-7. The data concerning the traces of faunalturbation are given in Tables 8-10. The quantitative results are displayed in Figures 2-4. Where the mean percentage coverage of a 1 cm deep area has exceeded 80% the area has been coloured black. Otherwise the area has been left unshaded. The cut off level of 80% was adopted as this is the point at which it becomes difficult to distinguish surviving archaeological material. In terms of the basic mineralogy there is very little variation from unit to unit within each site, even between to the two different types of unit identified. In overall compositional terms the main difference between the two types of units is that the fine matrix of the 'A' horizon type of unit contain a higher proportion of organic material. It is not possible to unequivocally state whether the deposits that would probably be identified in the field as ash deposits are in fact such on the basis of the micromorphological evidence. Given this uncertainty such deposits will be referred to as 'ash deposits'.

There is also a difference between the two types of units in terms of the traces of faunalturbation, as can be seen in Tables 8-10 and Figures 2-4. The majority of samples where

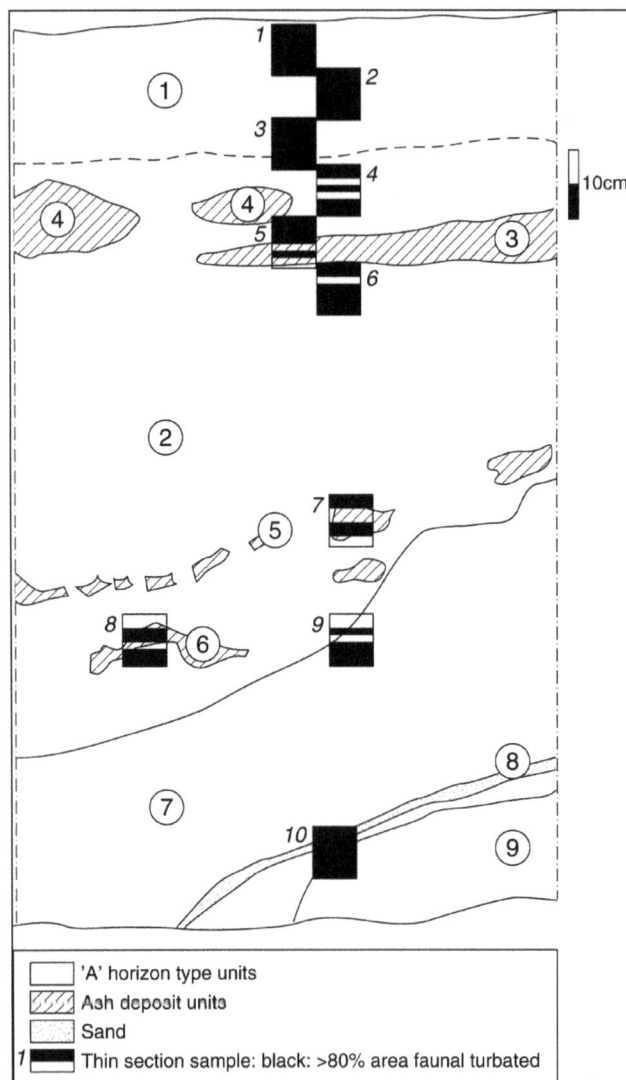

Figure 4. Stratigraphic sequence in test pit at Westbrough.

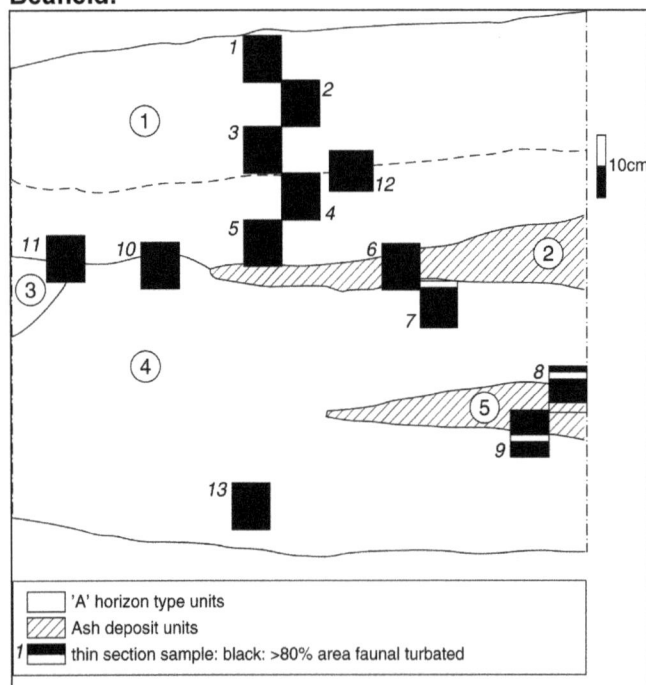

**Figure 2. Stratigraogic sequence in test pit at Beafield.**

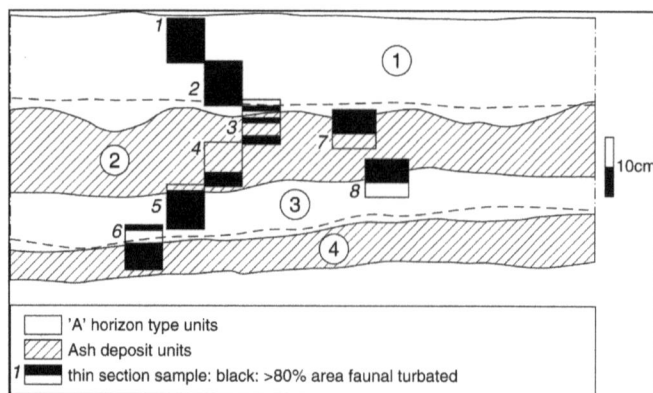

**Figure 3. Stratigraphic sequence in test pit at Tofts.**

the total coverage by faunalturbation features is less than 80% is in the ash deposit units. Of those areas with less than 80% coverage that fall within the 'A' horizon type deposits, a third lie near a boundary with an 'ash deposit' as depicted in Figures 2-4. These areas probably represent variation in the position of the unit boundaries in three dimensions: while each field section represents one 'slice' through a site at a given point, the thin sections in fact represent samples from 1-4 cm further back from the face of the profile. As such they may have been taken from ash deposit units. Thin sections of the 'A' horizon type units are largely or wholly composed of a total biological fabric containing fabric pedofeatures. The somewhat compacted nature of the material means that there are relatively few identifiable excremental pedofeatures. Those that are apparent generally have mammillated or bacillo-cylindrical forms; i.e. they are those types associated with earthworms and enchytraeid worms.

In contrast the areas of the thin sections covering the 'ash deposit' units tended to have a lower area coverage by traces of faunalturbation. There are a few limited areas showing no evidence of faunalturbation. A higher proportion of the excremental pedofeatures is associated with soil fauna that dwells in the uppermost level of the soil, such as the larvae of Coleoptera and Diptera. Some of these excrements are impregnated with iron, as is much of the unfaunalturbated material. The phenomenon of iron impregnation is not seen with the excremental pedofeatures that can be unequivocally associated with earthworms. It should be noted that despite exhibiting fewer traces of faunalturbation, all of the samples from ash deposit units have undergone significant faunalturbation, usually in a localised pattern. All the slides from these units contain areas of earthworm excrement or total biological fabric that is indistinguishable from the fabrics that characterise the 'A' horizon type deposits.

The 'A horizon' and 'ash deposit' layers essentially alternate through the site profiles.

Given the similarity of basic mineralogy between the two types of units on any given site, it seems probable that the 'ash deposit' units are the parent materials from which the 'A horizons' have developed. The occasional very small area of material that has not been heavily faunalturbated surviving in the 'A' horizon type deposits also points to this interpretation (e.g. as in sample Beafield 21-27). The greater levels of fine organic matter that characterise the 'A horizons' have been incorporated by faunal activity, as it continues to be in the modern 'A' horizon. This means that the other 'A' horizon type units constitute buried soils that have developed from anthropogenic sediments, i.e. archaeological stratigraphy, with faunalturbation as the primary mechanism of pedogenesis. For the alternating sequence of soils and archaeological stratigraphy to have occurred it is necessary that there should have been periods of deposition rapid enough for little faunalturbation to occur, interspersed with periods of much slower deposition or even a complete hiatus of deposition that would allow faunalturbation to occur to the point of a soil forming. Of the faunalturbation that has occurred it is notable that there are excrements attributable to the Diptera and Coleoptera (see Table 1), which are largely unknown in the 'A' horizon deposits. The Diptera and Coleoptera are likely to be the first groups to colonise a new deposit due to the dispersive capacity of the adult forms, the majority of which fly. As such these excrements can be interpreted as representing the first stages of faunalturbation.

While some earthworm and enchytraeid excrement is found in the 'ash deposits' it is essentially identical to that found in the 'A' horizon units, and is often contiguous with these units. As noted above, it is not impregnated with iron, although the remains of iron impregnated pedofeatures within the earthworm and enchytraeid excrements and the total biological fabric are common in some of the slides. This would suggest that pre-existing iron impregnated material has been incorporated into the earthworm and enchytraeid excrement. As such these types of excrements must post-date those of the surficial dwelling organisms. The survival of small areas of undisturbed material and evidence of the earliest phases of faunalturbation suggests that the 'ash deposit' units must have been covered to some depth fairly rapidly.

That the buried 'A' horizon type units have formed during a period of slow deposition or complete hiatus is undoubted – all the buried units are cognate with the modern, biologically active 'A' horizons that have formed on each site, where there has been no anthropogenic deposition of sediment on the sampling locations within living memory. While it is difficult to put a time scale on the time required to form these soils, one further relevant point should be noted. The modern 'A' horizons all have stone lines, created by the burial and undermining of stones and other small objects, such as shells, by earthworms (Edwards & Bohlen 1996). Only one of the buried units (no. Westbrough) exhibits such a feature. The other 'A' horizon units have fairly uniform distributions of clasts. This would suggest that these soils formed fairly rapidly, and that the sorting of the larger clasts that takes place over a longer period had not had time to occur in most cases. Investigation of local natural soils that had been ploughed about ten years before, thus disrupting any stone line, has shown that the stone lines had not reformed within that time period. Darwin's classic experiments, albeit in a rather different environmental setting suggests that stone lines can form within 15 years and may go on 'sinking' for a

further 15 years (Darwin 1881). Thus whilst no precise figure can be given for the pedogenesis time of the buried 'A' horizons, an estimate in the order of a few tens of years seems reasonable. This means that significant faunalturbation, and thus destruction of archaeological strata has occurred fairly rapidly.

Given that complete faunalturbation of the sediments that now compose the 'A' horizon units seems to have happened over a matter of decades, it seems reasonable to ask why the ash deposit units have survived for somewhere in the region of five centuries. The answer probably lies in the combination of the site formation history proposed above and the ecology of the earthworm. Two ecological classes of earthworm that can shift significant amounts of soil or sediment are routinely referred to: the endogeic and anecic groups. The endogeic species are the most constant burrowers, being true geophages. They also tend to be the most numerous group. The majority of this group lives in the top 15cm of the soil. The anecic species are litter consumers, but live in permanent burrows at greater depths, routinely down to 45 cm in the case of *Aporrectodea longa* and *Aporrectodea nocturna*, the two commoner species of this group and 1m in the case of *Lumbricus terrestris*. As such, each 'A' horizon unit represents the standard depth of penetration of the majority of species found on the sites. It is notable that the uppermost ash deposit units show the most signs of faunalturbation by earthworms: they fall within the main depth range of the incursions of the less intensively burrowing *L. terrestris* and the extended range for occasional incursions by the other anecic species (Edwards & Bohlen 1996).

## Conclusions

This paper has demonstrated a number of points. The first is that when a soil forms through faunalturbation on archaeological sediments the stratigraphic units within the 'A' horizon are lost. This loss of the later parts of a sequence of deposit has considerable implications for the reconstruction of site occupation sequences and in particular in the consideration of duration of use/occupation for sites affected by faunalturbation. Where a series of faunally driven pedogenic episodes have occurred throughout a sequence, as at the sites selected for the study, the problem becomes greater.

This is a conclusion that initially seems to verge on the catastrophic for the practice of stratigraphically based archaeology. Certain points need to be borne in mind in this regard. The first is that while the order and relationship of some units may be lost, some attributes of the lost deposits may be recoverable – for example combined mineralogy of the mixed deposits. It should also be noted that even in the most apparently faunalturbated units, small fragments of deposits might survive relatively intact, allowing further analysis of characteristics pertaining to that unit in itself.

With regard to ongoing faunalturbation, it should be noted that while the initial destruction of stratigraphic integrity in the upper deposits is rapid, subsequent faunalturbation is largely restricted to the already fully mixed horizon, which is effectively equivalent to the depth of activity of the endogeic earthworms. There is likely to be some ongoing mixing of deeper deposits, as the state of the currently surviving upper ash deposit units suggests. This is probably due to the activity of the deeper dwelling but less actively burrowing anecic species of earthworm. As such these processes are effective more gradually, over an extended period of time.

The final point to be made is that even archaeological deposits that may at first sight appear to be intact may contain significant quantities of interpenetrated, fully faunalturbated material, which may have come from almost anywhere else in the overlying deposit. This may not be a particular problem with regard to the overall recognition and recording of such deposits in the field: as noted above a unit may still be discernible for field recording which has up to 80% area coverage of faunalturbation related features at the microscopic scale. It does, however, have implications for the analysis of very small objects in such deposits, and also chemical and biochemical analyses.

## References

Armour-Chelu, M. and Andrews, P. (1994). Some Effects of Bioturbation By Earthworms (Oligochaeta) on Archaeological Sites. *Journal of Archaeological Science* **21** 433-443.

Barker, P. (1977). *Techniques of Archaeological Excavation.* London: Batsford.

Bertelsen, R. and Lamb, R. G. (1995). Settlement Mounds in the North Atlantic. In (C. E. Batey, J. Jesch and C. D. Morris Eds.) *The Viking Age in Caithness, Orkney and The North Atlantic.* Select papers from the Proceedings of the Eleventh Viking Congress, Thurso & Kirkwall, 1989. Edinburgh: Edinburgh University Press, pp 544-554.

Bullock, P., Fedoroff, N., Jongerius, A., Stoops, G., Tursina, T., and Babel, U. (1985). *Handbook for Soil Thin Section Micromorphology.* Wolverhampton: Waine Research Publications.

Carter, S. P. (1990) The Stratification and Taphonomy of Shells in Calcareous Soils: Implications for Land Snail Analysis in Archaeology. *Journal of Archaeological Science* **17** 495-507.

Darwin, C. (1881). *The Formation of Vegetable Mould through the Action of Worms with Observations on their Habits.* London: Faber & Faber.

Davidson, D. A., Harkness, D. D. and Simpson, I. A. (1986). The Formation of Farm Mounds on The Island of Sanday, Orkney. *Geoarchaeology* **1/1** 45-60.

Duffield, L.F. (1970). Vertisols and Their Implications for Archaeological Research. *American Anthropologist* **72** 1055-1062.

Edwards, C. A. and Bohlen, P. J. (1996). *Biology and Ecology of Earthworms.* London: Chapman & Hall.

Fitzpatrick, E.A. (1993). *Soil Microscopy and Soil Micromorphology.* Chichester: Wiley & Sons.

Harris, E. (1989). Principles of Archaeological Stratigraphy (2nd edition). London: Academic Press.

Hodgson, J. M. ed. (1974). Soil Survey Field Handbook: Describing and Sampling Soil Profiles. Harpenden.

Murphy, C. P. (1986). *Thin Section Preparation of Soils and Sediments.* Berkhampstead: Academic Publishers.

Rolfsen, P. Disturbance of Archaeological Layers by Processes in the Soil. *Norwegian Archaeological Review* **13/2** 110-118.

Schiffer, M. (1983). Toward the Identification of Formation Processes. *American Antiquity* **48** 675-706.

Villa, P. and Courtin, J. (1983) The Interpretation of Stratified Sites: A View from Underground. *Journal of Archaeological Science* **10** 267-281.

## Acknowledgements

Soil thin sections were manufactured by George MacLeod. Bill Jamieson and David Aitchison drew the figures. This research has been undertaken in the Department of Environmental Sciences, University of Stirling. The first named author is in receipt of a NERC award.

**Appendix : Tables**

| Pedofeature | Associated Organisms |
|---|---|
| Total biological fabric | Mainly associated with Lumbricidae, especially if fabric pedofeatures present, but formation may involve any soil dwelling mesofauna. |
| Textural pedofeatures | Lumbricidae, both endogeic and anecic. |
| Mammillated excrements | Lumbricidae, both endogeic and anecic. |
| Bacillo-cylindrical Excrements | Enchytraeidae. Also associated with Lumbricidae. |
| Spheroidal Excrements | Larvae of Diptera and Coleoptera. |
| Ellipsoidal Excrements | Orbatid mites. Possibly with larvae of Diptera and Coleoptera. |
| Tailed Conoidal Excrements | Isoptera. Possibly Coleoptera. |
| Cylindrical Excrements | Larvae of Diptera. |

Table 1. Micromorphological Pedofeatures Characteristic of Faunalturbation and Associated Agents of Formation.

| Unit No. | Description |
|---|---|
| 1 | Slightly sandy silt, colour 10YR2/2. Moderately to heavily rooted to 5-10 cm. Largely clast free in top 10-15 cm. Layer of clasts – 1-2 cm sub-rounded to sub-angular tabular sandstones and limpet shells, conforming to unit boundary. Strongly developed crumb structure. Basal matrix boundary diffuse. |
| 2 | Slightly sandy silt, colour 10YR3/2. Frequent clasts with an unsorted distribution. Clasts mostly 1-2 cm sub-angular tabular sandstones, with some limpet and cockle shells. Frequent orange mottling, 3-4mm and charcoal flecking, 3-5mm. Weakly developed crumb structure. Upper and lower boundaries diffuse. |
| 3 | Slightly sandy silt to silt, base matrix colour 10YR2.5/2, mottle colour 7.5YR9/8. Occasional clasts with an unsorted distribution. Clasts mostly 1-2 cm sub-angular tabular sandstones, with some limpet and cockle shells. Mottles very abundant, 2-3cm diameter. Weakly developed crumb structure. Upper and lower boundaries gradual. |
| 4 | Slightly sandy silt to silt, base matrix colour 10YR3/2.5, mottle colour 7.5YR9/8. Rare clasts with an unsorted distribution. Clasts mostly 1-2 cm sub-angular tabular sandstones, with some limpet shells. Mottles very abundant, 2-3cm diameter. Upper and lower boundaries gradual to clear. |
| 5 | Slightly sandy silt to silt, base matrix colour 10YR2.5/2, mottle colour 7.5YR9/8. Occasional clasts with an unsorted distribution. Clasts mostly 1-2 cm sub-angular tabular sandstones, with some limpet shells. Mottles very abundant, 2-3cm diameter. Weakly developed crumb structure. Upper and lower boundaries diffuse. |
| 6 | Silt, colour 2.5Y2.5/1. Some black flecking, 1-3 mm. Rare clasts; 1-2 cm sub-angular tabular sandstones. Upper and lower boundaries gradual to clear. |
| 7 | Slightly sandy silt, colour 2.5YR2.5/1. Largely clast free. Frequent black flecking, 5-10mm. Occasional orange mottling, c. 3mm diameter. Weakly developed crumb structure. Upper and lower boundaries gradual. |
| 8 | Pure coarse sand, colour 7.5YR2/2 Structureless. Upper and lower boundaries sharp. |
| 9 | Slightly sandy silt, colour 7.5YR4/3. Frequent orange mottles, c. 2-4 mm. Frequent black flecks, c. 2 mm. Largely clast free. Weakly developed crumb structure. Upper boundary abrupt. |

Table 2. Basic description of the soil/sediment units at Beafield, Sanday.

| Unit No. | Description |
|---|---|
| 1 | Silty clay loam, colour 10YR2.5/1. Heavily rooted to 2 cm. Clast free to 21 cm. At 21-22 cm layer of clasts; predominantly limpet shells, plus occasional tabular sub-rounded sandstone. Below this frequent clasts, compositionally as layer above, but unsorted. Strongly developed crumb structure. Lower boundary gradual to diffuse. |
| 2 | Silty clay loam, colour 10YR3/2. Occasional clasts; predominantly limpet shells. Abundant black flecks, c. 2-4 mm. Abundant mottles, 1-5 cm diameter, colour 7.5YR4/4. Moderately developed crumb structure. Upper and lower boundaries gradual to clear. |
| 3 | Silty clay loam, colour 10YR3.5/2. Occasional clasts; predominantly limpet shells. Occasional orange mottles, up to 1 cm diameter. Moderately developed crumb structure. Boundaries diffuse to clear distinct |
| 4 | Silty clay loam, colour 10YR3/2. Occasional clasts; stones, 1-10 cm, tabular sub-rounded to sub-angular; limpet shells. Occasional black flecks, 2-5 mm. Weakly developed blocky structure. Upper boundaries gradual. |
| 5 | Silty clay loam, colour 10YR3/2. Occasional clasts; predominantly limpet shells. Abundant grey mottles up to 2 cm, colour 10YR4/2. Abundant black flecks, c. 2-4 mm. Moderately developed sub-angular blocky structure. Upper and lower boundaries gradual. |

Table 3. Basic description of the soil/sediment units at Tofts, Sanday.

| Unit No. | Descriptions |
|---|---|
| 1 | Silty loam, colour 2.5Y2.5/1. Heavily rooted to 6 cm. Generally clast free, except for layer of angular, tabular stones and occasional shell, approximately coterminus with basal boundary. Boundary is moderately distinct to distinct. Boundary very irregular, interdigitating with unit below. Weakly developed sub-angular blocky structure. |
| 2 | Sandy silt loam, colour 10YR4/2.5. Occasional clasts; angular cuboidal/tabular sandstones, c. 10-15 mm with an unsorted distribution. Frequent orange flecks, c. 2-4 mm, colour 7.5YR5/8. Upper boundary clear to abrupt. Lower boundary moderaely distinct to moderately indistinct. Structureless. |
| 3 | Slightly sandy silt loam, colour 10YR2/2. Occasional clast; sub-angular prismoidal sandstone, 7-10 mm. Sorted – tending to form layer at base of unit. Occasional grey mottle, 10YR5/8, silt texture. Structureless. Upper boundary moderately distinct to indistinct. Lower boundary clear to gradual. |
| 4 | Clay silt, colour 10YR5/3. Occasional clast; sub-angular prismoidal sandstone, 10-40 mm, unsorted. Abundant mottles, colour 10YR3/1, 10-20 mm diameter and 7.5Y5/8 2-4 mm. Abundant black flecks, 2-4 mm. Structureless. Upper boundary clear. |

Table 4. Basic description of the soil/sediment units at Westbrough, Sanday.

| Slide No. | Zone | Quartz | Shell | Sandstone | Siltstone | Heated Stone | Compound Quartz Grains | Feldspar | FINE MINERAL MATERIAL | Organ | Tissue, Charred | Tissue, Uncharred | Fungal Sclerotia | Charcoal | Cell Residue | Amorphous (Reddish Brown) | Textural (Sand infill) | Amorphous (Nodule) | MICROSTRUCTURE | COARSE MATERIAL ARRANGEMENT | GROUNDMASS B-FABRIC | RELATED DISTRIBUTION |
|---|---|---|---|---|---|---|---|---|---|---|---|---|---|---|---|---|---|---|---|---|---|---|
| Beafield 1 | 1 | ••• | ••• | • | | | | | Brown; organo-mineral | ••• | | | • | • | | • | | | Massive, spongy | Random, unreferred | Crystallitic | Porphyric |
| | 2 | •• | ••• | • | | | | | Brown; organo-mineral | •• | | | • | • | | | | | Massive | Random, unreferred | Crystallitic | Porphyric |
| | 3 | •• | ••• | • | | | | | Brown; organo-mineral | • | • | | • | • | | | •• | • | Channel (locally spongy) | Random, unreferred | Speckled | Porphyric |
| Beafield 2 | 1 | ••• | •• | •• | | | | | Brown; organo-mineral | • | • | | • | • | | | | | Channel and vugh | Random, unreferred | Crystallitic | Porphyric (locally gefuric) |
| | 2 | •• | •• | | | | | | Brown; organo-mineral | • | • | | • | • | | | | | Channel and vugh | Random, unreferred | Crystallitic | Porphyric |
| | 3 | ••• | ••• | | | | | | Brown; organo-mineral | • | • | | • | • | | | | | Channel and vugh | Random, unreferred | Speckled | Porphyric |
| Beafield 3 | 1 | ••• | ••• | | • | | | | Brown; organo-mineral | • | • | | • | • | • | | ••• | •• | Spongy | Weakly clustered, unreferred | Crystallitic | Porphyric |
| Beafield 4 | 1 | ••• | | | • | | | • | Grey & brown (PPL); red & grey (OIL) organo-mineral | • | • | • | • | •• | | | • | • | Spongy | Random, unreferred | Crystallitic | Chitonic |
| | 2 | ••• | | • | • | | | | Grey & brown (PPL); red & grey (OIL) organo-mineral | • | ••• | | • | ••• | • | | ••• | | Spongy | Random, unreferred | Crystallitic | Chito-porphyric |
| | 3 | ••• | •• | | • | | • | | Brown; organo-mineral | • | • | | • | • | • | • | | | Spongy (massive) | Random, unreferred | Undifferentiated | Porphyric |
| | 4 | ••• | •• | | • | | | | Brown; organo-mineral | • | • | • | • | • | • | • | | • | Spongy (massive) | Random, unreferred | Undifferentiated | Porphyric |
| Beafield 5 | 1 | ••• | •• | • | | | • | | Brown; organo-mineral | • | • | • | • | • | • | • | • | | Spongy | Random, unreferred | Crystallitic | Porphyric |
| | 2 | •• | •• | | • | | • | | Grey & brown (PPL); red & grey (OIL) organo-mineral | •• | •• | •• | • | • | •• | • | ••• | | Vughy | Random, unreferred | Crystallitic | Porphyric/gefuric |
| | 3 | ••• | •• | | • | | • | | Brown; organo-mineral | •• | • | • | • | • | • | ••• | | ••• | Massive (locally vughy) | Random, unreferred | Crystallitic | Porphyric |
| Beafield 6 | 1 | ••• | •• | • | | | • | | Grey & brown (PPL); red & grey (OIL) organo-mineral | • | •• | • | • | • | • | • | • | • | Spongy | Random, unreferred | Crystallitic | Chito-porphyric |
| | 2 | •• | •• | | | | • | | Grey & brown (PPL); red & grey (OIL) organo-mineral | • | • | • | • | • | •• | • | • | | Spongy | Random, unreferred | Crystallitic | Chitonic |
| Beafield 7 | 1 | ••• | • | | | | • | | Brown; organo-mineral | •• | • | •• | • | • | •• | •• | | | Spongy | Random, unreferred | Undifferentiated | Porphyric |
| | 2 | •• | ••• | | | | • | | Grey & brown (PPL); red & grey (OIL) organo-mineral | • | • | ••• | • | • | • | • | ••• | ••• | Vughy | Random, unreferred | Crystallitic | Chito-porphyric |

Table 5. Basic soil thin section descriptions, Beafield, Sanday.

| Slide No. | Zone | Fine Mineral Material | Microstructure | Coarse Material Arrangement | Groundmass B-Fabric | Related Distribution |
|---|---|---|---|---|---|---|
| Beafield 8 | 1 | Brown; organo-mineral | Granular | Random, unreferred | – | Monic |
| | 2 | Grey & brown (PPL); red & grey (OIL) organo-mineral | Vughy | Random, unreferred | Crystallitic | Porphyric |
| | 3 | Brown; organo-mineral | Fragmented vughy | Random, unreferred | Crystallitic | Porphyric |
| Beafield 9 | 1 | Grey & brown (PPL); red & grey (OIL) organo-mineral | Fragmented, massive | Random, unreferred | Undifferentiated | Porphyric |
| | 2 | Grey & brown (PPL); red & grey (OIL) organo-mineral | Spongy | Random, unreferred | Crystallitic | Porphyric |
| | 3 | Grey & brown (PPL); red & grey (OIL) organo-mineral | Weakly developed crumb | Random, unreferred | Crystallitic | Porphyric |
| | 4 | Grey & brown (PPL); red & grey (OIL) organo-mineral | Granular | Random, unreferred | Crystallitic | Monic |
| | 5 | Brown; organo-mineral | Moderately developed crumb | Random, unreferred | Undifferentiated | Porphyric |
| Beafield 10 | 1 | Grey & brown (PPL); grey (OIL) mineral | Spongy | Random, unreferred | Crystallitic / Crystallitic | Porphyric / Chitonic |
| | 2 | Grey & brown (PPL); red & grey (OIL) organo-mineral | Moderately developed crumb | Random, unreferred | Crystallitic | Enaulic |
| | 3 | Brown; organo-mineral | Granular/crumb complex | Random, unreferred | Crystallitic | Monic |
| | 4 | Brown; organo-mineral | Spongy | Random, unreferred | Undifferentiated | Porphyric |
| Beafield 11 | 1 | Brown; organo-mineral | Spongy (massive) / Spongy | Random, unreferred | Undifferentiated | Porphyric |

**Table 5 (cont).** Basic soil thin section descriptions, Beafield, Sanday.

Frequency Scale: •: very few, ••: few, •••: frequent/common, ••••: dominant. Scale based on classes in Bullock *et al.* 1985.

| Slide No. | Zone | Quartz | Shell | Sandstone | Siltstone | Bone | Heated Stone | Compound Quartz Grains | Feldspar | Fine Mineral Material | Organ | Tissue, Charred | Tissue, Uncharred | Fungal Sclerotia | Charcoal | Cell Residue | Amorphous (Reddish Brown) | Textural (Sand Infill) | Amorphous (Nodule) | Microstructure | Coarse Material Arrangement | Groundmass B-Fabric | Related Distribution |
|---|---|---|---|---|---|---|---|---|---|---|---|---|---|---|---|---|---|---|---|---|---|---|---|
| | | | | COARSE MINERAL MATERIAL >20 m | | | | | | FINE MINERAL MATERIAL | | COARSE ORGANIC MATERIAL | | | | FINE ORGANIC MATERIAL | | PEDOFEATURES | | | | | |
| Tofts 1 | | .. | ... | | | . | | | . | Brown; organo-mineral | . | . | . | . | .. | .. | . | | | Weakly developed crumb | Random, unreferred | Undifferentiated | Porphyric/gefuric |
| Tofts 2 | | .. | ... | . | . | . | . | . | . | Brown; organo-mineral | . | . | . | . | | . | | | | Weakly developed crumb | Random, unreferred | Undifferentiated | Porphyric/gefuric |
| Tofts 3 | | ... | ... | . | . | . | . | . | . | Brown; organo-mineral | . | . | .. | . | .. | | | | . | Weakly developed crumb | Random, unreferred | Undifferentiated | Porphyric/chitonic |
| Tofts 4 | | ... | ... | . | . | . | . | . | . | Brown; organo-mineral | . | . | . | . | .. | . | . | | . | Weakly developed crumb | Random, unreferred | Crystallitic | Porphyric |
| Tofts 5 | 1 | ... | ... | . | . | . | . | | | Brown; organo-mineral | .. | . | . | . | | .. | | | | Weakly developed crumb | Random, unreferred | Undifferentiated | Chito-porphyric |
| Tofts 5 | 2 | ... | ... | . | . | . | | | | Grey & brown (PPL); red & grey (OIL) organo-mineral | . | . | . | . | . | | | | | Weakly developed crumb | Random, unreferred | Crystallitic | Chitonic |
| Tofts 6 | 1 | ... | .. | . | | | | | | Brown; organo-mineral | . | . | . | . | . | | | . | | Strongly developed crumb | Random, unreferred | Undifferentiated | Gefuric/chitonic |
| Tofts 6 | 2 | ... | ... | | . | | | | | Brown; organo-mineral | . | .. | . | . | .. | . | | | | Strongly developed crumb | Random, unreferred | Undifferentiated | Chitonic |
| Tofts 7 | 1 | ... | ... | . | . | | | | | Brown; organo-mineral | .. | .. | . | . | .. | . | . | | .. | Weakly developed blocky | Random, unreferred | Undifferentiated | Porphyric |
| Tofts 7 | 2 | ... | ... | . | . | | | | . | Brown; organo-mineral | .. | . | . | . | .. | .. | . | | | Strongly developed crumb | Random, unreferred | Crystallitic | Porphyric/gefuric |
| Tofts 8 | 1 | ... | ... | . | . | | | | | Brown; organo-mineral | .. | ... | . | . | ... | . | . | | .. | Moderately developed crumb | Random, unreferred | Undifferentiated | Porphyric/gefuric |
| Tofts 8 | 2 | ... | .. | | | | | | | Grey & brown (PPL); red & grey (OIL) organo-mineral | ... | . | . | . | .. | | | | . | Moderately developed crumb | Random, unreferred | Crystallitic | Gefuric |
| Tofts 9 | 1 | ... | ... | . | . | | | | | Brown; organo-mineral | ... | .. | . | . | ... | .. | . | | | Moderately developed blocky | Random, unreferred | Crystallitic | Porphyro-gefuric |
| Tofts 9 | 2 | ... | ... | . | . | | | | | Grey & brown (PPL); red & grey (OIL) organo-mineral | ... | .. | . | . | .. | .. | . | | .. | Granular/well developed crumb | Random, unreferred | Undifferentiated | Chitonic/gefuric |
| Tofts 10 | | ... | ... | . | . | | | | | Brown; organo-mineral | .. | .. | . | . | .. | .. | | | . | Moderately developed blocky | Random, unreferred | Undifferentiated | Porphyric |
| Tofts 11 | 1 | ... | ... | . | . | | | . | | Brown; organo-mineral | . | . | . | . | ... | .. | | . | | Moderately developed blocky | Random, unreferred | Undifferentiated | Porphyric |
| Tofts 11 | 2 | ... | | | | | | | | Grey & brown (PPL); red & grey (OIL) organo-mineral | ... | . | . | . | .. | .. | | | | Granular/moderately developed crumb | Random, unreferred | Undifferentiated | Gefuric |
| Tofts 12 | | . | ... | . | . | . | | | | Brown; organo-mineral | .. | .. | . | . | . | .. | | . | | Moderately developed blocky | Random, unreferred | Undifferentiated | Porphyric |
| Tofts 13 | | ... | .. | . | . | . | | | | Grey & brown (PPL); red & grey (OIL) organo-mineral | .. | .. | . | . | ... | | | | | Weakly developed blocky | Random, unreferred | Undifferentiated | Porphyric |

Table 6. Basic soil thin section descriptions, Tofts, Sanday.

Frequency Scale: .: very few, ..: few, ...: frequent/common, .....: dominant. Scale based on classes in Bullock *et al.* 1985.

| Slide No. | Zone | COARSE MINERAL MATERIAL >20 mm | | | | | | | FINE MINERAL MATERIAL | COARSE ORGANIC MATERIAL | | | | FINE ORGANIC MATERIAL | | | | PEDOFEATURES | MICROSTRUCTURE | COARSE MATERIAL ARRANGEMENT | GROUNDMASS B-FABRIC | RELATED DISTRIBUTION |
|---|---|---|---|---|---|---|---|---|---|---|---|---|---|---|---|---|---|---|---|---|---|---|
| | | Quartz | Shell | Sandstone | Siltstone | Bone | Heated Stone | Compound Quartz Grains | | Organ | Tissue, Charred | Tissue, Uncharred | Fungal Sclerotia | Charcoal | Cell Residue | Amorphous | Amorphous (Reddish Brown) | Amorphous (Nodule) | | | | |
| Westbrough 1 | 1 | ••• | | • | | • | | | Brown; organo-mineral | ••• | | ••• | ••• | | ••• | | • | • | Weakly developed crumb | Random, unreferred | Crystallitic | Porphyric |
| | 2 | ••• | | • | | | | • | Brown; organo-mineral | • | | ••• | ••• | | ••• | •• | • | | Weakly developed crumb | Random, unreferred | Crystallitic | Porphyric |
| Westbrough 2 | 1 | •••• | | | | • | • | • | Brown; organo-mineral | • | ••• | | • | • | | | • | | Apedal | Random, unreferred | Crystallitic | Porphyric |
| | 2 | •••• | | •• | | • | | | Grey & brown (PPL); red & grey (OIL) organo-mineral | •• | | | | | • | • | | •••• | Apedal | Random, unreferred | Crystallitic | Porphyric |
| Westbrough 3 | 1 | •••• | | • | | | | | Brown; organo-mineral | •• | •• | •• | •• | ••• | | | | | Apedal, occasional channels and chambers | Random, unreferred | Undifferentiated | Porphyric |
| | 2 | •••• | | • | | •• | | | Grey & brown (PPL); red & grey (OIL) organo-mineral | • | ••• | | • | | | | | ••• | Apedal, occasional vughs | Random, unreferred | Undifferentiated | Porphyric |
| Westbrough 4 | 1 | •••• | | • | | • | | | Brown; organo-mineral | •• | | ••• | •• | | • | | | | Apedal, occasional channels and chambers | Random, unreferred | Undifferentiated | Porphyric |
| | 2 | •••• | | • | | • | | | Brown; organo-mineral | ••• | | •• | • | • | • | •• | | • | Apedal, occasional vughs | Random, unreferred | Undifferentiated | Chito-porphyric |
| Westbrough 5 | 1 | •••• | | • | | • | | | Brown; organo-mineral | ••• | ••• | •• | • | ••• | ••• | • | | | Apedal, occasional channels and chambers | Random, unreferred | Undifferentiated | Porphyric |
| | 2 | •••• | | • | | •• | | | Grey & brown (PPL); red & grey (OIL) organo-mineral | ••• | ••• | •• | | ••• | ••• | | ••• | ••• | Apedal, occasional vughs | Random, unreferred | Undifferentiated | Chito-porphyric |
| Westbrough 6 | 1 | •••• | | •• | | • | | | Brown; organo-mineral | ••• | | ••• | ••• | | | | | | Apedal, occasional channels and chambers | Random, unreferred | Undifferentiated | Porphyric |
| | 2 | •••• | | • | | • | | | Grey & brown (PPL); red & grey (OIL) organo-mineral | ••• | | ••• | | | | | | ••• | Apedal, occasional channels | Random, unreferred | Undifferentiated | Porphyric |
| Westbrough 7 | 1 | ••• | | • | | • | | | Brown; organo-mineral | ••• | • | • | ••• | | | | • | | Apedal, occasional channels and chambers | Random, unreferred | Undifferentiated | Porphyric |
| | 2 | ••• | | • | | • | | | Grey & brown (PPL); red & grey (OIL) organo-mineral | ••• | | • | ••• | | | | ••• | | Apedal, occasional vughs | Random, unreferred | Undifferentiated | Porphyric |
| Westbrough 8 | 1 | ••• | | • | | • | | | Brown; organo-mineral | ••• | | • | •• | • | | | | | Apedal, occasional channels and chambers | Random, unreferred | Undifferentiated | Porphyric |
| | 2 | •••• | | • | | •• | | | Grey & brown (PPL); red & grey (OIL) organo-mineral | •• | | • | •• | | | | | ••• | Apedal, occasional vughs | Random, unreferred | Undifferentiated | Porphyric |

## Table 7. Soil thin section descriptions, Westbrough, Sanday.

Frequency Scale: •: very few, ••: few, •••: frequent/common, ••••: dominant. Scale based on classes in Bullock et al. 1985.

| Depth (cm) | Slide No. | TBF | Textural Pedofeature | Mammillated Excrement | Bacillo-cylindrical Excrement | Spheroidal Excrement | Ellipsoidal Excrement | Cylindrical Excrement | Tailed conoidal Excrement |
|---|---|---|---|---|---|---|---|---|---|
| 1 | 1 | 80 | - | x | x | - | - | x | - |
| 2 | 1 | 95 | - | 5 | x | - | x | - | - |
| 3 | 1 | 100 | - | x | - | - | x | - | - |
| 4 | 1 | 90 | 10 | - | - | - | - | - | - |
| 5 | 1 | 95 | x | 5 | - | x | - | - | - |
| 6 | 1 | 95 | 5 | x | x | - | - | - | - |
| 7 | 1&2 | 85 | 5 | 10 | x | - | x | - | - |
| 8 | 2 | 80 | - | 15 | 5 | - | - | - | - |
| 9 | 2 | 90 | - | 5 | 5 | - | - | - | - |
| 10 | 2 | 100 | - | x | x | - | - | - | - |
| 11 | 2 | 90 | - | 5 | 5 | - | - | - | - |
| 12 | 2 | 90 | - | 5 | 5 | - | - | - | - |
| 13 | 2 | 85 | - | 10 | x | - | - | - | - |
| 14 | 3 | 75 | 25 | x | x | - | - | - | - |
| 15 | 3 | 85 | 10 | 5 | x | - | - | - | - |
| 16 | 3 | 100 | x | x | x | - | x | - | - |
| 17 | 3 | 95 | x | 5 | x | - | - | - | - |
| 18 | 3 | 90 | - | 10 | x | - | - | - | - |
| 19 | 3 | 90 | - | 10 | x | - | - | - | - |
| 20 | 3 | 50 | - | 25 | 10 | - | - | - | - |
| 21 | 4 | 90 | - | 5 | 5 | - | - | - | - |
| 22 | 4 | 90 | - | 10 | - | - | - | - | - |
| 23 | 4 | 40 | x | 15 | 10 | - | - | - | - |
| 24 | 4 | 80 | - | 10 | x | - | - | - | - |
| 25 | 4 | 20 | - | 10 | x | - | - | - | - |
| 26 | 4 | 65 | - | x | x | - | - | - | - |
| 27 | 4 | 75 | - | 10 | 5 | - | - | - | - |

**Table 8. Mean Percentage Area Coverage of Slide by Faunalturbation Features, Beafield.**
T.B.F. = Total Biological Fabric    X<5% coverage

| Depth (cm) | Slide No. | TBF | Textural Pedofeature | Mammillated Excrement | Bacillo-Cylindrical Excrement | Spheroidal Excrement | Ellipsoidal Excrement | Cylindrical Excrement | Tailed Conoidal Excrement |
|---|---|---|---|---|---|---|---|---|---|
| 28 | 5 | 90 | - | 10 | x | - | - | - | - |
| 29 | 5 | 80 | x | 15 | 5 | - | - | - | - |
| 30 | 5 | 95 | - | 5 | x | - | - | - | - |
| 31 | 5 | 85 | - | 10 | 5 | - | - | - | - |
| 32 | 5 | 70 | - | X | 20 | - | - | - | - |
| 33 | 5 | 90 | x | 5 | x | - | - | - | - |
| 34 | 5 | 5 | x | 20 | 5 | - | - | - | - |
| 35 | 6 | 85 | - | 10 | x | - | - | - | - |
| 36 | 6 | 95 | - | 5 | - | - | - | - | - |
| 37 | 6 | 45 | - | 10 | 10 | - | - | - | - |
| 38 | 6 | 80 | - | 5 | 10 | - | - | - | - |
| 39 | 6 | 80 | - | 10 | 10 | - | - | - | - |
| 40 | 6 | 90 | - | 5 | 5 | - | - | - | - |
| 41 | 6 | 85 | - | 5 | 10 | - | - | - | - |
| 67 | 7 | 95 | 5 | X | x | - | - | - | - |
| 68 | 7 | 95 | 5 | X | x | - | - | - | - |
| 69 | 7 | 50 | x | 5 | 10 | - | - | - | - |
| 70 | 7 | 70 | x | 5 | x | - | - | - | - |
| 71 | 7 | 65 | x | X | x | - | - | - | - |
| 72 | 7 | 90 | x | X | 10 | - | - | - | - |
| 73 | 7 | 35 | - | 15 | 10 | - | - | x | - |
| 82 | 8 | 45 | x | 15 | 5 | - | - | - | - |
| 83 | 8 | 10 | - | 10 | 40 | - | x | - | - |
| 84 | 8 | 30 | x | 10 | 55 | - | - | x | - |
| 85 | 8 | 15 | - | 20 | 40 | - | - | - | x |
| 86 | 8 | - | - | 15 | 75 | - | - | - | - |
| 87 | 8 | 10 | x | 10 | 60 | - | x | - | - |
| 88 | 8 | 15 | - | 20 | 60 | 5 | - | - | - |

**Table 8 (cont.). Mean Percentage Area Coverage of Slide by Faunalturbation Features, Beafield.**
**T.B.F. = Total Biological Fabric    X<5% coverage**

| Depth | Slide No. | TBF | Textural Pedofeature | Mammillated Excrement | Bacillo-cylindrical Excrement | Spheroidal Excrement | Ellipsoidal Excrement | Cylindrical Excrement | Tailed Conoidal Excrement |
|---|---|---|---|---|---|---|---|---|---|
| 84 | 9 | 10 | - | 15 | 15 | x | x | - | 5 |
| 85 | 9 | 50 | x | 10 | - | x | - | - | - |
| 86 | 9 | 80 | x | 10 | x | - | - | - | - |
| 87 | 9 | 30 | - | 55 | x | - | - | - | - |
| 88 | 9 | 50 | - | 5 | x | - | - | - | 15 |
| 89 | 9 | 90 | - | 5 | 5 | - | - | - | x |
| 90 | 9 | 85 | - | 10 | 5 | - | - | - | - |
| 114 | 10 | 55 | 20 | 5 | 5 | x | x | - | - |
| 115 | 10 | 40 | - | 10 | 25 | - | - | - | - |
| 116 | 10 | 25 | - | 25 | 50 | - | x | x | x |
| 117 | 10 | 15 | - | 15 | 25 | - | 5 | 5 | x |
| 118 | 10 | 75 | - | x | 5 | - | 10 | - | - |
| 119 | 10 | 90 | 5 | x | 5 | - | - | - | - |
| 120 | 10 | 95 | 5 | x | x | - | - | - | - |
| 27 | 11 | 95 | x | x | 5 | - | - | - | - |
| 28 | 11 | 85 | - | x | 5 | - | x | - | x |
| 29 | 11 | 95 | x | 5 | x | - | - | - | - |
| 30 | 11 | 90 | - | 5 | x | x | - | - | x |
| 31 | 11 | 95 | - | x | 5 | - | - | - | - |
| 32 | 11 | 75 | - | 5 | x | - | - | - | - |
| 33 | 11 | 90 | - | x | 10 | - | - | - | - |

**Table 8 (cont.). Mean Percentage Area Coverage of Slide by Faunalturbation Features, Beafield.**
**T.B.F. = Total Biological Fabric    X<5% coverage**

| Depth | Slide No. | TBF | Textural Pedofeatures | Mammillated Pedofeatures | Bacillo-cylindrical Pedofeatures | Spheroidal Excrement | Ellipsoidal Excrement | Cylindrical Excrement | Tailed Conoidal Excrement |
|---|---|---|---|---|---|---|---|---|---|
| 1 | 1 | 50 | - | 35 | 10 | - | - | - | - |
| 2 | 1 | 80 | - | 15 | 5 | - | - | - | - |
| 3 | 1 | 95 | - | x | 5 | - | - | - | - |
| 4 | 1 | 90 | - | 5 | 5 | - | - | - | - |
| 5 | 1 | 90 | - | 5 | 5 | - | - | - | - |
| 6 | 1 | 80 | - | 10 | 10 | - | - | - | - |
| 7 | 1&2 | 95 | - | x | 5 | - | - | - | - |
| 8 | 2 | 95 | - | - | 5 | - | - | - | - |
| 9 | 2 | 95 | - | x | 5 | - | - | - | - |
| 10 | 2 | 90 | x | 5 | 5 | - | - | - | - |
| 11 | 2 | 95 | - | - | x | - | - | - | - |
| 12 | 2 | 95 | x | x | 5 | - | - | - | - |
| 13 | 2 | 90 | - | x | 10 | - | - | - | - |
| 15 | 3 | 95 | - | x | 5 | - | - | - | - |
| 16 | 3 | 95 | - | x | 5 | - | - | - | - |
| 17 | 3 | 90 | - | 5 | 5 | - | - | - | - |
| 18 | 3 | 90 | - | 5 | 5 | - | - | - | - |
| 19 | 3 | 90 | - | x | 10 | - | - | - | - |
| 20 | 3&4 | 90 | x | 5 | 5 | - | - | - | - |
| 21 | 3&4 | 90 | - | 5 | 5 | - | - | - | - |
| 22 | 4 | 80 | - | 20 | x | - | - | - | - |
| 23 | 4 | 95 | - | x | 5 | - | - | - | - |
| 24 | 4 | 90 | x | x | 5 | - | - | - | - |
| 25 | 4 | 90 | - | x | 10 | - | - | - | - |
| 26 | 4 | 95 | - | x | 5 | - | - | - | - |

**Table 9. Mean Percentage Area Coverage of Slide by Faunalturbation Features, Tofts.**
**T.B.F. = Total Biological Fabric   X<5% coverage**

| Depth | Slide No. | TBF | Textural Pedofeatures | Mammillated Excrement | Bacillo-cylindrical Excrement | Spheroidal Excrement | Ellipsoidal Excrement | Cylindrical Excrement | Tailed Conoidal Excrement |
|---|---|---|---|---|---|---|---|---|---|
| 27 | 5 | 95 | - | x | 5 | x | - | - | - |
| 28 | 5 | 100 | - | x | x | - | - | - | - |
| 29 | 5 | 95 | - | x | 5 | - | - | - | - |
| 30 | 5 | 95 | - | x | 5 | - | - | - | - |
| 31 | 5 | 55 | - | 5 | 40 | - | - | - | - |
| 32 | 5 | 90 | - | x | 10 | - | - | - | - |
| 33 | 5 | 85 | - | x | 10 | - | - | - | - |
| 34 | 6 | 80 | - | x | 20 | - | - | - | - |
| 35 | 6 | 90 | - | x | 10 | - | - | - | - |
| 36 | 6 | 85 | - | x | 10 | - | - | - | - |
| 37 | 6 | 95 | - | x | 5 | - | - | - | - |
| 38 | 6 | 95 | - | x | x | - | - | - | - |
| 39 | 6 | 85 | - | x | 15 | - | - | - | - |
| 40 | 6 | 100 | - | x | x | - | - | - | - |
| 41 | 7 | 65 | - | x | 10 | - | - | - | - |
| 42 | 7 | 80 | - | 5 | 15 | x | x | - | - |
| 43 | 7 | 80 | - | x | 10 | - | - | - | - |
| 44 | 7 | 80 | - | x | 15 | - | - | - | - |
| 45 | 7 | 70 | - | 15 | 15 | - | x | - | - |
| 46 | 7 | 80 | - | x | 20 | - | - | - | - |
| 47 | 7 | 90 | - | 5 | 5 | - | - | - | - |
| 57 | 8 | 100 | - | x | x | - | - | - | - |
| 58 | 8 | 50 | - | 5 | 15 | - | x | - | - |
| 59 | 8 | 80 | - | x | 15 | - | x | - | - |
| 60 | 8 | 90 | - | x | 5 | - | - | - | - |
| 61 | 8 | 95 | - | x | 5 | - | - | - | - |
| 62 | 8 | 95 | - | x | 5 | - | - | - | - |
| 63 | 8 | 30 | - | x | x | - | - | - | - |

**Table 9(cont.). Mean Percentage Area Coverage of Slide by Faunalturbation Features, Tofts.**
**T.B.F. = Total Biological Fabric    X<5% coverage**

| Depth | Slide No. | TBF | Textural Pedofeature | Mammillated Excrement | Bacillo-cylindrical Excrement | Spheroidal Excrement | Ellipsoidal Excrement | Cylindrical Excrement | Tailed Conoidal Excrement |
|---|---|---|---|---|---|---|---|---|---|
| 63 | 9 | 100 | - | x | x | - | - | - | - |
| 64 | 9 | 90 | - | 5 | 5 | x | - | x | - |
| 65 | 9 | 100 | - | x | x | - | - | - | - |
| 66 | 9 | 100 | - | x | x | - | - | - | - |
| 67 | 9 | 70 | - | x | x | - | - | - | - |
| 68 | 9 | 95 | - | x | 5 | - | - | - | - |
| 69 | 9 | 75 | x | x | x | - | x | x | - |
| 70 | 9 | 100 | - | x | x | - | - | - | - |
| 32 | 10 | 95 | - | x | 5 | - | - | - | - |
| 33 | 10 | 100 | - | x | x | - | - | - | - |
| 34 | 10 | 100 | - | x | x | - | - | - | - |
| 35 | 10 | 90 | x | x | 10 | - | - | - | - |
| 36 | 10 | 100 | - | x | 10 | - | - | - | - |
| 37 | 10 | 95 | - | x | 5 | - | - | - | - |
| 38 | 10 | 100 | - | x | x | - | - | - | - |
| 29 | 11 | 90 | - | x | 10 | - | - | - | - |
| 30 | 11 | 95 | - | x | 5 | - | - | - | - |
| 31 | 11 | 100 | - | x | x | - | - | - | - |
| 32 | 11 | 95 | - | x | x | - | x | - | - |
| 33 | 11 | 95 | - | x | x | - | - | - | - |
| 34 | 11 | 90 | - | x | 5 | - | - | - | - |
| 35 | 11 | 95 | - | x | x | x | - | - | - |
| 20 | 12 | 95 | 5 | x | x | - | - | - | - |
| 21 | 12 | 100 | x | x | x | - | - | - | - |
| 22 | 12 | 95 | 5 | x | x | - | - | - | - |
| 23 | 12 | 100 | x | x | x | - | - | - | - |
| 24 | 12 | 95 | x | 5 | x | - | - | - | - |
| 25 | 12 | 95 | 5 | x | x | - | - | - | - |

**Table 9(cont.). Mean Percentage Area Coverage of Slide by Faunalturbation Features, Tofts.**
**T.B.F. = Total Biological Fabric    X<5% coverage**

| Depth | Slide No. | TBF | Textural Pedofeatures | Mammillated Excrement | Bacillo-cylindrical Excrement | Spheroidal Excrement | Ellipsoidal Excrement | Cylindrical Excrement | Tailed Conoidal Excrement |
|---|---|---|---|---|---|---|---|---|---|
| 73 | 13 | 95 | - | x | x | - | - | - | - |
| 74 | 13 | 90 | - | x | 10 | - | - | - | - |
| 75 | 13 | 95 | - | x | 5 | - | - | - | - |
| 76 | 13 | 100 | - | x | x | - | - | - | - |
| 77 | 13 | 100 | - | x | x | - | - | - | - |
| 78 | 13 | 95 | 5 | x | x | - | - | - | - |
| 79 | 13 | 100 | - | x | x | - | - | - | - |

**Table 9 (cont.). Mean Percentage Area Coverage of Slide by Faunalturbation Features, Tofts.**
**T.B.F. = Total Biological Fabric    X<5% coverage**

| Depth | Slide No. | TBF | Textural Pedofeature | Mammillated Excrement | Bacillo-cylindrical Excrement | Spheroidal Excrement | Ellipsoidal Excrement | Cylindrical Excrement | Tailed Conoidal Excrement |
|---|---|---|---|---|---|---|---|---|---|
| 1 | 1 | 100 | - | x | x | - | - | - | - |
| 2 | 1 | 100 | - | - | - | - | - | - | - |
| 3 | 1 | 100 | - | x | x | - | - | - | - |
| 4 | 1 | 100 | - | x | x | - | - | - | - |
| 5 | 1 | 100 | - | x | x | - | x | - | - |
| 6 | 1 | 100 | - | x | x | - | - | - | - |
| 7 | 1&2 | 100 | x | x | x | - | - | - | - |
| 8 | 2 | 100 | - | x | x | x | - | - | - |
| 9 | 2 | 100 | - | x | x | - | - | - | - |
| 10 | 2 | 100 | - | x | x | - | - | - | - |
| 11 | 2 | 95 | - | x | x | - | - | - | - |
| 12 | 2 | 80 | - | 10 | 5 | - | - | - | - |
| 13 | 2&3 | 75 | - | x | x | - | - | - | - |
| 14 | 3 | 65 | - | x | - | - | - | - | - |
| 15 | 3 | 85 | - | x | x | - | - | - | - |
| 16 | 3 | 80 | - | x | x | - | - | - | - |
| 17 | 3 | 90 | - | 5 | 5 | - | - | - | - |
| 18 | 3 | 35 | - | x | x | - | - | - | - |
| 19 | 3 | 45 | - | x | 10 | - | x | - | - |
| 20 | 3 | 80 | - | x | 5 | - | - | - | - |
| 21 | 4 | 60 | - | x | x | - | - | - | - |
| 22 | 4 | 75 | - | x | 5 | - | - | - | - |
| 23 | 4 | 55 | - | x | 10 | - | - | - | - |
| 24 | 4 | 50 | - | x | 5 | - | - | - | - |
| 25 | 4 | 70 | - | 5 | x | - | - | - | - |
| 26 | 4 | 95 | - | x | x | - | - | - | - |
| 27 | 4 | 90 | - | x | x | - | - | - | - |

**Table 10. Mean Percentage Area Coverage of Slide by Faunalturbation Features, Westbrough.**
**T.B.F. = Total Biological Fabric    X<5% coverage**

| Depth | Slide No. | TBF | Textural Pedofeature | Mammillated Excrement | Bacillo-cylindrical Excrement | Spheroidal Excrement | Ellipsoidal Excrement | Cylindrical Excrement | Tailed Conoidal Excrement |
|---|---|---|---|---|---|---|---|---|---|
| 28 | 5 | 65 | - | x | 5 | - | - | - | - |
| 29 | 5 | 100 | - | x | x | - | - | - | - |
| 30 | 5 | 100 | - | x | x | - | - | - | - |
| 31 | 5 | 100 | - | x | x | - | - | - | - |
| 32 | 5 | 100 | - | x | x | - | - | - | - |
| 33 | 5 | 100 | - | x | - | - | - | - | - |
| 34 | 5 | 100 | - | x | x | - | - | - | - |
| 35 | 6 | 100 | - | x | x | - | - | - | - |
| 36 | 6 | 100 | - | x | x | - | - | - | - |
| 37 | 6 | 60 | - | x | x | - | - | - | - |
| 38 | 6 | 55 | - | 5 | x | - | - | - | - |
| 39 | 6 | 95 | - | x | x | - | - | - | - |
| 40 | 6 | 100 | - | x | x | x | - | - | - |
| 41 | 6 | 85 | - | x | 5 | - | - | - | - |
| 42 | 6 | 100 | - | x | x | - | - | - | - |
| 17 | 7 | 95 | - | x | - | - | - | - | - |
| 18 | 7 | 80 | - | x | x | - | - | - | - |
| 19 | 7 | 85 | - | x | x | - | - | - | - |
| 20 | 7 | 70 | - | x | x | - | - | - | - |
| 21 | 7 | 70 | - | x | x | - | - | - | - |
| 29 | 8 | 100 | - | - | - | - | x | - | - |
| 30 | 8 | 95 | - | 5 | - | - | x | - | - |
| 31 | 8 | 100 | - | x | x | x | - | - | - |
| 32 | 8 | 75 | - | x | x | - | - | - | - |
| 33 | 8 | 55 | - | x | x | x | - | - | - |
| 34 | 8 | 70 | - | x | x | x | - | - | - |

**Table 10 (cont). Mean Percentage Area Coverage of Slide by Faunalturbation Features, Westbrough. T.B.F. = Total Biological Fabric    X<5% coverage**

# The Dnieper Rapids region of Ukraine: A consideration of chronology, diet and dental pathology at the Mesolithic-Neolithic transition

Malcolm C. Lillie

Centre for Wetland Archaeology, Department of Geography, University of Hull, Hull HU6 7RX, England

**Abstract:**

This paper presents new insights into cultural developments in Ukraine during the Mesolithic to Neolithic periods. Twenty-three recently obtained radiocarbon determinations on human skeletal remains facilitate a complete revision of the periods in question. The results of the new chronology show that numerous cultural traits originally thought to be of Neolithic derivation, such as burial inventories, cranial surgery, 'art' and population movements actually have their genesis at the end of the Mesolithic period. The combination of palaeopathological analyses and bone collagen stable carbon isotope values obtained from late Mesolithic and earlier Neolithic skeletal remains from the Dnieper Rapids region of Ukraine confirm an overall dietary equivalence occurring across these periods.

It appears that the indigenous populations consumed fisher-hunter-gatherer diets throughout the period *c.* 10,000-3500 cal. BC, with some limited archaeological evidence for the exploitation of domesticated animals occurring towards the end of the Neolithic period. In addition, analysis of dental pathologies from both periods establishes the protein-based nature of the dietary regimes. No secure evidence for the integration of cereal-based dietary regimes during either period was forthcoming from the study, thereby contradicting previous conclusions relating to subsistence strategies at the Mesolithic-Neolithic transition. The precise nature of the observed variability in the stable isotopic evidence for diet remains to be established by future collaborative studies in both Russia and Ukraine.

Keywords: Ukraine, Mesolithic-Neolithic Transition, Dental Pathology, Stable Isotopes $\delta^{13}$C, $\delta^{15}$N, Palaeodietary Reconstruction.

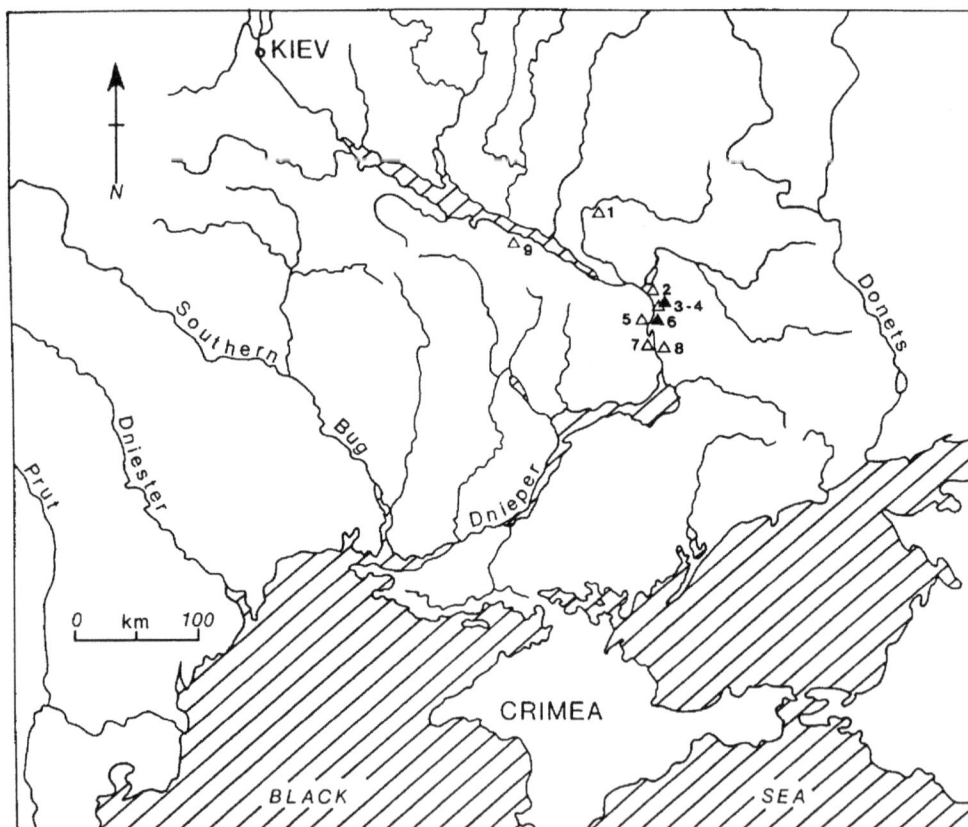

Figure 1: The Dnieper Rapids region, showing location of cemeteries discussed in text. 1. Osipovka, 2. Igren VIII, 3. Vasilyevka V, 4. Vasilyevka III and II, 5. Nikolskoye, 6. Marievka, 7. Vovnigi II, 8. Yasinovatka, 9. Dereivka I and II. ▲ = Mesolithic, + = Neolithic

# Introduction

The current research emerged due to the growing awareness of an East-West dichotomy in the reporting of pathological markers on archaeological skeletal material (e.g. Meiklejohn and Zvelebil 1991). Indeed, recent palaeopathological analyses of the transition from the Mesolithic-Neolithic periods in the Dnieper Rapids region of Ukraine (Figure 1) had indicated that a dietary shift towards the exploitation of cereal-based subsistence strategies, away from the traditional Mesolithic fisher-hunter-gatherer subsistence regimes, was occurring towards the end of the Mesolithic in Ukraine (Jacobs 1993, 1994).

The Dnieper Rapids contains a significant number of cemeteries dating from the Epipalaeolithic through to the Eneolithic periods between *c.* 10,000 and 3500 cal. BC (Gokhman 1966, Konduktorova 1974, Telegin and Potekhina 1987.). The availability of a data set that contains the skeletal remains of *c.* 310 individuals from a broad temporal range, that essentially covers 6500 years of human evolution, is clearly fundamental when attempting to reconstruct socio-economic developments across significant cultural horizons such as the Mesolithic-Neolithic transition.

The importance of this study is highlighted by the fact that recent attempts to reconstruct the mechanisms behind the shift away from food extracting to food producing societies have indicated that this process is both spatially and temporally diverse in Europe (e.g., Ammerman and Cavalli-Sforza 1971, 1973, 1979, 1984, Armit and Finlayson 1992, Bonsall *et al.* 1997, Dennell 1985, Lillie 1996, 1997, Lillie and Zvelebil 1999, Lubell *et al.* 1994, van Andels and Runnels 1995, Zvelebil 1986, Zvelebil and Rowley-Conwy 1984, Zvelebil and Dolukhanov 1991). In order to model such significant dietary and social developments we, as archaeologists and anthropologists, clearly need to investigate a wide range of parameters, and a comparatively broad temporal range, when attempting studies concerned with such reconstructions.

## Chronology

In contrast to the conventional European understanding of 'Neolithic' society, such as the major socio-economic transformations associated with the shift from forager-based societies, the Ukrainian term 'Neolithic' is generally used to denote the presence of pottery (*cf.* Jacobs 1993:312, Lillie 1996:137, 1998a:185). Conversely, despite this methodological premise, it has been shown that the early Neolithic cemeteries of Mariupol-type (Telegin 1987) such as Marievka and Vasilyevka V are in fact aceramic. Similarly, the cemetery of Vovnigi II has only two sherds of Dnieper-Donets pottery in association, and the earliest phase of interment at Yasinovatka is also aceramic (*cf.* Lillie 1996:136).

Telegin (1968:175-80) had used the rite of extended burial to characterise the Neolithic Mariupol-type cemeteries. This typological criterion is supplemented by similarities in artefact types, such as pottery and flint, imports from the adjacent Tripolye farming culture and a limited number of

radiocarbon determinations from the Kiev conventional radiocarbon facility (Potekhina and Telegin 1995). These determinations consisted of eight dates obtained from human bone from the cemeteries of Nikolskoye, Yasinovatka and Osipovka (Table 1, prefix Ki-), which suggested use between *c.* 5400-3900 cal. BC. Recent reconsideration of the available evidence (Lillie 1998*a* and *b*) has shown that a number of the cemeteries (Figure 1), or discrete phases within them, whilst designated as Neolithic by Telegin (1968, 1987), either failed to fulfill the basic criteria as set, or had little secure evidence for their attribution to the Neolithic period (Lillie 1998*a*).

This has led to a complete revision of the Ukrainian cemetery series (Table 1) (Lillie 1998a and b), with numerous revisions occurring in the periodisation of such 'Neolithic' cultural markers as the rite of extended burial. It is now apparent that this custom has it genesis in what is essentially an Epipalaeolithic context at the cemetery of Vasilyevka III, which is dated to between 10,230-9000 cal BC (OxA-3807-9). At this cemetery seven of the forty-four individuals buried at the site were in the extended position, with the remaining thirty-seven being in the crouched (flexed) position (Telegin 1982). The new radiocarbon dates obtained by Jacobs (1993) for Vasilyevka II indicate that this cemetery is late Mesolithic in age at 7300-6220 cal. BC, as opposed to the earlier Neolithic position inferred by Telegin (1987) on typological criteria. Similarly, the cemetery of Marievka which was originally though to follow Vasilyevka II in Telegin's (1968) earlier Neolithic sequence, now has an age that would conform to a late Mesolithic context at 7000-6050 cal BC (OxA-6199, -6200 and 6269).

The thirty-two individuals interred at Vasilyevka II and the fifteen individuals interred at Marievka are all buried in the extended position. This indicates that in contrast to Telegin's (1968, 1987) assertion that the extended burial ritual represents a wholly Neolithic cultural trait, this form of burial is in fact Epipalaeolithic in origin, and it actually supercedes burial in the crouched position as the dominant burial ritual during the Mesolithic period. This observation has further implications in that the associated artefacts from the cemeteries of Vasilyevka II and Marievka, which include microlithics and Cyprinidae (carp) and Pearl Roarch tooth pendants and necklaces, must now be considered to represent an integral part of the Mesolithic cultural repertoire. Additionally, research by Kozlowski (1989) had identified an apparent lacuna in terms of Mesolithic art from the Ukrainian region. The new dating of Vasilyevka II has redressed this imbalance due to the fact that there are a number of engraved bone arm bands, clearly an expressive 'art' form, from this particular cemetery (Lillie *in press*, Telegin and Potekhina 1987:12).

Four determinations for Vasilyevka V place this cemetery at *c.* 5738-5059 BC (the 6th millennium BC). This cemetery is again considerably older than has been supposed from burial inventory and mode of interment. Discrepancies occur within the internal seriation of this cemetery. While the general assumption that microlithic flint artefacts are older than more massive flint implements is borne out by the

| Cemetery | Laboratory number | Material | Burial number | Uncalibrated determination (b.p.) | Calibrated date-range (BC) |
|---|---|---|---|---|---|
| Marievka | *OxA-6199 | Human bone | 4 | 7955±55 | 7036-6604 |
| | *OxA-6200 | Human bone | 10 | 7620±160 | 6989-6060 |
| | *OxA-6269 | Human bone | 14 | 7630±110 | 6615-6189 |
| Vasilyevka V | *OxA-6171 | Human bone | 8 | 6470±60 | 5479-5273 |
| | *OxA-6172 | Human bone | 10 | 6805±60 | 5738-5531 |
| | *OxA-6268 | Human bone | 20 | 6710±90 | 5711-5440 |
| | *OxA-6198 | Human bone | 29 | 6280±70 | 5369-5059 |
| Osipovka | Ki-519 | Human bone | 53 | 5940±100 | 5199-4588 |
| | Ki-517 | Human bone | 53 | 6075±125 | 5308-4723 |
| | *OxA-6168 | Human bone | 20 | 7675±70 | 6604-6376 |
| Yasinovatka | Ki-1171 | Human bone | 36 | 5650±70 | 4810-4470 |
| | Ki-3032 | Human bone | 18 | 5900±90 | 5044-4580 |
| | Ki-3033 | Human bone | 65 | 6240±100 | 5430-4930 |
| | OxA-5030 | Human bone | 64 | 6330±90 | 5435-5068 |
| | OxA-5057 | Human bone | 36 | 6260±180 | 5521-4788 |
| | *OxA-6163 | Human bone | 5 | 6465±60 | 5476-5271 |
| | *OxA-6166 | Human bone | 17 | 6360±75 | 5437-5090 |
| | *OxA-6167 | Human bone | 18 | 6255±65 | 5313-5052 |
| | *OxA-6165 | Human bone | 19 | 6370±60 | 5434-5221 |
| | *OxA-6164 | Human bone | 45 | 6360±60 | 5432-5148 |
| Nikolskoye | Ki-3284 | Human bone | 115 | 5200±30 | 4216-3976 |
| | Ki-3283 | Human bone | 125 | 5460±40 | 4450-4220 |
| | Ki-523 | Human bone | N/A | 5640±400 | 4950-4000 |
| | OxA-5029 | Human bone | 125 | 6300±80 | 5429-5057 |
| | OxA-5052 | Human bone | 137 | 6145±70 | 5244-4910 |
| | *OxA-6155 | Human bone | 94 | 6225±75 | 5286-4947 |
| Derievka I | OxA-5031 | Human bone | 109 | 6110±120 | 5273-4771 |
| | *OxA-6162 | Human bone | 33 | 6175±60 | 5256-4940 |
| | *OxA-6159 | Human bone | 42 | 6200±60 | 5263-4950 |
| | *OxA-6160 | Human bone | 49 | 6165±55 | 5245-4940 |
| | *OxA-6161 | Human bone | 84 | 7270±110 | 6361-5879 |

**Table 1: Accelerator radiocarbon determinations from the Dnieper Rapids, Mariupol-type cemeteries of Ukraine (\* new dates obtained July 1996 from the Oxford AMS facility). OxA dates without \* from Hedges *et al*. 1995, Kiev dates obtained from Potekhina and Telegin 1995. All dates are calculated at the 2 sigma level using the OxCal calibration program of C. Bronk Ramsay and the 1993 bi-decadal calibration curve in *Radiocarbon* 35.**

dating of burials 8 and 10 (OxA-6171 and OxA-6172), with both containing microlithic artefacts, the youngest burial 29, contained a fragment of a larger, and typologically later, flint knife. As these artefacts are attributable to the Mesolithic and Neolithic periods respectively, Vasilyevka V must be considered to be of transitional later Mesolithic-earliest Neolithic age. This observation is consistent with the overlap of the later radiocarbon determinations from Vasilyevka V with the earliest dates from the cemeteries of Derievka, Yasinovatka and Nikolskoye (Table 1). In essence, Vasilyevka V is a sub-Neolithic stage cemetery, somewhat older than Telegin's typological seriation suggests.

The recently obtained determinations from the Dereivka and

Yasinovatka cemeteries accord with the previous six dates (Lillie 1996:136-7), and with a number of conventional radiocarbon determinations from Kiev. Kiev date Ki-3033 on burial 65 (grave pit A-4) at Yasinovatka, at 5430-4930 BC corresponds with date OxA-5030 from the same Stage A burial phase, 5440-5060 BC (grave pit A-1). The other determinations obtained by Telegin for Yasinovatka also match the chronological sequence indicated by the Oxford dates. One of the new dates from Nikolskoye (OxA-6155), at 5286-4947 BC, again fully overlaps with the dates of 5429-4910 BC from OxA-5029 and OxA-5052 (Table 1).

It is clear from the new determinations that the 'Neolithic' cemetery sequence as developed by Telegin (1968, 1987) on the basis of limited radiocarbon determinations and typological seriation is fundamentally flawed. The chronological span of the Mariupol-type cemeteries must be extended back towards the seventh millennium cal BC, with the associated burial rituals and artefact inventories also being in need of re-periodisation on the basis of this data.

### Stable Isotopes and Diet

The paucity of reliable information relating to past dietary regimes in the Dnieper region of Ukraine necessitates a reliance on stable isotope and dental pathology to provide a realistic assessment of the foods consumed across the Mesolithic to Neolithic periods (*cf.* Bonsall *et al.* 1997, Iacumin *et al.* 1998, Keegan 1989, Lubell *et al.* 1994, McGovern-Wilson and Quinn 1996, Pate 1997, Richards 1998, Richards *et al.* 1998).

In the Dnieper Rapids region, Jacobs (1993, 1994) has argued that differences in $\delta^{13}C$ values between Vasilyevka III and II reflect a dietary shift in the later Mesolithic, towards the exploitation of either $C_3$ plants such as wheat, or the consumption of grazing domesticates such as cattle, or both. Variations in the barium levels between both sites are also used to support this argument. Reconsideration of this evidence (Lillie 1996:135-6, 1998*a*) in light of preliminary stable isotope data from the cemeteries outlined above, initially corroborated a shift towards more terrestrial oriented diets, which was presumed to have been occurring at both Vasilyevka II and Marievka between 7300-6060 BC (OxA-3806: 8020±90 BP; OxA-6200: 7620±160 BP) (Lillie 1998*a*). However, it is argued below that this evidence does not support the assertion of an agricultural transition occurring during the late Mesolithic in Ukraine, and in fact, the new stable isotope data refines the earlier conclusions relating to dietary change (Lillie 1998*a*), suggesting overall dietary equivalence across the Mesolithic-Neolithic transition.

### Material and Methods: Human bone

In the present analysis, twenty-one individuals, from six cemeteries dating to the Mesolithic and Neolithic periods and a single interment (Igren VIII) in the vicinity of the Dnieper Rapids region of Ukraine, have been assessed for their $\delta^{13}C$ and $\delta^{15}N$ ratios. The stable isotope analysis of the human bone collagen was carried out by Mike Richards at the Research Laboratory for Archaeology and the History of Art, University of Oxford.

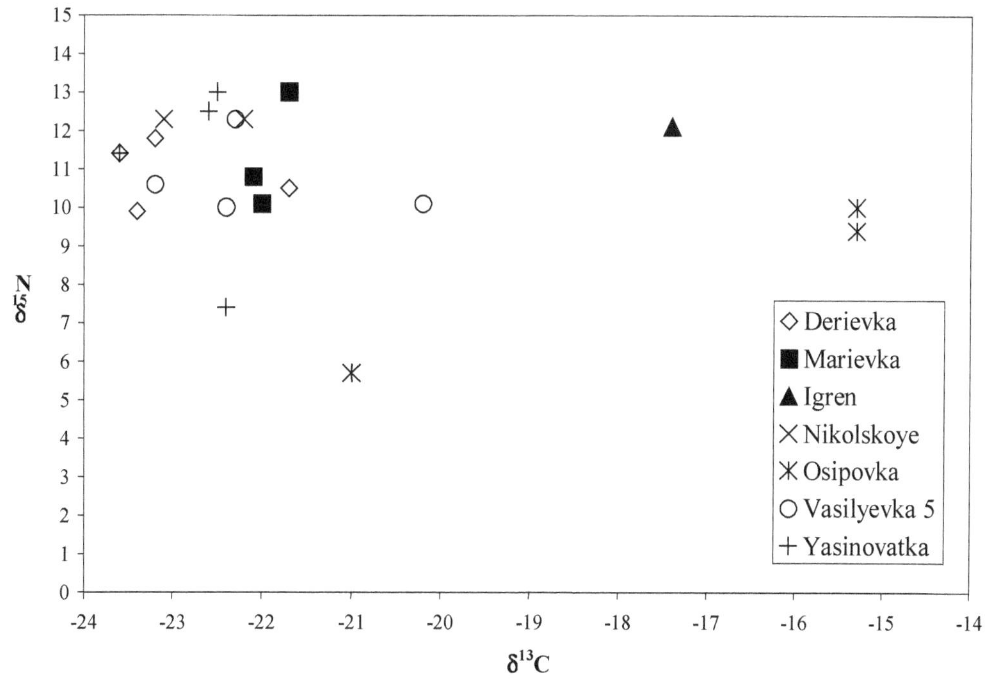

Figure 2: Human collagen $\delta^{13}C$ and $\delta^{15}N$ values from various Ukrainian sites.

## Sample Preparation

Collagen was extracted from the human bone samples following the protocol outlined in Richards (1998). This method is similar to other published methods of collagen extraction (e.g. Ambrose 1990, Brown *et al*. 1988), with some variation, and is summarised as:

1) For each sample a solution of 0.5M HCl was added to approximately 100-300 mg of cleaned whole bone (cortical bone only), and the bone was left to demineralise at approximately 5 °C for 3-5 days

2) The remaining solid was rinsed in $H_20$ and then gelatinised in a sealed sample holder (in a pH3 HCl solution and heated at approximately 70 °C for 24 hours).

3) This solution was then filtered through an 8 μm polyethylene filter, and then centrifuged at 65 °C for 15 hours under a vacuum in order to evaporate water and acid.

4) The resultant residue was then rehydrated in 2-3 ml of distilled $H_2O$, and then lyophilised for 48 hours.

5) The $\delta^{13}C$ and $\delta^{15}N$ values of the extracted 'collagen' was then measured at the Research Laboratory for Archaeology and the History of Art, Oxford, using a Roboprep CHN Analyser coupled with an Europa 20/20 isotope ratio monitoring mass spectrometer.

## Isotope Results

The stable isotope ratios obtained from the Ukrainian human skeletal material are presented in Table 2 and Figure 2. As can be seen in Table 1 all of the collagen was fairly well preserved (as defined in the criteria given in Ambrose 1990) with C:N ratios between 3.3 and 3.6.

A number of samples have $\delta^{13}C$ values that are between –22 ‰ and –24 ‰, which is more negative than one would expect for a purely terrestrial $C_3$ diet (*c*. –20 ‰ to -21‰). These more negative values are indicative of the addition of aquatic resources, most likely river fish, to the diets. This interpretation is supported by the associated higher $\delta^{15}N$ values for these individuals. These $\delta^{15}N$ values are not as high as those observed by Bonsall *et al*. (1997) for Mesolithic humans from the Danubian Iron Gates region. Bonsall *et al*. (1997) interpret the humans with collagen $\delta^{15}N$ values of *c*. 14 or 15 ‰, associated with $\delta^{13}C$ values of *c*. –23 ‰ as being indicative of a diet in which almost all of the protein was from river fish. The values observed here are more indicative of diets in which the majority of protein came from $C_3$ terrestrial-based resources with the addition of a significant amount of river fish. Without associated faunal collagen $\delta^{13}C$ and $\delta^{15}N$ values it is difficult to assess the relevant proportions of plant, terrestrial mammal and river fish protein in the diets.

Other samples (Der 33, Vas 29) have collagen $\delta^{13}C$ and $\delta^{15}N$ values that probably do not indicate any significant amounts of river fish in the diets. Again, further interpretation is difficult without associated faunal isotope values, but the high $\delta^{15}N$ values are indicative of diets with significant amounts of animal, rather than plant, protein in them.

Two individuals, Osip 20e and Yas 19 have unusually low $\delta^{15}N$ values, although they are within the range of values observed for other European humans (Richards 1998). These samples are clearly from human samples, and are not misidentified faunal remains. The low $\delta^{15}N$ values for these individuals indicate that much of the dietary protein came from plant foods.

There are three individuals with unusual isotope values and equally unusual radiocarbon dates. The Igren VIII individual has a $\delta^{13}C$ value of –17.4 ‰, while two individuals from Osipovka have $\delta^{13}C$ values of –15.3 ‰. These values are indicative of either a significant input of marine foods into the diet, which while highly unlikely due to the location of the cemeteries, could reflect influences occurring from the Black Sea transgression (Ryan *et al*. 1998), or an input of $C_4$ plants into the diet. The most obvious $C_4$ plant would be millet, which was not available in Europe until the Iron Age. Murray and Schoeninger (1988) report human $\delta^{13}C$ values close to –13 ‰ for samples from Iron age sites in central Europe which they interpret as being due to millet in the diets. Given the similarities in isotope ratios from Igren VIII and Osipovka to those reported by Murray and Schoeninger (1988), it seems likely the three individuals from the Ukrainian cemeteries also had an equivalent dietary input, with this being from millet consumption. If accurate, this data would strongly suggest that these individuals are later, intrusive burials, but obviously the possible influences from the Black Sea transgression cannot be ruled out in this context.

There are no clear chronological differences in isotope values between the Mesolithic and Neolithic periods in the current analysis, as the earliest samples from the Marievka Mesolithic cemetery have isotope values that are similar to those of later Neolithic individuals. In fact, if there is any chronological trend occurring it is within the earlier Neolithic period itself. It appears that there may be an increased input of river fish in the diets of the subsequent Neolithic period, as the individuals dating to this period have a tendency to have $\delta^{13}C$ values that are between –23 ‰ and –24 ‰, while earlier individuals tend to have $\delta^{13}C$ values >-23 ‰. This however is not the case for all samples considered, and indicates that diets were somewhat varied in this region throughout the Mesolithic and Neolithic periods.

Within the whole dataset there are no clear differences in diets that can be related to sex or age differences. However, in the case of the Derievka samples, there does seem to be a difference in isotope values between males and females, with females having higher $\delta^{15}N$ values, perhaps indicating more river fish in their diets.

## Dental Evidence for Diet

A range of dental pathologies such as caries levels, dental calculus expression and rates of enamel hypoplasia were investigated on the intra- and inter-cemetery levels of analysis. The analysis of the incidence of dental pathologies

| Site | Sample No. | Sex | Age | $\delta^{13}C$ | $\delta^{15}N$ | C:N | %Coll. | %C | %N | OxA | $^{14}C$ Date |
|------|-----------|-----|-----|------|------|-----|--------|-----|-----|-----|----------|
| Dereivka I | Der 42 | F | 18-20 | -23.2 | 11.8 | 3.5 | 9.8 | 22.7 | 7.8 | 6159 | 6200 ± 60 |
| Dereivka I | Der 49 | M | 20-30 | -23.4 | 9.9 | 3.4 | 4.2 | 30.8 | 10.5 | 6160 | 6165 ± 55 |
| Dereivka I | Der 84 | F | 35-55 | -23.6 | 11.4 | 3.3 | 17.6 | 33.1 | 11.7 | 6161 | 7270 ± 110 |
| Dereivka I | Der 33 | M | 18-25 | -21.7 | 10.5 | 3.6 | 3.7 | 34.4 | 11.2 | 6162 | 6175 ± 60 |
| | | | | | | | | | | | |
| Igren VIII | Igr 4 | F | 18-25 | -17.4 | 12.1 | 3.3 | 20.0 | 40.3 | 14.2 | 6270 | 630 ± 60 |
| | | | | | | | | | | | |
| Marievka | Mar 4 | ?M | 50-60 | -22.0 | 10.1 | 3.3 | 3.4 | 15.7 | 5.6 | 6199 | 7955 ± 55 |
| Marievka | Mar 10 | M | 35-45 | -21.7 | 13.0 | 3.3 | 5.4 | 36.2 | 12.7 | 6200 | 7620 ± 160 |
| Marievka | Mar 14 | I | 35-45 | -22.1 | 10.8 | 3.2 | 2.6 | 30.3 | 11.1 | 6269 | 7630 ± 110 |
| | | | | | | | | | | | |
| Nikolskoye | Nik 94 | F | 50-60 | -23.1 | 12.3 | 3.3 | 7.4 | 36.5 | 13.0 | 6155 | 6225 ± 75 |
| Nikolskoye | Nik 58 | M? | 35-55 | -22.2 | 12.3 | 3.4 | 6.4 | 33.5 | 11.7 | 6156 | 2305 ± 45 |
| | | | | | | | | | | | |
| Osipovka | Osip 20b | M? | 20-35 | -21.0 | 5.7 | 3.3 | 2.3 | 31.0 | 11.0 | 6168 | 7675 ± 70 |
| Osipovka | Osip 31a | F | 35-45 | -15.3 | 9.4 | 3.3 | 3.8 | 32.4 | 11.4 | 6169 | 2895 ± 50 |
| Osipovka | Osip 34b | I | adult | -15.3 | 10.0 | 3.4 | 9.3 | 37.3 | 13.0 | 6170 | 2780 ± 55 |
| | | | | | | | | | | | |
| Vasilyevka V | Vas 8 | M | 50-60 | -22.4 | 10.0 | 3.3 | 2.3 | 24.4 | 8.6 | 6171 | 6470 ± 60 |
| Vasilyevka V | Vas 10 | F | 40-50 | -23.2 | 10.6 | 3.4 | 6.4 | 15.1 | 5.2 | 6172 | 6805 ± 60 |
| Vasilyevka V | Vas 29 | M? | 25-35 | -20.2 | 10.1 | 3.3 | 5.4 | 35.0 | 12.4 | 6198 | 6280 ± 70 |
| Vasilyevka V | Vas 20 | I | 20-30 | -22.3 | 12.3 | 3.3 | 9.3 | 37.8 | 13.5 | 6268 | 6710 ± 90 |
| | | | | | | | | | | | |
| Yasinovatka | Yas 45 | M | 20-25 | -23.6 | 11.4 | 3.3 | 4.8 | 35.8 | 12.8 | 6164 | 6360 ± 60 |
| Yasinovatka | Yas 19 | F | 20-25 | -22.4 | 7.4 | 3.4 | 2.1 | 36.7 | 12.4 | 6165 | 6370 ± 60 |
| Yasinovatka | Yas 17 | F | 20-30 | -22.5 | 13.0 | 3.4 | 9.9 | 27.5 | 9.5 | 6166 | 6360 ± 75 |
| Yasinovatka | Yas 18 | M | 20-35 | -22.6 | 12.5 | 3.4 | 9.2 | 38.0 | 13.1 | 6167 | 6255 ± 65 |

**Table 2: Stable isotope values, and various attributes of collagen extracted from various Ukrainian Mesolithic and Neolithic human samples. The errors on the $\delta^{13}C$ values are ± 0.3 ‰, and the errors on the $\delta^{15}N$ values are ± 0.4 ‰.**

such as dental caries and dental calculus (which, in turn, reflect the relative frequencies of carbohydrates versus proteins in the diet), ante-mortem tooth loss and abscesses, coupled with general systemic stress indicators such as enamel hypoplasias and the more specific stress indicator, porotic hyperostosis (indicative of an anaemic disorder), have been used in numerous investigations of the transition to a production economy in both archaeological and modern ethnographic studies (Alexandersen 1988, Angel 1966, Frayer 1987, Goodman *et al.* 1984, Larsen *et al.* 1991, Littleton and Frohlich 1993, Lubell *et al.* 1994, Macchiarelli 1989, Meiklejohn *et al.* 1988, Meiklejohn and Zvelebil 1991, Molnar and Molnar 1985, y'Edynak 1978, 1989). These pathologies can therefore be used to enhance the general picture of the dietary spectrum exploited by the human populations of the Dnieper Rapids region across bothMesolithic and Neolithic periods (Lubell *et al.* 1994).

## Materials and Methods: Human dentition

The dentitions from all 309 adult individuals, with 3,050 teeth in evidence from the Mesolithic and Neolithic cemeteries outlined above were studied on the macroscopic level by Lillie during research visits to St. Petersburg and Kiev in 1993, and additional analyses were carried out in Kiev in 1995. Methodologies, identification and classification of dental diseases followed those of Goodman *et al.* (1980), Goodman and Armelagos (1985), Goodman and Rose (1991), Hillson (1979, 1986), Littleton and Frohlich (1993), Meiklejohn and Zvelebil (1991), Mensforth (1991), Nikiforuk (1985), Stuart-Macadam (1989, 1991), Wei *et al.* (1986) among others.

## Dental Caries and Calculus

Caries, indicative of the consumption of dietary carbohydrates, is completely absent from the entire dental sample studied. Conversely, dental calculus, which in this context is clearly indicative of the consumption of dietary protein, is consistently recorded on the dentitions from all of the cemeteries considered in this analysis. Consideration of the expression of calculus using a Chi-square test ($x^2$) indicates that a significant difference occurs between males and females in the Mesolithic period (Chi-square=161.21, df=4, $P < 0.005$). Males exhibit higher observed incidences of calculus throughout the skeletal series, thus reflecting the fact that males may well have been in the favoured position regarding access to protein-based dietary resources during the Mesolithic of Ukraine as heavy plaque deposits probably reflect consumption levels. However, as reported by Lillie (1997:223), this expression does not appear to have resulted in a significant reduction in the quality of female dietary intakes, as the overall expression of pathological markers in the Mesolithic period is not indicative of elevated levels of sub-optimal health for females during this period.

Chi-square analysis ($x^2$) of the occurrence of dental calculus in the Neolithic period has highlighted variability in expression, with the cemeteries of Vasilyevka V, Osipovka, Igren VIII and Dereivka II having too few teeth for use in statistical consideration on the intra-cemetery level of analysis. However, at Vovnigi II a statistically significant difference between males and females (Chi-square=50.78, df=4, $P <0.005$) in calculus expression is interpreted as reflecting the higher incidence of heavy deposition visible on the dentitions of males in this cemetery. This scenario mirrors that observed in the earlier Mesolithic cemetery of Vasilyevka III, possibly suggesting some degree of inequality in the frequencies of access to dietary protein sources within this cemetery population, with males consuming higher levels of protein-rich foodstuffs.

The main area of divergence from the Mesolithic trend is intimated by the analysis of the dentitions from Yasinovatka and Nikolskoye, and confirmed by the statistical consideration of the Dereivka I populations. The assessment of male-female calculus expression at Yasinovatka and Nikolskoye is thought to indicate broadly equivalent levels of food consumption between the sexes. This suggestion contradicts the general model of Mesolithic expression whereby males tend to exhibit higher incidence of heavy calculus deposition than females, a level of expression visible in the early Neolithic cemetery of Vovnigi II. The analysis of the Dereivka I dentitions supports the observed equivalence suggested by Yasinovatka and Nikolskoye, with a null hypothesis ($P >0.005$) indicating broadly coequal levels of calculus expression, and therefore presumably dietary protein consumption, between males and females.

The stable isotope evidence from Dereivka I (individual Der 33) and Vasilyevka V (Vas 29) suggests that certain males were consuming higher levels of animal protein, but the general picture of increasing fish consumption during the earlier Neolithic may provide insights into the mechanism whereby females were unaffected by differential access to animal proteins. In addition, individual Yas 29, from the cemetery of Yasinovatka, has been shown to have had a diet, with a protein base derived from plant food resources. This evidence highlights the potential range of resources that can be utilised to provide the protein based element of the hunter-fisher-gatherer diet, and introduces us to the potential equalising mechanisms acting to reduce inequalities in access to specific resources.

## Discussion

The above scenario appears to augment recent suggestions of the non-egalitarian nature of hunter-gatherer subsistence patterns (Speth 1990), and may indicate that in an area of reliable resources, such as has been suggested for the Dnieper region (Lillie 1997, 1998*b*), access to dietary proteins is reflecting some degree of equality in access to a broad range of resources between the sexes. Low levels of enamel hypoplasia in the Mesolithic and Neolithic periods coupled with the limited incidence of porotic hyperostosis at the Neolithic site of Dereivka I (Lillie 1998*c*) lends weight to the argument that the populations of the Dnieper Rapids region have an overall expression of dental and cranial pathology consistent with minimal dietary stressors, and the exploitation of protein dominated diets across this transition. In a similar vein to the results of Bonsall *et al* (1997), there is no unequivocal evidence for nutritional stressors indicative of preferential male health across the Mesolithic-Neolithic transition in Ukraine.

The dating evidence has shown that the reliance upon artefact typologies, with little emphasis on absolute dating, created an unsound seriation from which a consideration of the Mesolithic-Neolithic transition could be based. Within the new chronological framework, the combined stable isotope and dental evidence for diet at the Mesolithic-Neolithic transition in Ukraine has shown that in both the Mesolithic and earlier Neolithic periods fishing, hunting and gathering were combined to produce the main elements of the protein based subsistence strategies along the Dnieper.

## References

Alexandersen, V. (1988). Description of the Human Dentitions from the Late Mesolithic Grave-Fields at Skateholm, Southern Sweden. In L. Larsson (Ed.) *The Skateholm Project: Man and Environment.* Sweden: Almqvist and Wiksell Int. pp. 106-63.

Ambrose, S.H. (1990). Preparation and characterization of bone and tooth collagen for stable carbon and nitrogen isotope analysis. *Journal of Archaeological Science* **17**, 431-451.

Ammerman, A.J., and Cavalli-Sforza.L.L. (1971). Measuring the Rate of Spread of Early Farming in Europe. *Man* **6**, 674-88.

Ammerman, A.J., and Cavalli-Sforza. L.L. (1973). A Population Model for the Diffusion of Early Farming in

Europe. In C. Renfrew (Ed.) *The Explanation of Culture Change: models in prehistory.* London: Duckworth. pp. 343-57.

Ammerman, A.J., and Cavalli-Sforza, L.L. (1979). The Wave of Advance Model for the Spread of Agriculture in Europe. In C. Renfrew, C., and K.L. Cooke (Eds.) *Transformations, mathematical approaches to culture change.* New York: Academic Press. pp. 275-93.

Ammerman, A.J., and Cavalli-Sforza, L.L. (1984). *The Neolithic Transition and the Genetics of Populations in Europe.* Princeton: University Press.

Angel, J.L. (1966). Porotic Hyperostosis, Anemias, Malarias, and Marshes in the Prehistoric Eastern Mediterranean. *Science* **153**, 760-3.

Armit, I., and Finlayson, B. (1992). Hunter-Gatherers Transformed: The transition to agriculture in northern and western Europe. *Antiquity* **66**, 664-76.

Bonsall, C., Lennon, R., McSweeney,,K., Stewart, C., Harkness, D., Boroneant, V., Bartosiewicz, L., Payton, R., and Chapman, J. (1997). Mesolithic and Early Neolithic in the Iron Gates: a palaeodietary perspective. *Journal of European Archaeology* **5** (1), 50-92.

Brown, T.A., Nelson,D.E., and Southo, J.R. (1988). Improved collagen extraction by modified Longin method. *Radiocarbon* **30**, 171-177.

Dennell, R. (1985). *European Economic Prehistory: A new approach.* London: Academic Press.

Frayer, D.W. (1987). Caries and Oral Pathologies at the Mesolithic Sites of Muge: Cabeço Da Arrunda and Moita Do Sebastião. *Trabalhos de Antroplogia e Etnologia* **27** (fasc. 1-4), 9-25.

Gokhman, I.I. (1966). Naselenie Ukrainy v Epokhu Mezolita i Neolita: Anthropologicheskiy ocherk. (The Population of the Ukraine in the Mesolithic and Neolithic Periods: An anthropological outline). Nauka: Moscow.

Goodman, A.H., and Armelagos, G. J.. (1985). Factors Affecting the Distribution of Enamel Hypoplasias Within the Human Permanent Dentition. *American Journal of Physical Anthropology* **68**, 479-93.

Goodman, A.H., and Rose, J.C. (1991). Dental Enamel Hypoplasias as Indicators of Nutritional Status. In M.A. Kelley and C.S. Larsen (Eds.) *Advances in Dental Anthropology.* New York: Wiley-Liss, Inc. pp. 279-93.

Goodman, A.H., Armelagos, G.J. and Rose, J.C. (1980). Enamel Hypoplasias as Indicators of Stress in Three Prehistoric Populations from Illinois. *Human Biology* **52** (3), 515-28.

Goodman, A.H., Armelagos, G.J. and Rose, J.C. (1984). The Chronological Distribution of Enamel Hypoplasias from Prehistoric Dickson Mounds Populations. *American Journal of Physical Anthropology* **65**, 259-66.

Hedges, R.E.M., Housley, R.A., Bronk Ramsey, C. and Van Klinken, G.J. (1995). Radiocarbon dates from the Oxford AMS system: *Archaeometry* datelist 20, *Archaeometry* **37**, 417-30.

Hillson, S.W. (1979). Diet and Dental Disease. *World Archaeology* **11** (2), 147-62.

Hillson, S.W. (1986). *Teeth.* Cambridge: University Press.

Iacumin, P., Bocherens, H., Chaix, L., and Marioth, A. (1998). Stable carbon and nitrogen isotope as dietary indicators of ancient Nubian populations (Northern Sudan). *Journal of Archaeological Science* **25**, 293-301.

Jacobs, K. (1993). Human Postcranial Variation in the Ukrainian Mesolithic-Neolithic. *Current Anthropology* **34**, 311-24.

Jacobs, K. (1994). Human Dento-Gnathic Metric Variation in Mesolithic/Neolithic Ukraine: Possible Evidence of Demic Diffusion in the Dnieper Rapids Region. *American Journal of Physical Anthropology* **95**, 1-26.

Keegan, W.F. (1989). Stable Isotope Analysis of Prehistoric Diet. In M.Y. Iscan and K.A.R. Kennedy (Eds.) *Reconstruction of Life from the Skeleton.* New York: Alan R. Liss. pp.223-36.

Konduktorova, T.S. (1974). The Ancient Population of the Ukraine: From the Mesolithic Age to the first centuries of our era. *Anthropologie BRNO* **XII** (1and2), 5-149.

Kozlowski, S.K. (1989). A survey of early Holocene cultures of the western part of the Russian plain. In C. Bonsall, (Ed)., the *Mesolithic in Europe: Papers presented at the third International symposium.* Edinburgh: John Donald Publishers Ltd, pp.424-441.

Larsen, C.S., R. Shavit and MGriffin, M.C. (1991). Dental Caries Evidence for Dietary Change: An archaeological context. In M.A. Kelley and C.S. Larsen (Eds.) *Advances in Dental Anthropology.* New York: Wiley Liss. pp. 179-202.

Lillie, M.C. (1996). Mesolithic and Neolithic Populations of Ukraine: Indications of Diet from Dental Pathology. *Current Anthropology* **37**, 135-42.

Lillie. M.C. (1997). Women and Children in Prehistory: Resource Sharing and Social Stratification at the Mesolithic-Neolithic Transition in Ukraine. In: J. Moore and E. Scott (Eds.) *Invisible People and Processes: Writing Gender and Childhood into European Archaeology.* London: Leicester University. Press. pp.213-28.

Lillie, M.C. (1998a). The Mesolithic-Neolithic transition in Ukraine: new radiocarbon determinations for the cemeteries of the Dnieper Rapids region. *Antiquity* **72**, 184-88.

Lillie, M.C. (1998b). The Dnieper Rapids Region of Ukraine: A Consideration of Chronology, Dental Pathology and Diet at the Mesolithic-Neolithic Transition. Sheffield University: Unpublished PhD Thesis.

Lillie, M.C., *in press*. 'Mesolithic Cultures of Ukraine: Observations on cultural developments in light of new radiocarbon determinations from the Dnieper Rapids cemeteries'. B.A.R. (Int. Series). Proceedings of Prehistoric Society Conference held in Sheffield 1999.

Lillie, M.C. and Zvelebil, M. (1999). L'Adoption de L'Agriculture en Europe de L'Est: Le cas d'étude de la région des cascades du Dniepr en Ukraine. (The transition to farming in eastern Europe: a case study from the Dnieper Rapids region of Ukraine). In A. Thévenin (Ad.). *L'Europe des Derniers Chasseurs: Épipaéolithique et Mésolithique.* Paris: Éditions du CTHS. pp.429-39.

Littleton, J., Frohlich, B. (1993). Fish-Eaters and Farmers: Dental Pathology in the Arabian Gulf. *American Journal of Physical Anthropology* **92**, 427-47.

Lubell, D., Jackes, M., Schwarcz, H., Knyf, M., and Meiklejohn, .C. (1994). The Mesolithic-Neolithic Transition in Portugal: Isotopic and dental evidence of diet. *Journal of Archaeological Science* **21**, 201-16.

Macchiarelli, R. (1989). Prehistoric "Fish-Eaters" Along the Eastern Arabian Coasts: Dental variation, morphology, and oral health in the Ra's al-Hamra community (Qurum, Sultanate of Oman, 5th-4th Millennia BC). *American Journal of Physical Anthropology* **78**, 575-94.

McGovern-Wilson, R., and Quinn, C. (1996). Stable isotope analysis of ten individuals from Afetna, Saipan, Northern Mariana Islands. *Journal of Archaeological Science* **23**, 59-65.

Meiklejohn, C., and Zvelebil, M. (1991). Health Status of European Populations at the Agricultural Transition and the Implications for the Adoption of Farming. In H. Bush, and M. Zvelebil (Eds.) *Health in Past Societies: Biocultural Interpretations of Human Skeletal Remains in Archaeological Contexts.* Oxford: B.A.R. (Int. Ser.) **567**, 129-44.

Meiklejohn, C., Baldwin, J.H. and Schentag, C.T. (1988). Caries as a Probable Dietary Marker in the Western European Mesolithic. In B.V. Kennedy and G.M. LeMoine (Eds.) *Diet and Subsistence: Current archaeological perspectives.* Proceedings of the. 19th. Chacmool Conference, Calgary: University Press. pp. 273-9.

Mensforth, R.P. (1991). Palaeoepidemiology of Porotic Hyperostosis in the Libben and Bt-5 Skeletal Populations.

*Kirtlandia* **46**, 1-47.

Molnar, S., and I. Molnar (1985). Observations of Dental Diseases Among Prehistoric Populations of Hungary. *American Journal of Physical Anthropology* **67**, 51-63.

Murray, M., and Schoeninger, M. (1988). Diet, status, and complex social structure in Iron Age Central Europe: Some contributions of bone chemistry. In D. Gibson and Geselowitz (Eds.) *Tribe and Polity in Late Prehistoric Europe*: pp. 155-176. London: Plenum Press.

Nikiforuk, G. (1985). *Understanding Dental Caries: Etiology and mechanisms, basic and clinical aspects.* New York: S. Karger.

Pate, F.D., (1997). Stable carbon isotope assessment of hunter-gatherer mobility in prehistoric South Australia. *Journal of Archaeological Science* **22**, 81-7.

Potekhina, I.D., and Telegin, D.Ya.. (1995). On the dating of the Ukrainian Mesolithic-Neolithic transition. *Current Anthropology* **36** (5), 823-6.

Richards, M.P. (1998). Palaeodietary Studies of European Human Populations Using Bone Stable Isotopes. Unpublished D.Phil. Thesis, University of Oxford.

Richards, M.P., Hedges, R.E.M., Molleson, T.I., and Vogel, J.C. (1998). Stable isotope analysis reveals variations in human diet at the Poundbury Camp cemetery site. *Journal of Archaeological Science* **25**, 1247-52.

Ryan, W.B.F., Pitman, W.C. III,Major, C.O., Shimkus, K., Moskalenko, v., Jones, G.a., Dimitrov., P., Gorür, N., Sakinç, M., and Yüce, H. (1997). An Abrupt Drowning of the Black Sea Shelf. *Marine Geology* **138**, 119-26.

Speth, J.D. (1990). Seasonality, Resource Stress and Food Sharing in So-called 'Egalitarian' Foraging Societies. *Journal of Anthropological Archaeology* **9** (2), 332-33.

Stuart-Macadam, P. (1989). Porotic Hyperostosis: Relationship between orbital and vault lesions. *American Journal of Physical Anthropology* **80**, 187-93.

Stuart-Macadam, P. (1991). Anaemia in Roman Britain: Poundbury Camp. In H. Bush and M. Zvelebil (Eds.) *Health in Past Societies: Biocultural interpretations of human skeletal remains in archaeological contexts.* Oxford: B.A.R. (Int. Ser.) **567**, 101-13.

Telegin, D.Ya. (1968). *Dnipro-donetska kultura.* (The Dnieper-donets culture). Kiev: Naukova Dumka.

Telegin, D.Ya. (1982). *Mesolitichni pamyatki Ukraine (9-6 tisyacholitta do n.e.).* (Mesolithic Populations of Ukraine (9-6 millennia)). Kiev: Naukova Dumka. pp. 236-43.

Telegin, D.Ya. (1987). Neolithic Cultures of the Ukraine and

Adjacent Areas and their Chronology. *Journal of World Prehistory* **1** (3), 307-31.

Telegin, D.Ya., and I.D. Potekhina. (1987). *Neolithic Cemeteries and Populations in the Dnieper Basin.* Oxford: B.A.R. (Int. Ser.) **383**.

van Andel, T.H., and Runnels, C.N. (1995). The Earliest Farmers in Europe. *Antiquity* **69**, 481-500.

Wei, S.H.Y., JCrall, J.J., and Wefel, J.S. (1986). Dental Caries: Resistance factors - enamel chemistry and saliva. In L. Granath and W. D. McHugh (Eds) *Systematized Prevention of Oral Disease: Theory and practice.* Florida: CRC Press, Inc. pp. 43-59.

y'Edynak, G. (1978). Culture, Diet, and Dental Reduction in Mesolithic Forager-Fishers of Yugoslavia. *Current Anthropology* **19** (3), 616.

y'Edynak, G. (1989). Yugoslav Mesolithic Dental Reduction. *American Journal of Physical Anthropology* **78**, 17-36.

Zvelebil, M. (1986). *Hunters in Transition: Mesolithic societies of temperate Eurasia and their transition to farming.* Cambridge: Cambridge University Press.

Zvelebil, M., and P. Dolukhanov, P. (1991). The Transition to Farming in Eastern and Northern Europe. *Journal of World Prehistory* **5**, 233-78.

Zvelebil, M., and Rowley-Conwy, P. (1984). Transition to Farming in Northern Europe: A hunter-gatherer perspective. *Norwegian Archaeological Review* **17** (2), 104-28.

# Sampling for phosphorus over a grave site: Theory and practice

Andy Owen and David A. Jenkins

School of Agriculture and Forest Science, University of Wales, Bangor

## Abstract

In the acid soils of western and upland UK, bones do not survive physically. However, their phosphorus content is fixed *in situ* due to the relative immobility of the phosphate anion and its fixation by iron/aluminium hydrous oxides in these soils, so preserving traces of the original occupant of the grave. The strategy necessary to detect such cryptic traces has been investigated theoretically by "sampling" data from a whole body X-ray scan at a range of grid intervals. The results suggest that a 10cm grid interval should be adequate to detect a body shape in enhanced soil phosphorus. This strategy has been tested in a 5th-9th century Christian cemetery on Ynys Mon, North Wales. A body silhouette was not detected yet soil phosphorus values of up to 3% were obtained. These results are discussed in terms of the subsequent agricultural liming causing loss of definition of the phosphate anomaly through homogenisation by soil mesofauna, the burial type and the sampling style.
(3750 words text+12 references, 8 Figures and 1 table)

## I. Introduction

Phosphorus analysis is a well documented technique of archaeological survey (Bethel and Mate 1989) and is particularly useful for the examination of cryptic features, e.g. suspected inhumations in acidic soils where there has been the complete dissolution of bone. Under these conditions it is difficult to visually establish whether there was an actual inhumation, and the measurement of soil phosphorus can help to clarify this. The preservation of bone within soil is dependent on the age of the bone at interment, (Gordon and Buikstra 1981) and soil conditions, notably the soil pH. Hydroxy-apatite ($Ca_5(PO_4)_3OH$), the main inorganic component of bone, is relatively insoluble at pH values above 6.5-7.0, so in soils at this pH, bone is well preserved. However, as the pH drops, protons replace the Ca in hydroxy-apatite that can then be leached from the soil, causing the bone to undergo dissolution. At pH values of <5.0, the rate of dissolution is accelerated by an increase in H+ ions and the removal of phosphate ions, (18.5% of hydroxy-apatite), by adsorption onto Fe and Al oxides and hydroxides in soil, so under acidic conditions complete dissolution occurs and no physical trace of the bone is left. Under these conditions soil phosphate analysis can reveal the chemical trace of bone, because P released during its dissolution is fixed locally at concentrations greatly elevated above natural 'background' levels.

Grave sites are often located in association with other archaeological features, and once discovered merit a separate sampling strategy. If the soil conditions are such that an inhumation cannot be visibly identified, then phosphate analysis is a useful technique to ascertain whether the feature is an inhumation, or whether the grave was never 'occupied' or perhaps if a body was removed at some stage following burial. The sampling strategy utilised, while being designed to suit the sampling area, can still remain problematic, the central problem being the choice of interval of sampling required to achieve a pattern of results that enable the distribution of P arising from an inhumation to be clearly displayed. Soil analyses are expensive, and excavation time often limited, so the smallest number to achieve the required results is usually preferred. This paper examines a number of sampling strategies using data collected from a whole body bone density scan, and the results are compared to those from initial test samples collected during the excavation of an early Christian burial site. The work presented in this paper forms part of a larger study of the examination of the spatial distribution of P in soil (Owen *et al.*, 1999)

## 2. Grid sampling of a grave utilising a whole body bone density scan

### 2.1 Methods

A whole body radiograph is used in hospitals to assess bone density using a whole body, X-ray scan. The image produced (Figure 1) is composed of 172 columns, and 338 rows of pixels (58136 pixels in total).

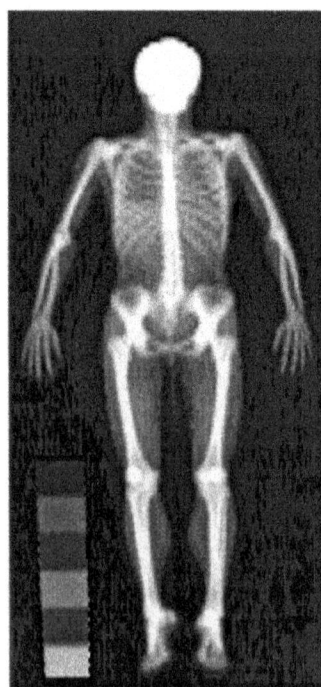

**Figure 1. Whole body bone density scan.**

Each pixel has an associated figure representing the attenuation of the signal, and the level of shading at that position, which is directly related to the bone density. This unique sample set composed of 58136 'samples' collected from an area approximately 190cm x 95cm (each sample represents 0.55cm x 0.55cm), could never be obtained as actual samples. It is used here to examine sampling strategies across this area.

A program was written in Perl (Wall 1997) to pick out samples from this data set on a grid basis. The size of the sampling interval, the starting row, and the starting column, were all fed into the program, and the sampled cells were displayed with their accompanying co-ordinates. A block of 4x4 pixels were collected for each point to represent the area of soil that an auger would sample ($\sim$5cm$^2$). This data-set was then used to generate distribution maps which were compared to the original body scan to see at what sampling interval the samples collected produce an image that is representative of the bone density. The distribution maps were plotted using Winsurf, surface mapping for windows package (Golden software, 1993) with a 'minimum curvature' data interpolation method.

## 2.2 Results and discussion

Data sets are generated for four different sampling intervals; every 20, 15, 10 and 5cm, over the sample area of 190 x 95cm. The distribution patterns of these data sets are then plotted and are produced in Figures 2-5 of the Appendix. The resolution of the image increases as a greater number of sample points is used to generate the image. At a 20cm sampling interval there are only 45 sampling points and the image shows a concentration in the upper central area of the map. This does correspond with the position of the head of a skeleton, where the greatest concentration of P is likely to be found, but at this scale the area of concentrated P could not be related to an inhumation. At the 15cm sampling interval there are 72 sampling points and an image is generated which is closer to a body shape, in which a head and torso can be identified. However, no limb areas have been identified, as these have obviously all been missed at this size of sampling interval; the shape might not be positively identified as a body unless it was associated with a stone-lined grave or cist. At the 10cm sampling interval there are 153 sample points and the image becomes clearer. There is no doubt that this image would be positively identified as an inhumation; the head shoulders, torso and thighs are identifiable, however, the shins and feet, and the forearms and hands are still missed by the sampling at this scale. The final image, at a sampling interval of every 5cm has a much greater concentration of sampling points -578. At this sampling density the skeleton's image is clear, and even the hands and feet can be identified.

This method of theoretical sampling provides a useful illustration of the distribution patterns of P that may be expected when sampling grave sites, however, it cannot be expected to accurately mirror the distribution patterns one might uncover in the field for a number of reasons. The whole body bone density scan gives a value for bone density of the skeleton, set against a blank background surrounding the body. The range effectively goes from a zero value to one of high bone density in the skull area of the skeleton. In comparison, any grave site sampled in an archaeological phosphate survey would be set against background values of total phosphorus ($P_{tot}$) in the soil. These can range from 200 to 5000+$\mu$g g$^{-1}$ (Barber, 1984) which could be a considerable proportion of the value of $P_{tot}$ resulting from dissolution of a skeleton. The results for any P survey would therefore not be as distinctive as this theoretical distribution suggests, as the values of P measured from the skeletal P will be adding to a background concentration inherent in the soil. This background concentration of P in the relevant soil fabrics can vary naturally by up to 50% (Owen *et al.*, 2000) which will add to the background 'noise' of the P distribution making any discernible 'pattern' increasingly blurred.

The level of background P present in the soil would not be a problem if all the P that was present in the bone at the time of burial was 'fixed' in the soil, remaining in this fixed form until the archaeologist measured it many years later. The P content of bone has been measured at between 16% (Eastoe 1961) and 20% (Dojlido and Best 1993), whereas the $P_{tot}$ content of soils could be roughly 0.2%, a 100 fold difference. However, many processes take place to reduce the amount of P from the bone, which is actually fixed in the soil. P is gradually released as bone is broken down by the soil microbial population, and becomes part of the soluble P pool. In this form it can be fixed in the soil inorganic pool or assimilated by plants and micro-organisms into the organic pool. A small proportion will be leached from the soil if there is excess water, a condition that exists for most months of the year under the North Wales climate. The component which enters the organic P pool can also be lost from the system, as plants are harvested or grazed. These processes serve to reduce the amount of P which is fixed in the soil. Diffusion will also take place from the point source of P at the surface of the bone and as the mineral P becomes soluble it will diffuse away into the soil matrix. Many grave sites investigated are over 1000 years old, some being much older, which allows considerable time for movement away from the point P source. The dispersion of P within soil is exacerbated by mesofaunal homogenisation. The activity of earthworms under suitable conditions mixes the soil thoroughly, and therefore the chances of a P trace exhibiting a pattern similar to that of a skeleton's layout will depend on there being negligible mesofaunal activity. Any grave sites located in brown earth soils with a pH of 5.5 or greater are likely to have earthworm activity and therefore a reduced possibility of retaining an identifiable P pattern.

It is unlikely that many grave sites contain bodies which would be laid out in the symmetrical position used for bone density scanning, so the theoretical images generated are of limited applicability. It would perhaps be possible to obtain further total body scans of people in a variety of positions, but that remains as work for a future study.

# 3. Investigation of an early Christian burial site

## 3.1 Site locations

The field work for this study took place at Ty Mawr farm, Anglesey (GR SH252814). The site consisted of a number of stone cists and stone-lined graves similar in style to other excavated burial sites dated to the early Christian period 400-800AD (Ian Grant *pers. comm.*). Samples were collected from a number of cists at this site and the results from two of these are examined in this paper. The recent history of the field is not recorded, however the land had been improved and at the time of excavation it was utilised for cattle and sheep grazing with annual fertiliser applications. The soil at this site is mapped as *East Keswick 1* series (Rudeforth *et al.*, 1984) and is a brown earth developed on local drift material.

## 3.2 Sampling strategy

Soil samples were collected from two horizontal layers within a stone cist (feature No.170). The first set of samples was collected from 15cm depth within the cist, on a 10cm grid, using a 1cm Ø soil auger. Each sample was bulked from a 5cm depth of soil on the auger, thus comprising of roughly 2-3g soil, which was air-dried and hand-ground in the laboratory with a sub-sample taken for P analysis as described below. The second set of samples was collected using the same procedure and grid layout but from the bottom 5cm of soil fill within the grave. A background set of samples was collected from alongside the grave at 10cm intervals along a 150cm line, at a depth of 15cm using the same soil auger.

A stone lined grave (feature No.304) was also sampled which had been partially excavated to reveal a clear dark stain covering approximately 5% of the excavated surface, thought to be a relic of the decomposed body, and several areas of paler colour thought to be imparted by the bone. At this level the remains of a single tooth were also visible. A systematic 10cm grid interval sampling strategy was used to collect 91 samples for $P_{tot}$ analysis from the excavated surface over an area of 190cm x 40cm. Samples were collected using a metal scoop designed to take about 1g soil from each grid node.

## 3.3 Phosphorus analysis

Total phosphorus was measured in the dried, ground soil samples using a rapid perchloric acid digestion procedure (Sommers and Nelson 1972). Phosphate was then measured colorimetrically in each digest using a Perstorp 'Flow Solution 3000' flow injection analyser, incorporating the ascorbic acid reduced molybdate method of Murphy and Riley (1962).

## 3.4 Results

The means and selected descriptive statistics for cist 170 (Figure 6 and 7 of the Appendix), for grave 304 and for the background samples are presented in table 1. The mean $P_{tot}$ results for the two sets of samples collected from cist 170 were considerably lower (420-1170 µg g$^{-1}$) than those for grave 304 (500-30810 µg g$^{-1}$). Generally, values from cist 170 were only slightly enhanced above background values (300-670 µg g$^{-1}$), but $P_{tot}$ results collected from the basal layer

of the cist are significantly greater (P=0.01) than those collected from the upper layer. A much greater mean value would be expected if there was a large portion of skeletal P still present fixed in the soil, values of >1% (10,000 µg g$^{-1}$) having been reported (Keeley *et. al.*, 1977). The significant (P=0.01) differences present between the two layers does suggest that the $P_{tot}$ levels in the basal layer have been enhanced, perhaps by skeletal P from the grave's 'occupant'.

The distribution of $P_{tot}$ levels in cist 170 at each layer have been plotted using the Winsurf mapping package (Golden software, 1993) and are displayed in Figures 6 and 7 of the Appendix. No pattern is discernible in either distribution, and certainly no 'skeletal' image can be detected, but they both reach their maximum $P_{tot}$ concentration at a position roughly one third of the total length of the grave, at the narrow end. This does not correspond to any skeletal $P_{tot}$ maximum, which would be at the head end of a body, assuming the body would be laid in the grave conventionally with the feet at the narrow end. The slight increase in $P_{tot}$ values to the base of the grave indicates that it is likely that a body had occupied the grave, but the high values of P which would be associated with a skeleton, if all its P content were fixed in the soil, have not been detected.

The $P_{tot}$ results from grave 304 are higher than those for cist 170. The high concentrations measured in a number of samples collected from grave 304 indicate that the soil $P_{tot}$ has been enhanced, perhaps by skeletal P fixed during the dissolution of the bones. P concentrations in grave 304 reach 3%, which is close to the value that might be expected if all the P from a skeleton was fixed within a 1cm thick layer of soil (~4%). However, high values of P are sporadic and the mean value over the whole grave is 0.35%. The distribution of $P_{tot}$ results for grave 304 has again been plotted (Figure 8 of the Appendix), and does not conform to a 'classical body' shape. While there are areas of definite P enhancement, these are not located in any distinct pattern, and it is surprising that there is no anomaly in the region where the body's head should be, especially considering a tooth was visible and a sample was collected from within a couple of centimetres from this.

## 3.5 Discussion

The values of $P_{tot}$ measured at the base of cist 170 and from grave 304 are enhanced relative to background samples collected at this site. Skeleton-derived P has been fixed within the soil fill of each grave to increase the P concentration. These P concentrations are not as great as those reported in the literature, or those which might be expected if the majority of skeletal P was fixed in the soil, a result which could be due, in part, to the problem of sampling at the correct depth within the grave. The enhanced P concentration in soil derived from a burial is likely to accumulate in a particular layer, which could be only a few millimetres thick, and is not necessarily planar, so it is difficult to sample this layer completely. If a method collects only a small sample from a particular depth, it could easily miss the P enhanced layer, however coarse sampling could significantly dilute the P 'signal'. Ideally 2-4 sample

| | CIST 170 | | GRAVE 304 | BACKGROUND |
|---|---|---|---|---|
| | Upper layer | Basal layer | | |
| Mean | 597 | 679 | 3522 | 487 |
| Std dev | 109 | 138 | 5819 | 101 |
| Range | 450 | 720 | 30314 | 370 |
| Min-Max | 420-870 | 450-1170 | 496-30810 | 300-670 |
| Count (n) | 60 | 60 | 91 | 26 |
| CV (%) | 18 | 20 | 165 | 21 |

**Table 1. Descriptive statistics of $P_{tot}$ results for cist 170 and grave 304**

cores should be collected of the grave fill and analysed prior to an excavation to assess at what depth the greatest amounts of $P_{tot}$ are located, however constraints of time often preclude this and at Ty Mawr no initial sampling could be carried out. Without this initial prospecting, samples were collected from cist 170 at the depth within the grave where $P_{tot}$ levels would be expected to be highest, i.e. at the basal surface, with another layer of samples being collected at half this depth for comparison. A second method was used for grave 304 where samples were collected when excavation of the grave revealed features that could have been imparted by a decomposed body. The method of burial also has a considerable effect on the $P_{tot}$ trace uncovered and the type of graves examined at Ty Mawr suggests two main scenarios. A body would be interred within the empty stone lined cist (grave 170), the top stones replaced and the cist covered with soil. In this situation it is likely that the body will decompose before the percolating water transports enough soil material into the grave through the gaps between the capstones to cover the body, the P will accumulate on the surface of the basal stones and, under conditions of high rain infiltration/percolation, could be easily removed from the grave. Fixation of P will take place on the soil material, which is carried into the grave, but this will only occur in a thin layer of soil at the basal surface, and it is therefore vital that this layer is sampled if the $P_{tot}$ trace is to be detected. The majority of soil that will eventually fill the grave will do so after the P has been fixed and so will not have an unusually high P content. For grave 304 a second scenario is envisaged where the body is placed in a grave which is back-filled with soil, in this situation the body decomposes and as P is slowly released from the bones it will be fixed within the soil material; only a small amount would be leached from the system. When sampling this sort of burial, the P will be relatively more diffuse but should still be concentrated at a specific layer within the soil which, if sampled, should yield an informative $P_{tot}$ body trace. The large differences in $P_{tot}$ content between cist 170 and grave 304 could be due to these two different burial methods. The lower P concentration in cist 170 could be due to the body decomposing before the in-fill of the grave, with soil carried in by percolating water contrasted to, perhaps, the body being buried in soil in grave 304, thus leaving more soil fixed P.

The $P_{tot}$ concentrations measured at Ty Mawr could also have been reduced due to the effect of the soil conditions in the years following burial, which are important primarily for the effect they have on the soil fauna. The organisation of a

$P_{tot}$ skeletal trace will be destroyed if the soil within the grave is homogenised by mesofauna. If at some stage after burial the soil pH rises above pH 5.5, perhaps with the 20th century application of agricultural lime, conditions become suitable for the mesofauna, especially earthworms (*Lumbricus terrestris*), which homogenise the soil disturbing the trace of the skeleton. Only if conditions have remained acidic since burial is there likely to be an undisturbed skeletal P trace. The soil pH at this site was 6.8, which indicates liming and is favourable for mesofauna thus homogenising distribution of $P_{tot}$ in the graves examined.

## 4. Conclusions

Phosphate analysis of soil samples collected from graves under acidic conditions where there has been no bone preservation is a useful technique to aid the interpretation of burial sites. The selection of a suitable sampling strategy and method of sample collection is essential, and careful consideration must be given to the depth of sample collection. If possible initial sampling to ascertain the depth at which $P_{tot}$ is most concentrated should be undertaken. The analysis of sampling strategies over a data-set collected from a whole body bone density scan illustrated a number of sampling grid intervals and at a 10cm interval the 'image' of a body, in elevated $P_{tot}$ values became apparent. The analysis of samples collected from two graves from an Early Christian burial site were not so clear and highlighted the problems of sample depth, and soil homogenisation by mesofauna. Differences in $P_{tot}$ values were clearly possible due to the method of interment. Only two initial tests of the model sampling have been carried out so far and there is now a need to examine further graves under low pH soil conditions in a non-rescue excavation situation.

## Acknowledgements

We wish to acknowledge Dr Michael Worfold, Robert Jones and Agnes Hunt Orthopaedic Hospital, Oswestry, for providing us with a whole body bone density scan. Karina Kuchowski and Ian Grant, Gwynedd Archaeological Trust for assistance in sample collection from Ty Mawr burial site and Mr Paul Wood, Information Services, University of Wales, Bangor for his assistance with computer programming.

## References

Barber, S. A. (1984). *Soil Nutrient Bioavailability - A mechanistic approach*. New York: Wiley - Interscience.

Bethel, P. and Mate, I. (1989). The use of phosphate analysis in archaeology: a critique. In: J. Henderson (Ed) *Scientific Analysis in Archaeology,* pp. 1-29, Oxford: OUC for Archaeology, Oxbow.

Dojlido, J. R. and Best, G. A. (1993). *Chemistry of Water and Water Pollution.* Hemel Hempstead: Ellis Horwood Limited.

Eastoe, J. E. (1961). The chemical composition of bone. In: C. Long (Ed) *The Biochemists Handbook*, pp.715-720. London: E and F. N. Spon Ltd.

Golden Software inc., (1993). *Winsurf surface mapping for windows*. Release 3.1.

Gordon, C. C. and Buikstra, J. E. (1981). Soil pH, bone preservation and sampling bias at mortuary sites. *American Antiquity*, **46**,566-571.

Keeley, H. C. M., Hudson, G. E. and Evans, J. (1977). Trace element contents of human bones in various states of preservation. *Journal of Archaeological Science*, **4**, 19-24.

Wall, L. (1997). *PERL: Practical Extraction and Report Language.* O'Reilly and Associates Inc. USA

Murphy, J. and Riley, J. P. (1962). A modified single solution method for the determination of phosphorus in natural waters. *Analytical Chimica Acta*, **27**, 21-26.

Owen, A. G., Jenkins, D. A. and Kelso, W. I. (1999). Sampling strategies for phosphorus in archaeological sites. *Proceedings of the Archaeological Sciences Conference*, 1997, B.A.R.

Rudeforth, C. C., Hartnup, R., Lea, J. W., Thompson, T. R. E. and Wright, P.S. (1984). *Soils and Their Use in Wales*. Soil Survey of England and Wales Bulletin 11, Harpendon Press.

Sommers, L. E. and Nelson, D. W. 1972. Determination of total phosphorus in soils: a rapid perchloric acid digestion procedure. *Soil Science Society of American Proceedings*, **36**, 902-906.

# Appendix

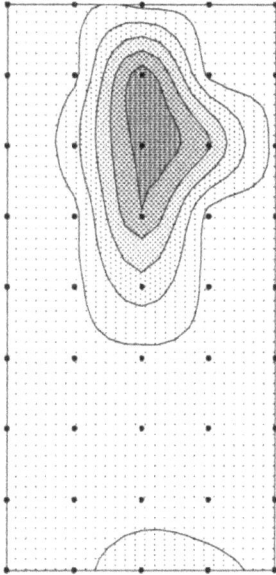

**Figure 2. 20cm grid**

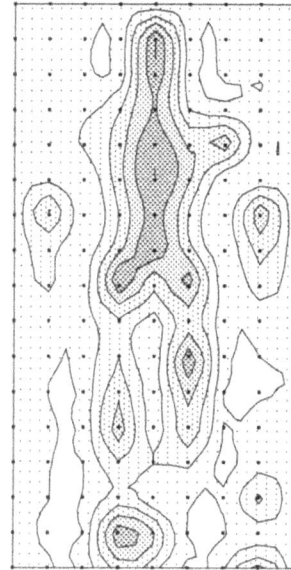

**Figure 4. 10cm grid**

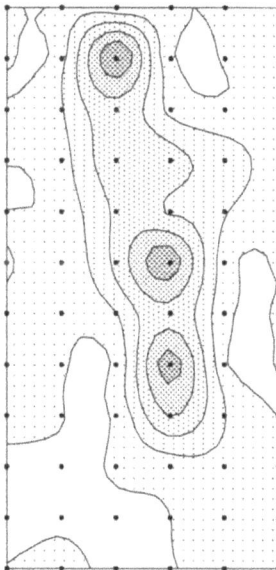

**Figure 3. 15cm grid**

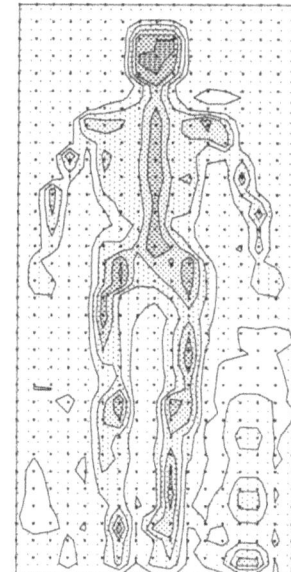

**Figure 5. 5cm grid**

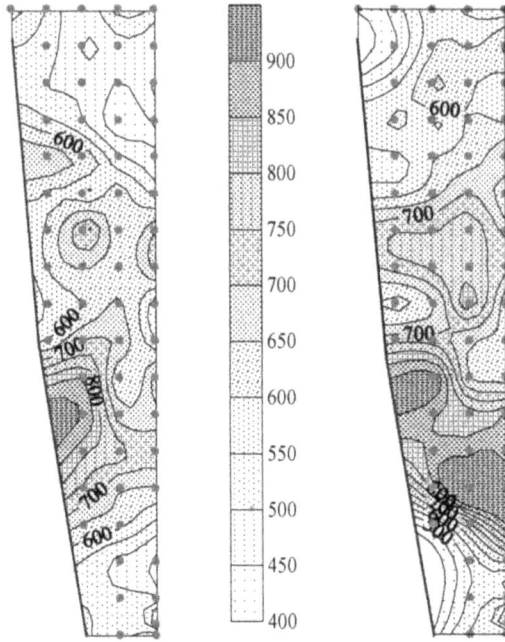

**Figure 6.**
**Cist 170 Upper layer**

**Figure 7.**
**Cist 170 Basal layer**

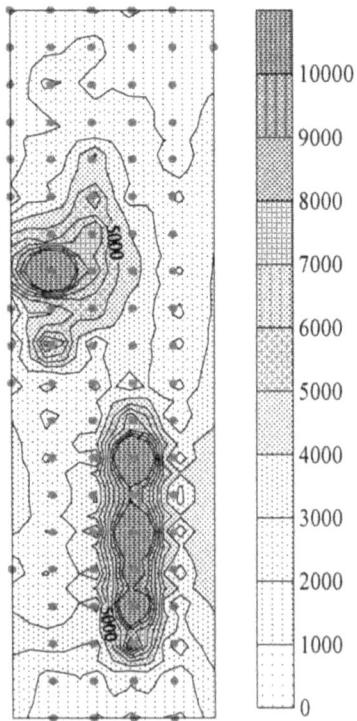

**Figure 8. Grave 304**

# Early Saxon cultivation of Emmer wheat in the Thames Valley and its cultural implications

Ruth Pelling

Institute of Archaeology, University College London, 31-34 Gordon Square, London, WC1H 0PY, UK.

## Introduction

The final withdrawal of Roman administration from Britain and the cessation of control of economic organisation and trade routes had an impact on the localised rural economy. The precise nature of the response to changes in administration in terms of agriculture is not yet fully understood, especially as the number of sites producing good macrofossil evidence is still limited and the problems of residual contamination are many. In addition, the influx and settlement of Germanic immigrants must have had a great impact on crop husbandry regimes. While some continuity in cereal cultivation may be demonstrated, the available evidence for lowland southern Britain indicates change, or even abandonment, of arable cultivation was more widespread. Much useful material has been generated in recent years as a result of the excavation of rural early to mid-Saxon sites, although the evidence is still limited.

To enable a fully comprehensive study of this period and the changes in the arable economy and husbandry methods, analysis of more large, well preserved, charred assemblages is necessary. In addition it is necessary to pull together all the available evidence to identify regional patterns as well as the gaps in the data set, both chronological and spatial, in order to target these gaps. To understand fully the impact of potential immigrant populations it is also necessary to look at the continental data. This paper attempts to explore the evidence for a possible introduction of a new arable tradition into the Thames Valley by populations derived from the Ems Estuary region of Northern Germany in the light of recent discoveries from sites at Dorney in Berkshire and Yarnton in Oxfordshire.

### The Botanical Background

The established view of Saxon cereal cultivation in southern, lowland, Britain is that the principle wheat cultivated was a *Triticum aestivum*, bread-type wheat. *Triticum aestivum* grains are recorded sporadically from the Neolithic onwards but always in small numbers until the Saxon period when it appears quite suddenly in the archaeological record in large quantities. Grains of *Triticum turgidum* (rivet wheat) cannot be distinguished from *Triticum aestivum*, but the earliest record of *Triticum turgidum* rachis from Britain is from the late Saxon period (Campbell 1994). *Triticum aestivum* and *Triticum turgidum* are free-threshing wheats in which the grain is held loosely within the ear and are consequently easily shaken free with no, or only limited, threshing once ripe. Conversely the proceeding centuries had seen a hulled wheat, *Triticum spelta* (spelt), as the principle wheat cultivated, the earliest records of which now appear to be Middle Bronze Age (for example at Black Patch, East Sussex, Hinton 1982; Princes Street Dartford, Pelling *forth*.

a; Yarnton, Oxfordshire, Robinson, 2002). Some evidence exists for the continued cultivation of spelt wheat into the early Saxon period from West Stow, Suffolk (Murphy 1985) and Mucking, Essex (Van der Veen 1981-3), although generally archaeological examples seem to stop quite abruptly with the final departure of Roman administration. A third wheat species, *Triticum dicoccum* (emmer wheat) is known from the Neolithic and Bronze Age as a major cereal (Grieg 1991, Campbell and Straker this volume). While not the principal wheat cultivated, it continues to appear occasionally, and often in significant quantities, during the Iron Age, for example at Hascombe, Surrey (Murphy 1977), Ham Hill, Somerset (Ede 1990). Roman period finds also occur, such as from Gravelly Guy, Oxfordshire (Moffett 1989). Saxon records of *Triticum dicoccum* have generally been interpreted as residual. Both *Triticum spelta* and *Triticum dicoccum* are hulled wheats in which the grain is held within tight adhering grains. In order to process the grains it is necessary to render the spikelets (pairs of grain and glume) brittle, usually done by subjecting the ears to heat, prior to threshing. Sieving or winnowing is then necessary to separate the grain from the chaff. The hulled wheats are usually processed within or near the settlement or storage facilities, hence the chaff is more likely to be used within that settlement, while the increased contact with fire results in an increased likely-hood of the chaff and grain being charred. There is therefore an increased possibility of the hulled wheats entering the archaeological record, especially the chaff.

Of the other cereals, hulled barley is most frequently encountered on early and middle Saxon sites while oats and rye are also known. Rye has occasionally been recorded in significant numbers on Roman sites, for example at Ellesmere Road, Shrewsbury (Robinson, 2002) and Melford Meadows, Brettenham (Robinson, *unpubl.* b). The first evidence of widespread cultivation of rye is, however, from the Saxon period, although its adoption tends to be regional. It is only rarely recorded from the Hampshire basin, for example, and never seems to have been successfully introduced there (Green 1994), while its early and successful adoption in East Anglia is demonstrated at sites such as West Stow in Suffolk (Murphy 1985).

### The Evidence from Dorney, Berkshire

Excavations at Lake End Road, Dorney in Berkshire in 1996 and 1997 revealed a substantial number of deep Saxon rubbish pits in addition to other features including sunken feature buildings. The excavations were undertaken by the Oxford Archaeological Unit in advance of the construction of a flood relief channel in the region of Maidenhead. The pits contained large quantities of early to middle Saxon pottery and small finds, and considerable quantities of articulated animal bone and charcoal. Samples of pit fills were taken for the extraction of charred plant remains. Twenty-one of these samples were subsequently analysed; nine from the 1996 excavations (DOLER), and 12 from the 1997 excavations (LERW). The detailed results of the analysis are discussed in an Oxford Archaeological Unit monograph (Pelling 2002). The cereals form the basis of discussion here.

**Figure1: Emmer grain and glume bases from Lake End Road, Dorney**

The 1996 samples, derived from six pits, produced unusually large assemblages for Thames Valley sites of this period, but with a fairly typical 'Saxon' suit of cereals. Free-threshing bread type wheat dominated, while barley formed the second cereal and oats and rye were present as minor species. Occasional grains of hulled wheat (*Triticum dicoccum/spelta*) and glume bases of both emmer (*Triticum dicoccum*) and spelt wheat (*Triticum spelta*) were interpreted as residual.

The 1997 samples, also derived from pits, were again dominated by wheat and barley, with some oats and rye. In these assemblages, however, a significant proportion of the wheat grain was identified as *Triticum diccocum* or *Triticum* cf. *dicoccum* (emmer). Hulled wheat (including *Triticum dicoccum/spelta*) was actually more numerous than free-threshing wheat in one of the pits (pit 40356). The emmer grain (Fig. 1) was generally narrow with a flat or slightly concave ventral surface, a prominent dorsal keel, and a humped back with the widest point situated just behind the embryo. The embryo and dorsal ends were slightly pointed. Some grain was more bluntly rounded at the dorsal end and much wider, characteristic of 'drop-shaped' emmer. A substantial number of glume bases were recovered, 1363 in total, forming by far the greatest category of cereal chaff. Of these, 397 glume bases were identified as emmer, being narrow with a strongly developed primary keel, fairly prominent secondary dorsal keel and poorly developed tertiary veins. An additional 84 glume bases displayed less

well developed secondary keels, or were less angular, and were therefore recorded as *Triticum* cf. *dicoccum*. Only one glume base was recorded as *Triticum spelta* (spelt). It is likely that the majority of the remaining glumes (recorded as *Triticum dicoccum/spelta*) are also in fact of emmer. The distribution of the emmer wheat was by no means universal; finds were concentrated in two pits in particular (pits 40356 and 40697), although smaller numbers were found across the site. Importantly, the emmer was always found in association with free-threshing bread-type wheat and rye, the widespread cultivation of which, as mentioned above, can be regarded as a Saxon innovation.

Given the intrinsic problems of contamination often encountered on Saxon sites, great care was taken in the selection of samples. For example, samples from Saxon pits clearly shown to cut prehistoric features were avoided and isolated, discrete pits were targeted where possible. The shear number of emmer glumes and grains identified from the samples would further suggest their presence as residual contaminants was unlikely. Emmer was rarely present in earlier deposits and only ever in low numbers. To confirm the date, glume bases were submitted for radiocarbon dating. Five glume bases from sample 54 (pit 40697) gave a radiocarbon date of 1487+-58BP (NZA-9206) (cal 543AD to 642AD at 1 sigma, or 435AD to 663AD at 2 sigma), which indeed suggests it to be early Saxon.

The Lake End Road samples therefore provide good evidence for the early Saxon cultivation of emmer wheat within an otherwise characteristic Saxon cereal economy, including rye and *Triticum aestivum* type wheat.

**Worton Rectory Farm, Yarnton**
The Dorney assemblages were interpreted as being of quite high status with the cereals perhaps representing imported goods. Evidence from the site of Worton Rectory Farm, Yarnton, Oxfordshire, indicates that the site was not in isolation. A sample from a Saxon post hole produced an assemblage which contained 70 grains and 19 glume bases of hulled wheat (Pelling and Robinson 2001. A sub-sample of this material was examined in more detail prior to radiocarbon dating (Pelling and Robinson, *forth*). Most of the glumes were identified as *T. dicoccum* and none could be identified with certainty as *T. spelta* L. (spelt wheat). Grains were tentatively attributed to both *T. dicoccum* and *T. spelta*. A calibrated radiocarbon date of AD 670-900 at two sigma (OxA-7365) was obtained on four glume bases and one spikelet fork of *T. dicoccum*. In the light of this evidence it would appear, therefore, that emmer was being cultivated here too, albeit at a slightly later, middle-Saxon date.

**Emmer Wheat in the National Record**
A search through the archaeological literature has revealed a limited number of additional lowland British sites, which have also produced evidence of emmer wheat in Saxon deposits (Appendix A and Figure 2). While these finds have in most cases been dismissed as residual, the recent evidence from Dorney and Yarnton must raise the possibility that at least some are of genuine Saxon date. Barton Court Farm (Jones 1984) and Hurst Park, East Mosley, Surrey (Hinton

1996) both produced Iron Age and Roman deposits of hulled wheat, including emmer. In these cases, therefore, it must be accepted that there is a high risk that the occasional Saxon finds of *Triticum dicoccum* or *T.* cf. *dicoccum* do represent residual contamination. Other sites could be more open to discussion.

Glynis Jones (1989) examined a large number of samples from Wraysbury, Berks., most of which were recorded as Saxon although dating of the site was not very secure. A total of 40 grains of *Triticum dicoccum,* and a further 24 of *Triticum* cf. *dicoccum*, were identified. Although this forms only 0.6% of the grain overall, the species does appear in 32 (23.5%) of the samples. Chaff was entirely absent from the site, hence no glume bases, the more reliable diagnostic part of the plant, were recovered. Earlier features were present on the site but no convincing prehistoric cereal assemblages have been identified.

A site on a tributary of the Thames, at Prospect Park, Harmondsworth in Hillingdon, Greater London, produced eight early Saxon samples of charred plant remains (Hinton 1996b). Several glume bases, and occasional grain, of hulled wheats, of 5th to 6th century date, were recovered. The glume bases included 27 examples identified as *Triticum* cf. *dicoccum*, while the majority were identified as *Triticum* cf. *spelta* or *Triticum dicoccum/spelta*. Earlier deposits had been recognised on the site, although the concentrations of remains were very low and the total hulled wheats recorded were one *Triticum* cf. *spelta* grain and one *Triticum dicoccum/spelta*

glume base. It is therefore plausible that both emmer wheat and spelt wheat were present at this site from the early Saxon period.

A site recently excavated by Bedfordshire County Archaeology Service at Stewartby Millennium Park, has also produced evidence of emmer wheat (Pelling, *forth* b). Pre-Saxon features were present on the site but produced only very limited charred remains and no evidence of emmer. Three early to middle Saxon samples contained occasional hulled wheat, including in two grains identified as *Triticum dicoccum* and three as *Triticum* cf. *dicoccum*, alongside a single glume base identified as *Triticum dicoccum*.

From Essex there is evidence of emmer wheat from Springfield Lyons (Murphy 1994). Small amounts of *Triticum* cf. *dicoccum* were recorded with *Triticum spelta* and *Triticum aestivum* type grains from the early Saxon cemetery. Perhaps more significant were several spikelet forks of *Triticum spelta* and one of *Triticum dicoccum* from the late Saxon settlement. The dates of these finds were thought to be genuine and their presence was interpreted as either the result of continued cultivation of spelt and emmer, or of their persistence as contaminants of free-threshing wheat.

Finally, samples of late Roman or early Saxon date from Alington Avenue in Dorchester, Dorset, produced both emmer and spelt wheat (Jones and Straker 1989). Of the 260

**Figure 2: Saxon records of emmer wheat in southern lowland Britain**

105

grains recovered 23 were of *Triticum* cf. *dicoccum*, while glume bases dominated the chaff element and included *Triticum dicoccum* and *Triticum spelta*. The samples were derived from the late infilling of a Roman corn-drier. In this case, therefore, it does appear most likely that the assemblages represent continuity of cultivation of the Roman British cereals by native populations.

Figure 2 shows that, with the exception of the (possibly Roman) Dorchester material, the distribution of finds of emmer in Lowland Britain is very much centred on the Thames Valley, and Thames Estuary. No finds have been recorded from other major rivers such as the Humber for example. Occasional records of emmer exist from Dark Age Scotland, where they are the result of its continued cultivation throughout prehistory and the early historic period north of the border. This is part of the entirely separate agricultural tradition of the highland zone, and based on the present distribution is not likely to be the source of the Thames valley material. It must be pointed out, however, that the data on which this distribution is based is still limited. As more large scale assemblages become available this pattern may change. On the basis of the present evidence however, it is proposed that there may have been a re-introduction of emmer wheat in association with more characteristic Saxon cereals, notably free-threshing bread type wheat and rye, into the Thames Valley. Furthermore, by the late Saxon period emmer wheat seems to have almost disappeared from cultivation again.

On the continent, the Roman evidence is strongest in the Netherlands (Bakels 1991) and Germany (Knörzer 1991). Here, both north and south of the Limes, the northern frontier of the Roman Empire, emmer wheat was being cultivated. Bread wheat and spelt wheat appear to be Roman cereals brought into the region from further south. The post Roman evidence suggests that across the bulk of the coastal region of France, the Netherlands, Germany and into Denmark, rye had become the dominant cereal and that emmer wheat had all but disappeared from France and the Netherlands. In Northern Germany however, particularly in the region between the Ems Estuary and the Elbe (Fig. 3), emmer wheat did continue to be cultivated as the principle wheat into the early medieval period. The distribution of known finds of emmer wheat in the Saxon period both in lowland England and in northern Europe, would suggest that it is from Germany, and specifically the Ems Estuary region, that the emmer wheat was bring re-introduced. The present evidence suggests that it was not being re-introduced from Wales in the west or from areas where emmer wheat is known to have continued in cultivation in the northern and western 'highland zone'.

**Cultural versus Ecological**
There are perhaps two issues to discuss here. Firstly, can the widespread shift from the cultivation of spelt wheat to bread type wheat be attributed to ecological factors, or was it purely cultural. Secondly, could the cultivation of emmer

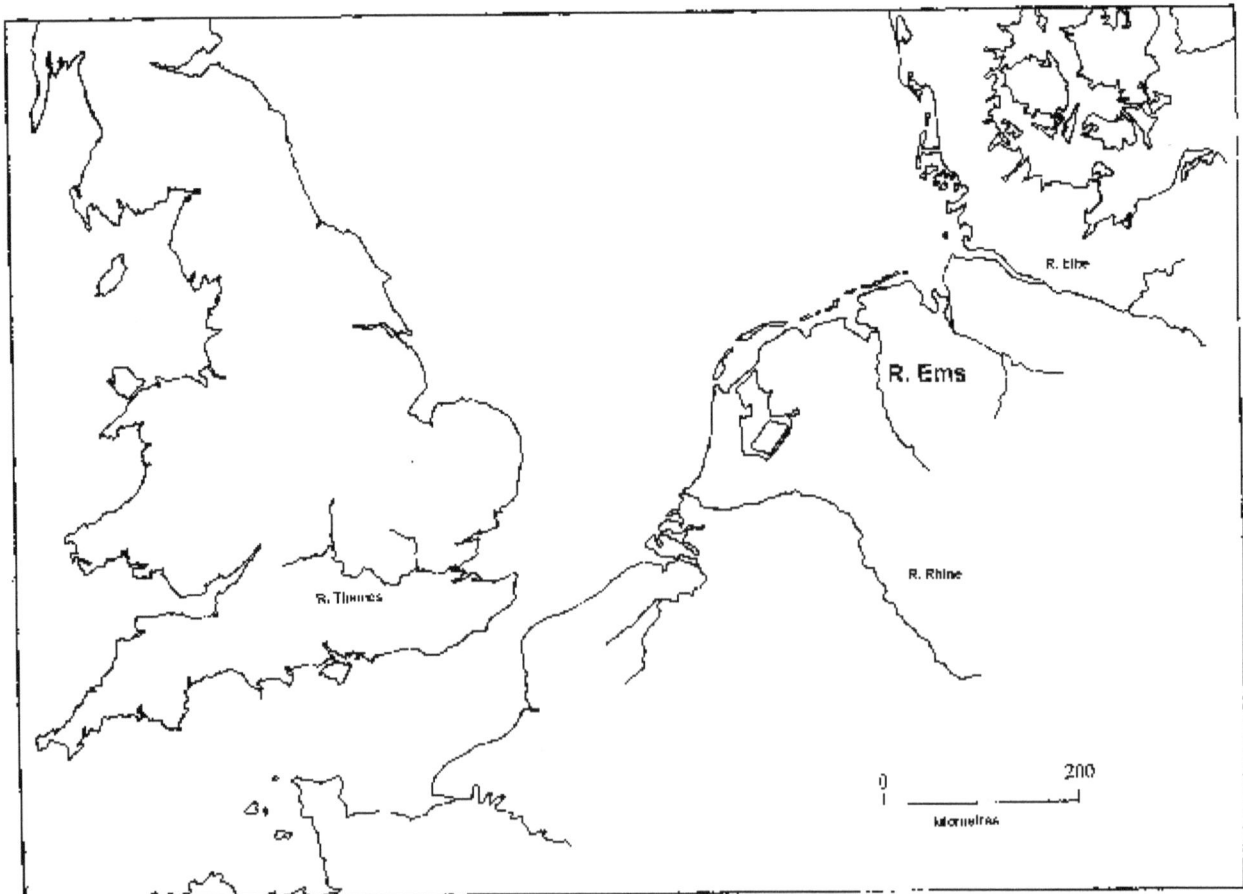

**Figure 3: Map of Northern Europe showing the River Ems**

wheat in the Thames Valley be a localised response to ecological conditions, or, again, can it be attributed to cultural choice?

Emmer wheat is well suited to light and dry soils, but along with spelt wheat and bread type wheats it is also suited to heavy soils with a higher silt or clay content. Emmer is possibly more susceptible to frost than spelt wheat or bread wheat (Percival 1921), but it can be grown as an autumn sown crop in most areas of Britain. Bread wheat and spelt are well suited to autumn sowing. Emmer and spelt wheat are both hulled wheats, which means their grain is held within tightly adhering glumes. While this provides protection against loss due to fungal attack or birds, it does mean an increase in labour requirement in terms of processing. Bread type wheat is free-threshing, which reduces processing time, although the grain is more exposed in the ear, so being more open to insect or fungal attack. Bread type wheat is also a poor competitor with weeds and modern varieties respond better to the application of fertilisers than spelt wheat (Jones 1989), although this appears to be due to modern breading and could equally apply to spelt wheat (Miller quoted in Pelling and Robinson, 2001). Analysis by Van der Veen and Palmer (1997), based on a national wheat growing experiment, demonstrated that spelt wheat was generally higher yielding than emmer and also club wheat (a modern bread wheat). They also demonstrated that emmer and spelt wheat benefited from higher summer (July) rainfall, while the yield of emmer was adversely affected by increased altitude and cold autumn temperatures. Club wheat, however, was adversely affected by increasing temperature. They concluded, however, that while these relationships are statistically significant they are very weak. If the ecological and climatic preferences dictated the type of wheat cultivated, one would assume that bread type wheat was better suited to the north and higher altitudes, while the cultivation of emmer wheat may be less labour intensive, and would also be more suited to the lighter soils of the Thames Valley gravel terraces.

The replacement of spelt wheat by bread type wheats in southern, lowland Britain can not be because of better suitability to the soils or increased yields. Jones (1989) suggests that bread wheat was not favoured until such time as it was possible and desirable to invest the greater amount of fertiliser and man hours in the form of cultivation and weeding. Since Jones made this statement there has been a significant increase in the archaeobotanical data set, such that it is now clear that the widespread shift from spelt to bread wheat occurred quite rapidly with the early Saxon period, rather than being a late Roman adoption (Campbell and Straker, this volume). The early Saxon period cannot be regarded as one of increased organisation of the rural economy and investment in cereal cultivation. Rather, it appears to be a period of decreased arable production, possibly with a shift to a more livestock based economy in which the bulk of the cereal production (mostly barley) is concerned with animal feed. Neither can the preference for an autumn sown wheat crop (as opposed to spring sown barley) be a reason, given that spelt is likely to be an autumn sown cereal. It must therefore be proposed that the relatively

sudden shift to the cultivation of bread wheat was largely related to cultural factors.

At no time in the Saxon period does emmer wheat appear to have been cultivated as the sole wheat crop. Bread type wheat is present in the Dorney and the Yarnton samples from the earliest deposits onwards, and even at Dorney it is clear that emmer wheat was grown as an addition to the bread wheat, not instead of it. Both species clearly can be cultivated very successfully throughout the region as the prehistoric records of emmer wheat confirm (Robinson and Wilson 1987; Campbell and Straker this volume). The choice to cultivate emmer must then be due to cultural preference. It would seem quite plausible that emmer wheat (and rye) seed corn was introduced with Germanic settlers and cultivated alongside the newly adopted bread type wheat. The eventual demise in emmer wheat in the region may equally be due to choice, given that ecologically there is no reason why it should not compete well with bread wheat. This could be due to taste, its preferred bread making qualities, its higher yield, its ease of processing, or a preference for autumn sowing, especially given the importance of barley at his time, usually a spring sown crop.

## Discussion

Perhaps the most important conclusion to draw from the recent findings of emmer wheat is that our knowledge of early and middle Saxon agriculture is still limited and much more thorough research of the archaeobotanical data is required. In particular the evidence from certain areas such as Kent and Sussex is almost entirely lacking. The evidence from Dorney does suggest very strongly that emmer wheat was being cultivated in the 5th to the 7th centuries AD as part of an otherwise characteristic 'Saxon' cereal economy which includes both rye and oats. In addition to this, the dated emmer from Yarnton raises the possibility that finds of emmer wheat at other sites are also the result of early or middle Saxon cultivation and must not be automatically regarded as relics of earlier periods or as residual contamination. The sites on which emmer has most convincingly been recorded appear to centre on the Thames Valley, a well established communications link with the continent into the heart of England.

The continental evidence would suggest that this particular agricultural tradition was imported from the Ems Estuary area of Germany. On a wider scale, it would appear that quite distinct regional patterns in the cereal economy of the 5th to the 8th/9th centuries may be beginning to emerge. The particular tradition of the Thames Valley may include and be characterised by emmer wheat as well as bread type wheat, oats and rye. Furthermore, cultural factors must be a major determinant in the nature and extent of the adoption of such regimes. The exact nature of such regional variation in the arable economy, and the relative roles of any cultural influences, the extent of influence of Germanic immigrants, of existing native traditions, and of ecological conditions, can only be understood when placed in the wider context. Large, perhaps national, scale synthetic studies of the existing botanical evidence in relation to the known archaeological and cultural data and the identification and consequent targeted sampling of the temporal and spatial gaps in the data set are of paramount importance.

# References

Bakels, C. C. (1991). Western Continental Europe. In W. Van Zeist, K. Wasylikowa and K-E. Behre (Eds) *Progress in Old World Palaeoethnobotany*, Balkema, Rotterdam, pp. 279-298

Campbell, G. V. (1994). The preliminary archaeobotanical results from Anglo-Saxon West Cotton and Raunds. In J. Rackham (Ed). Environment and Economy in Anglo-Saxon England , CBA Research Report **89**, pp.65-68.

Campbell, G. and Straker, V. (2003). Early Saxon cultivation of emmer wheat in the Thames Valley and its cultural implications. In Robson Brown (Ed). *Archaeological Sciences 1999*, pp. 14-30. BAR.

Ede, J. (1990). Carbonised seeds. In G. Smith (Ed) Excavations at Ham Hill, 1983. pp. 39-43 in *Proc. Somerset Archaeol. Nat. Hist. Soc.* **134** (1991), 27-45.

Green, F. (1994). Cereals and plant food: a reassessment of the Saxon economic evidence from Wessex. In J. Rackam (Ed) *Environment and economy in Anglo-Saxon England* Council for British Archaeology, Research Report **89**, pp. 83-88

Greig, J. (1991). The British Isles. In W. van Zeist, K. Wasylikowa and K-E, Behre (Eds) *Progress in Old World Palaeoethnobotany*, Balkema, Rotterdam, pp. 299-334

Hinton, P. (1996a). The plant remains at Hurst Park, East Mosley, Surrey. In P. Andrews and A. Crocket (Eds) *Three Excavations Along the Thames and its Tributaries, 1994: Neolithic to Saxon Settlement and Burial in the Thames, Colne and Kennet Valleys, Wessex* Archaeological Report No 10.

Hinton, P. (1996b). The plant remains at Prospect Park. In P. Andrews and A. Crocket (Eds) *Three Excavations Along the Thames and its Tributaries, 1994: Neolithic to Saxon Settlement and Burial in the Thames, Colne and Kennet Valleys, Wessex* Archaeological Report No 10.

Hinton, P. (1982). Carbonised seeds, 382-90. In P. Drewitt (Ed) Late Bronze Age downland economy and excavations at Black Patch, East Sussex, *Proceedings of the Prehistoric Society* **48**, 321-400

Jones, M. (1989). The Development of Crop Husbandry. In M. Jones and G. Dimbleby (Eds) *The Environment of Man: the Iron Age to the Anglo-Saxon Period*. British Archaeological Reports, **87**, 95-128

Jones, G. (1989). The Charred Plant Remains, 124-128. In G. G. Astil and S. J. Lobb Excavation of Prehistoric, Roman, and Saxon Deposits at Wraysbury, Berkshire. The *Archaeological Journal* **146**, 68-134

Jones, J. and V. Straker (1989). *Alington Avenue, Dorchester Dorset, 1984-1985: Macroscopic Plant remains from Deposits of Prehistoric to Post Roman Date.* Ancient Monuments Laboratory Report 44/8914.

Jones, M. (1984). The carbonised plant remains in D. Miles (Ed) *Archaeology at Barton Court Farm, Abingdon, Oxon.* Oxford Archaeology Unit Report 3, CBA Research Report 50.

Knorzer, K-H, (1991). Deutschland nordlich der Donau (Germany north of the Danube). In W. Van Zeist, K. Wasylikowa and K-E. Behre (Eds) *Progress in Old World Palaeoethnobotany*, Balkema, Rotterdam, pp. 189-206.

Moffett, L. C. (1989). *The evidence for crop processing products from the Late Iron Age and Romano-British periods at Gravelly Guy and some earlier prehistoric plant remains.* AML Report 46/89.

Murphy, P. (1977). Early agriculture and environment on the Hampshire chalklands, c. 800BC-400AD. Unpublished M.Phil. thesis: University of Southampton.

Murphy, P. (1985). The cereals and crop weeds in S. West, West Stow. *The Anglo-Saxon Village, Vols. 1 and 2, East Anglian Archaeology* **24**, 100-108 (Ipswich, Suffolk County Planning Department).

Murphy, P. (1994). The Anglo-Saxon landscape and rural economy: some results from sites in East Anglia and Essex. In J. Rackam (Ed) *Environment and economy in Anglo-Saxon England,* Council for British Archaeology, Research Report **89**, 23-39.

Pelling, R. (2002).. The Saxon and medieval charred assemblages from Lake End Road West, Lake End Road East and Lots Hole. In Foreman, S., Hillier, J. and Petts, D. (Eds) *Gathering the people, settling the land: The archaeology of a middle Thames landscape: Anglo-Saxon to post-medieval.* Oxford Archaeology, Thames Valley Landscapes Monograph 14, CD-ROM.

Pelling, R. *forthcoming.* The charred plant remains. In P. Hutchings (Ed). Ritual and riverside settlement: Excavation of a multiperiod site at Princes Road, Dartford 1997-98. *Archaeologia Cantiana.*

Pelling, R. unpublished report. a. *Princes Road Dartford: the middle Bronze Age Charred Plant Remains,* for Canterbury Archaeological Trust

Pelling, R. unpublished report b. *Stewartby Millennium Park, Bedfordshire: The Saxon Plant Remains,* for the Bedfordshire County Archaeology Service.

Pelling, R. and Robinson, M. (2001). Saxon Emmer Wheat from the Upper and Middle Thames Valley, England,

*Environmental Archaeology,* **5**, 117-119.

Pelling, R., Robinson M. and Stevens C. *forthcoming.* The Saxon Plant Remains. In G. Hey (Ed) *Yarnton: Saxon and Medieval Settlement and Landscape,* Thames Valley Landscape Monograph.

Percival, J. (1921). *The Wheat Plant, A Monograph.* New York: Dutton and Co.

Robinson, M. (2002). Plant remains. In A. Mudd (Ed) *Excavations at Melford, Meadows, Brettenham, 1994: Romano-British and early Saxon occupations.* East Anglian Archaeology Report **99**, 108-110. Oxford: Archaeological Unit.

Robinson, M and B. Wilson (1987). A survey on environmental archaeology in the south midlands. In H.C. Keeley (Ed) Environmental Archaeology: A Regional Review Vol. II, 16-100, HBMC occasional paper No 1.

Van der Veen, M. and Palmer C. (1997). Environmental Factors in the yield Potential of Ancient Wheat Crops. *Journal of Archaeological Science* **24**, 163-182.

Van der Veen, M. (1981-3). *Grain impressions in Early Saxon Pottery from Mucking, Essex. Interim reports 1-3, Ancient Monuments Laboratory Report Series Nos.* **3833** *and* **3834**, (London, HBMC).

# Appendix A

| Site | Location | Date Range | T dicoccu grain | T cf dicoccu grain | T dicoccum glume | T cf dicoccu glume | Features | Number of samples | Total volume (l) | Total grain | Total chaff | Reference |
|---|---|---|---|---|---|---|---|---|---|---|---|---|
| Allington Aveneue | Dorchester, Dorset | | 0. | 23 | 66 | 0 | Oven, building | 8 | | 260 | 610 | Jones and Straker 1989 |
| Barton Court Farm | Abingdon, Oxon | | 5 | 0 | 0 | 0 | SFB, pit | 2 | 30 | 53 | 1 | Jones, M. 1984 |
| Lake End Road | Dorney, Berks | 5-8thC AD | 156 | 27 | 397 | 84 | Pits | 21 | 710 | 6880 | 4150 | Pelling, forth a. |
| Hurst Park | East Mosley, Surrey | 6-7th C AD | 2 | - | 2 | - | Pit, SFB | 4 | 41 | 167 | 111 | Hinton, P 1996 |
| Prospect Park | Harmondsworth, Greater London | 5-6th C AD | 0 | 0 | 0 | 27 | Well, pits, SFB | 8 | 64 | 164 | 205 | Hinton, P. 1996 |
| Springfield Lyons | Essex | Early Saxon | 0 | 0 | 0 | 2 | Cremation | 23 | - | 65 | 36 | Murphy, 1994 |
| Springfield Lyons | Essex | Late Saxon | 0 | 0 | 1 | 0 | Post holes, pits, ditches | 96 | - | 3154 | 184 | Murphy 1994 |
| Stewartby Millennium Park | Beds | Early-mid Saxon | 2 | 3 | 1 | 0 | Pits, layer | 3 | 56 | 429 | 20 | Pelling, forth b. |
| Wraysbury | Berks | 40 | 24 | 0 | 0 | 0 | Pits, ditches, PH, gullies | 163 | 9849 | 10640 | 0 | Jones, G. 1989 |
| Yarnton (phase 1-3) | Oxfordshire | 700-900AD | 6+ | 68+ | 6+ | 0 | SFB, pits PHs, hearths | 42 | 550 | 5647 | 363 | Pelling, Robinson, Stevens, *forth* |

SFB = sunken feature building

PH = post hole

# Antique to early Medieval copper-alloy metallurgy in Palestine

Matthew Ponting

Department of Archaeology, University of Nottingham, University Park, Nottingham, NG7 2RD, UK.

## Introduction

This paper presents an overview of current scientific research into copper-alloy metallurgy in ancient Palestine, specifically the area of modern Israel. In 1996 a project was initiated to investigate the first century Roman military metalwork from the excavations of the sites of Masada and Gamla. A preliminary report of one of these sites (Masada) appeared in Archaeometry (1998). Opportunities to study additional material allowed the project to gradually become diachronic. Material from the well-established excavations at Bet She'an (Hellenistic Scythopolis) was made available which all came from reliable archaeological contexts spanning the Roman through to Early Islamic periods (Ponting 1999). Byzantine period metalwork of sixth century date from recent excavations at the Jewish settlement site of Ein Gedi (Ponting, forthcoming) complemented the late antique material and added another cultural dimension.

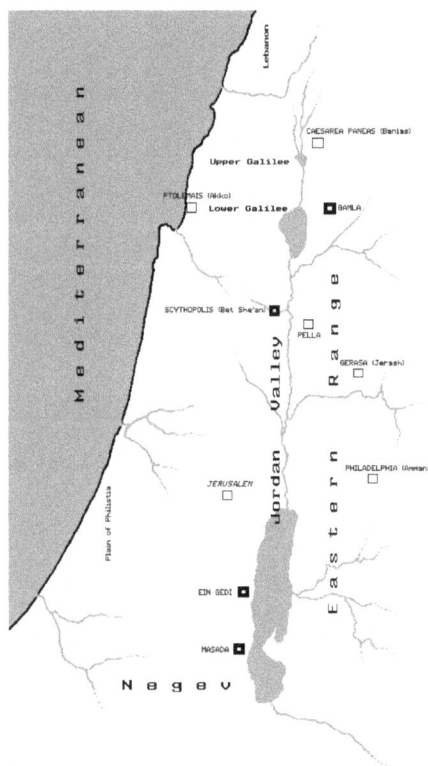

**Figure 1. Map showing sites mentioned in text (thick-walled squares).**

Copper-alloy artefacts from the Jewish civilian contexts at Gamla (Ponting, forthcoming) provide an interesting comparison for both the later material from Ein Gedi and the contemporary Roman military metalwork from Gamla.

The artefacts chosen for analysis were, as far as possible commonly represented types from the assemblages of each site. Common utilitarian or decorative types were selected across the sites, such as fibulae, buckles, weights and cosmetic implements, to allow direct comparison of similar artefact types. Inevitably, the military material form distinct typological groups, however, overlaps exist which enable comparisons with non-military artefacts, such as fibulae and buckles.

## Method

All the compositional data discussed are bulk chemical analyses conducted on approximately 25mg samples drilled out from the 'heart-metal' of the artefacts. In all cases the first millimetre or two of metal was discarded to minimise any contamination by corroded or otherwise unrepresentative material. The drillings were prepared in the standard way described in Hughes et al. (1976) and analysis was by either inductively coupled plasma atomic emission spectrometry (ICP-AES) or atomic absorption spectrometry (AAS). In both cases standard reference materials (BCS 183/3 and BAM 211) were always run alongside each batch of samples to monitor accuracy and precision. Furthermore, duplicate samples from a selection of sites were analysed by both techniques, confirming excellent agreement. The differences that were noticed related to the differences in limits of detection; ICP is generally a more sensitive technique, especially for the elements tin and arsenic. Typically, the precision of AAS is ± 1–2% for major elements (>1%), ± 5-10% for minors (0.1 – 1%) and ± 20-50% or less for traces (<0.1%), with precision worsening as the detection limits are approached. For ICP the precision is somewhat better, with typical figures being ± 1-2% for majors and ± 3-5% for minors and trace, again worsening as the detection limits are approached. The detection limits vary from element to element, typical examples would be arsenic which is poor by AAS at about 1ppm and 0.1ppm by ICP, iron at 0.05ppm by AAS and 0.05ppm by ICP and lead at 0.6ppm by AAS and 0.2ppm by ICP.

### Discussion of the data

Masada and Gamla were both the sites of famous sieges during the First, or Great, Revolt of the Jews against Rome that lasted from AD 63 to 74. The sites are quite different in their origins and functions; Gamla was a substantial walled town situated up in the Golan Heights, Masada was a purpose built palace/fortress constructed on the summit of an impregnable mountain close to the shores of the Dead Sea. A massive programme of excavations was conducted at Masada from 1963 to 1965 and at Gamla from 1976 to 1989; work continues on both sites today. Furthermore, the First Revolt was documented in great detail by one of the Jewish generals involved, Flavius Josephus, who was captured by the future Emperor Vespasian and allowed to live out his life in exile in Rome. During his exile he wrote his account of 'The Jewish War'. Josephus' history includes graphic accounts of the sieges of Masada and Gamla with considerable detail about which legions were involved and how they were deployed. Excavation has recently substantiated (as far as is possible) much of what Josephus reports (Aviram et al. 1988) and suggests that (at least for his descriptions of locations and military deployment) the account is reliable, although, like most ancient historians, he had his own agenda. For this reason, material from the siege contexts (as identified by excavation) provides military metalwork which in many cases can be attributed to a particular legion and which entered the archaeological record in a particular year. Gamla was the first casualty of the revolt and fell in October AD 67, never to be re-occupied. Three legions were involved in the siege; *Legio X Fretensis*, *Legio XV Apollinaris* and the *Legio V Macedonica*. Masada was the last stronghold of the rebels, finally being stormed in April AD 74, and thereafter deserted except for a short-lived monastic community in the sixth century (a Roman military camp was maintained below the mountain until *c*. AD 105). Only one legion was involved at Masada, the *Legio X Fretensis*. Of these three legions, only the *X Fretensis* can be regarded as 'local'. The *Legio XV Appollinaris* and the *Legio V Macedonica* had been moved from Southern Central Europe to fight the Parthians a short while before the revolt, whilst the *Legio X Fretensis* had been the *locally* recruited garrison legion of Syria since at least AD 6 (Cotton and Geiger 1989).

Current thinking on the logistics of Roman military supply sees the involvement of local artisans and of the individual units themselves in re-cycling and even manufacturing equipment (Bishop and Coulston 1993, 184). It is suggested that to view the Roman army – in terms of its equipment - as a single, culturally homogeneous entity is a mistake. However, much of this debate is based on studies of the Roman army in northern Europe, the situation in the East could well have been different. The composition of the military brasses from Masada and Gamla is remarkably consistent and, furthermore, virtually identical to the composition of contemporary military brasses from Europe. This may suggest that much, if not all, of the military brasses used by the Roman legions in Palestine was produced in Europe. This rather controversial view is supported by the fact that much of the equipment has typological parallels from European sites. In particular, at both Masada and Gamla, the most prevalent fibula type was the *Aucissa*. This type of fibula has long been shown to have strong military associations in Europe and to be commonly made of brass (Bayley 1998, 15) (Table 1).

| | No. | Zinc % | Tin % | Lead % |
|---|---|---|---|---|
| British sites | 16 | 19.54 +/- 2.54 | 1.72 +/- 1.83 | 0.15 +/- 0.18 |
| Masada and Gamla | 19 | 20.35 +/- 3.21 | 1.01 +/- 1.37 | 0.85 +/- 0.70 |

**Table 1. Compositions of *Aucissa* type fibulae. British sites data after Bayley (1998).**

The type has its origins in Southern Gaul in the first half of the first century, and occurs predominantly on military sites (de la Bédoyère 1989, 121). Regardless of whether the fibulae formed a part of compulsory military uniform, or whether wearing a particular type of fibula was down to personal whim, the fact that soldiers in a locally recruited

legion (*X Fretensis*) in Palestine did so is significant[1]. It suggests a degree of 'cultural' homogeneity within the Roman army of the first century at a remarkable level. Either scenario has to see the *Aucissa* fibulae being brought into Palestine along with the 'official' uniform fittings. If their use by the soldiers of the *X Fretensis* was down to fashion amongst the troops, the scenario is more remarkable. It suggests that European made fibulae were brought in to satisfy a demand by the local soldiery – and that the local soldiery saw the Gallic fibula as, in some way, a badge of their status – of 'belonging' to the Roman system and of marking them out as being different from the civilians who shared their ethnicity. Their ethnicity was no longer 'Syrian' or 'Semitic' but 'Roman soldier'.

The trace elements associated with the technology of brass production indicate that the military brasses from Masada and Gamala were made in the classic Roman fashion using a zinc carbonate ore (calamine or smithsonite) which is not found in economic quantities in Palestine or surrounding areas. The nearest smithsonite source would probably have been in western Anatolia, but the production technology there was different, resulting in a characteristically low level of trace element contamination (Craddock, Burnett and Preston 1980, 60-61). The levels of the principal contaminants related to the production technology in the Israeli brasses, iron and manganese, are relatively high and consistent with those found in contemporary European Roman military brasses and coins (Table 2). This indicates the use of a solid-state cementation method, where calcined smithsonite ore is in direct contact with the copper during the process. Only in this way can the iron and manganese present in the ore pass directly into the copper along with the zinc (Carradice and Cowell 1987, 35-38; Craddock 1995, 298).

| | Brasses | | Bronzes/coppers | |
|---|---|---|---|---|
| | *Mn (Wt.%)* | *Fe (Wt.%)* | *Mn (Wt.%)* | *Fe (Wt.%)* |
| Masada and Gamla | 0.0030 | 0.29 | 0.0005 | 0.19 |
| Camerton | 0.0011 | 0.32 | <0.0005 | 0.27 |
| Coinage | 0.0035 | 0.28 | <0.0005 | 0.20 |

**Table 2. Camerton data after Cowell (1990) and Coinage data after Carradice and Cowell (1987).**

The exceptions to this finding are the brass armour scales. These are all made of primary cementation brass, the same as the Roman brasses, but form a uniquely homogeneous group with significantly higher levels of manganese (Figure.2). This marks the armour scales out as being chemically

---

[1] Auxilliary troops would also have been present at both sieges and could arguably have come from Western provinces. However, it appears that at the time of the Revolt the auxilliary troops were largely recruited from the gentile populations of Caesarea and Sebaste (Millar 1993, 69). Thus the question over the prevalence of *Aucissa* type fibulae remains regardless.

different from the clearly Roman military equipment. This also fits in with the archaeological context of some of these pieces; many were found associated with the skeleton of a young man who was almost certainly one of the defenders. Typological studies of scale armour also suggest that, morphologically, the Masada scale armour is inconsistent with Roman military issue. Furthermore, Josephus mentions that supplies of weapons, unwrought iron, bronze and lead were found by the Sicarii when they seized Masada (BJ VII, 288). Taken on balance, this may suggest that the brass scales are not of Roman manufacture, but perhaps represent indigenous brass, presumably manufactured for the Royal troops of Herod's regime (who, as citizens of a 'client' kingdom, were also heavily influenced by Rome).

Given the apparent compositional homogeneity of the Roman military equipment and its similarity to that from European sites, it was important to compare the military copper-based metalwork with civilian products. The site of Gamla provided an ideal assemblage of metalwork which is largely contemporary with the military material and which all has firm archaeological contexts.

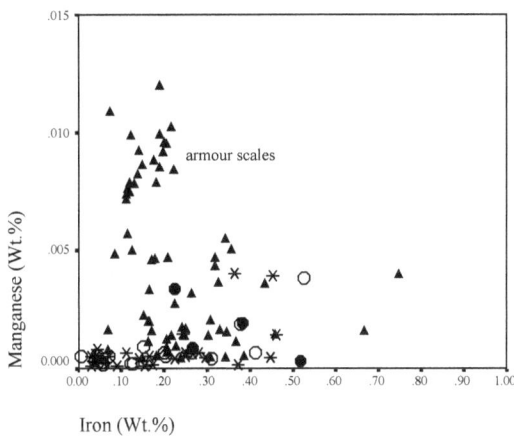

**Figure 2. Scatter plot of manganese and iron for Masada and Gamla data. ⬈, brass; ⬊, bronze; ⬇'gunmetal'; ⬇, un-alloyed copper.**

The difference to the military metalwork is quite profound; none of the civilian pieces were found to contain appreciable levels of zinc. Indeed, the zinc concentrations measured are so low as to suggest that there had been no brasses at all circulating within the metal re-cycling 'pool' accessed by the local population. The apparent lack of any zinc containing alloy in the civilian assemblage from Gamla stands in stark contrast to the Military metalwork, and, furthermore, is different to comparable assemblages from first century settlements on the Roman periphery in the West. Analyses of pre-Roman copper-alloy metalwork from European and British sites show that zinc containing alloys were known and used (Dungworth 1996, Hamilton 1996). Furthermore, there appears, in certain cases, to be a link between the use of brass and 'Romanisation', although the over simplicity of this as a universal model has rightly been challenged (Dungworth 1997). However, it remains very likely that the use of brass was in some way linked to a desire to 'buy into' the Roman 'cultural system'; that the metal was viewed as both exotic (gold coloured) and symbolic of Roman values.

An example of this, the *Aucissa* fibulae, has already been discussed above.

This evidence therefore suggests that there was little or no metal exchange between the people using copper-alloy objects at Gamla and the Roman military. This may not, on the face of it, seem surprising. However, given the evidence from Europe, we would expect some contamination of the local scrap 'pool' by recycled Roman military brasses, as has been demonstrated at the Tittelburg in Luxembourg (Hamiliton, 1996). Indeed, given that the Roman military had been in the area since the middle of the first century BC (Millar 1993, 2), we would expect as much, if not more, evidence of 'Roman contamination' in Palestine as in Gaul. This is clearly not the case; at the Tittelburg 30% of copper-alloy artefacts dated to between 100 and 50 BC are brass, and this trend continues during the following period (50 to 1 BC); from AD 1 to 70 this figure then rises to 44% (Hamilton 1996, 44). Clearly, at Gamla at least, a distinct effort must have been made to ensure a supply of 'uncontaminated' metal. This selection procedure was presumably related, to some extent, to the alloy's golden colour, although low (residual) levels of zinc would not have had any noticeable effect on this. How this would have worked is unclear, but may suggest that metal was only procured from specific (traditional/non-Roman) sources.

The evidence of the trace elements associated with the copper also supports this idea of 'mutual exclusivity'; higher levels of cobalt and arsenic are noted in the Gamla civilian

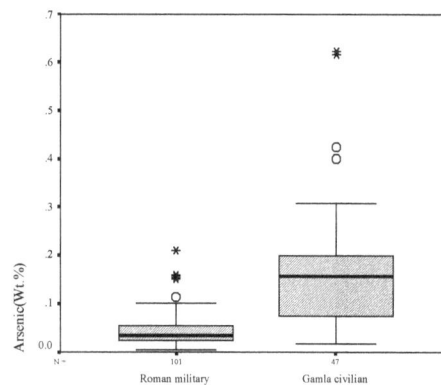

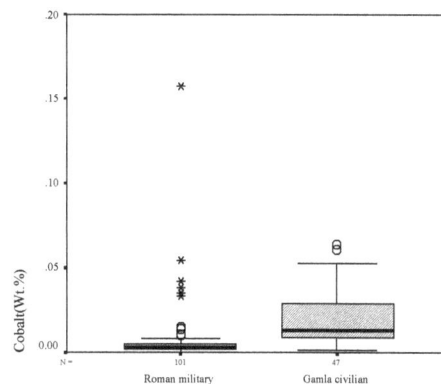

**Figures 3 and 4. Box-and-Whisker plots of arsenic and cobalt for Masada and Gamla military metalwork against the Gamla civilian metalwork. Dilution effects caused by differences in alloying constituents have been taken into consideration.**

copper-alloys than in the Roman material, as can be seen in the Box-and-Whisker plots (Figures 3 and 4).

This seems to suggest a basic chemical difference between European and Near Eastern coppers, or perhaps, between locally produced metalwork and Roman military metalwork. It is perhaps significant that very similar trace element differences have been reported between first century Roman military copper-alloys and indigenous Iron Age copper-alloys from Britain (Cowell, 1990), suggesting, perhaps, technological differences rather than differences in the chemical characteristics of the copper sources. Indeed, it is well established that the re-cycling of copper (repeated re-melting) will result in a gradual reduction in impurity levels (Merkel 1990,116-118).

In north-western Europe it seems that zinc containing alloys gradually replaced bronzes, with ternary alloys, often called 'gunmetals' (alloys containing appreciable amounts of tin and zinc), becoming the norm and 'true' brasses being reserved for specific (luxury?) applications (Craddock 1985; Dungworth 1997). A working model for the adoption of 'gunmetals' would be the increasingly frequent contamination of local 'bronze-based' scrap-metal pools by Roman military brasses. However, this model is probably overly simplistic, with a degree of fashion creeping in, as has been suggested by Dungworth in his study of copper-alloys in Northern Britain (1997, 909). With the collapse of Roman administration in the northwestern provinces it appears that the trend towards the use of 'gunmetals' continued, but with the zinc content declining and primary brasses becoming rare (Bayley 1998, 20). This may indicate that zinc-containing alloys were becoming increasingly rare or less popular. In Palestine it is likely that a similar initial process of 'zinc infiltration' occurred during the centuries of Roman rule. However, Roman rule continued for longer there, the Christianisation of the Roman state in the mid-fourth century merely providing a suitable point for modern scholars to indicate this change by using the term Byzantine where Roman had previously been used. Changes in material culture are somewhat less dramatic, only a steady increase in Christian symbols chart a gradual change from classical Rome to Medieval Byzantium. Other aspects of material culture also changed slowly, reflecting the continuity of the local people and their traditions

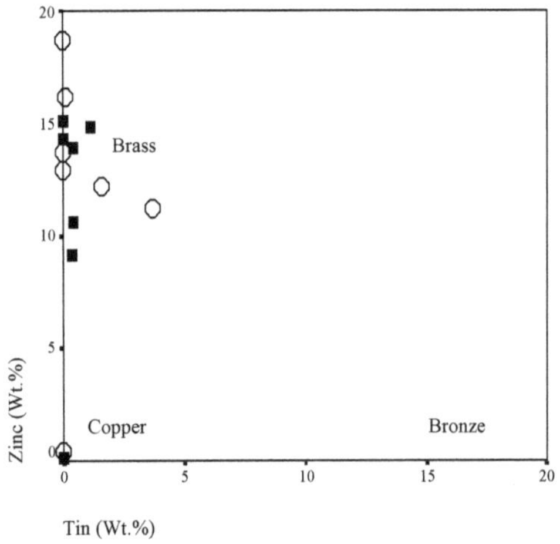

**Figure 5. Scatter plot of zinc and tin for Ein Gedi metalwork; O, scrap metal; ■, artefacts.**

The analysis of copper-alloy artefacts from the Byzantine settlement at Ein Gedi show that by the sixth century the use of bronze had been totally replaced by brasses (Fig. 5). This was presumably the result of five hundred years of gradual change that remains to be charted. Like Gamla, the settlement at Ein Gedi was distinctly Jewish, yet the predominant copper-alloy used had changed in a remarkable way. If we see the first century population of Gamla actively preserving their traditional use of bronze as a statement of their identity against the perfidious contamination by Roman brass, then to find this situation turned on its head five centuries later is surely significant. Yet, where the earlier Gamla copper-alloys have almost no zinc in them, the Ein Gedi brasses quite frequently contain up to a percent or even two of tin. This, presumably reflects the composition of the available scrap; where the bronzes had been successively mixed with brasses until the tin content had be diluted to the levels seen here. This continuous process of re-cycling and mixing is also apparent from the zinc contents. The cementation process is capable of producing brasses with a maximum zinc content of 28% (Haedecke, 1973) with 20% to 25% being more common in antiquity, yet each re-melting will cause the loss of about 10% of the zinc through volatilisation (Caley 1964, 19). Thus re-cycled brasses will tend to have zinc contents of less than 18%. The study of copper-alloy lamps in the British Museum showed two distinct groups of brass lamps having zinc contents of around 22% for one and between 8% and 14% for the other. These have been identified as primary and secondary (re-cycled) brasses respectively (Hook and Craddock 1996, 151). It is therefore significant that the Ein Gedi brasses have zinc contents of between 9% and 17% and are therefore clearly consistent with the re-cycled or 'secondary' brasses postulated by Hook and Craddock.

A similar pattern of copper-alloy use was found in the analyses of the copper-alloy artefacts from the recent excavations at Bet She'an in Israel. This site was an important Late Classical settlement, the classical city of Scythopolis, one of the cities of the Decapolis. Here a limited diachronic study of 50 samples was conducted, hoping to identify broad general trends in copper-alloy usage from the Late Antique to the Early Medieval periods (Ponting 1999). As at Ein Gedi, brass was the most predominant alloy in Byzantine period with predominantly secondary brasses being identified. But in 634 AD, Scythopolis fell to the Ummayad Arabs shortly after the battle of Ajnadayn and remained in Muslim hands until 1917. The copper-alloy metalwork that can be dated to the first Arab dynasty shows a remarkable break with Byzantine tradition in terms of alloy recipe (Figure 6).

There are no proper brasses; the majority of objects are made of a low tin bronze, often highly leaded, with a small number of ternary alloys containing low levels of both zinc and tin. This finding agrees with the only other published analyses of Ummayad copper-alloy artefacts, the material from Umm El-Walid in Jordan, but these only consist of the analyses of nine artefacts (Schwiezer 1994). The Ummayad period is particularly well represented at Bet She'an and is archaeologically well defined with the city being substantially destroyed by an earthquake in AD 749.

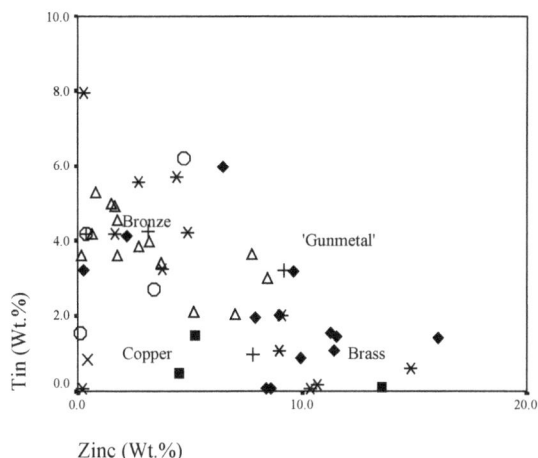

**Figure 6. Scatter plot of zinc and tin contents of Bet She'an metalwork. ⊕ ,Mamluk; +, Crusader/Ayyubid; ×, Fatimid; *, Abbasid; ↖, Ummayad; ⇦, Late Byzantine; ■, Early Byzantine; ○, Roman.**

In later periods brasses begin to re-appear with almost equal percentages of bronze and brass by the Abasid period (750-950 AD). The use of brass apparently re-gained its ascendancy by the 9th century, as has been reported by the survey of the Islamic metalwork in the British Museum collection (Craddock, LaNiece and Hook 1998).

## Conclusion

The analytical work to date and its interpretation presents a picture where alloying practice and culture are closely aligned. The motivations behind technological changes are inevitably complex and cannot be addressed solely by scientific means; comprehensive understanding of the social and cultural constraints of the societies involved needs to be brought to bear. Scientific analyses of archaeological material can identify trends and the significant points of change in a technology, but, as this paper has demonstrated, the interpretation of these data in their correct context requires an archaeological training.

The present work has identified important questions that need addressing;
1) When did the local brass industry begin? Sometime between the first and sixth century clearly. It apparently has the same beginnings as in Europe; through the Roman military and Administration, but this technology clearly had a different development which requires charting.
2) Why did the Ummayad smiths return to the use of bronze? Does this merely reflect local availability of zinc ores; Anatolia was still Byzantine until 9th century, or is this fashion or the cultural biases of the inhabitants? After all, brasses would still have been available for re-cycling, as they had been for centuries. This 'technological choice' needs explaining.

Clearly more sites need to be studied to establish the viability of the models suggested here, however, the close relationship between technology and culture remains apparent.

## References

Aviram, J., Foerster, G. and Netzer, E. (1988).*Masada I.* Jerusalem: Israel Exploration Society.

Bayley, J. (1998). The Production of Brass in Antiquity with Particular Reference to Roman Britain. In P.T. Craddock (Ed). *2000 Years of Zinc and Brass.* (Revised edition). pp. 7-27. London: British Museum Occasional Paper No.

de la Bédoyère, G. (1989). *The Finds of Roman Britain.* London: Batsford.

Bishop, M. C. and Coulston, J. C. N. (1993). *Roman Military Equipment.* London:Batsford.

Caley, E. R. (1964). The Analysis of Ancient Metals. London: Pergamon press.

Carradice, I., and Cowell, M.R. (1987). The Minting of Roman Imperial Bronze Coins for Circulation in the East:Vespasian to Trajan. *Numismatic Chronicle* **147**, 26-50.

Cotton, H. M., and J. Geiger, J. (1989). *Masada II; the Latin and Greek Documents.* Jerusalem: Israel Exploration Society.

Cowell, M. R. (1990). Scientific Report. In Jackson, R. (Ed). *Camerton: The Late Iron Age and Early Roman Metalwork.* pp. 69-80. London: British Museum Press.

Craddock, P. T. (1985). Three Thousand Years of Copper Alloys:From the Bronze Age to the Industrial Revolution. In P. England and L. van Zelst. (Eds). *The Application of Science in the Examination of Works of Art.* pp. 59-67. Boston: Museum of Fine Arts.

Craddock, R.T. (1995). *Early Metal Mining and Metal Production.* Edinburgh.: Edinburgh University Press.

Craddock, P. T., Burnett, A.M., and Preston, K. (1980). Hellenistic Copper-Based Coinage and the Origins of Brass. In W.A. Oddy (Ed). *Scientific Studies in Numismatics.* pp. 53-64. London: British Museum Occasional Paper 18.

Craddock, P. T., La Niece, S.C., and D. R. Hook, D.R. (1990). Brass in the Medieval Islamic World. In P.T. Craddock (Ed). *2000 Years of Zinc and Brass.*pp. 73-102. London: British Museum Occasional Publication No. 50.

Dungworth, D.(1996).The Production of Copper-Alloys in Iron Age Britain. *Proceedings of the Prehistoric Society.* **62**, 399-421.

Dungworth, D. (1997). Roman Copper Alloys: Analysis of Artefacts from Northern Britain. *Journal of Archaeological Science* **24**:901-910.

Haedeke, K. (1973). Gleichgewichtsverhaeltnisse bei der Messingherstellung nach dem Galmeiverfahren. *Erzmetall,* **25**; 229-251.

Hamilton, E. G.(1996). *Technology and Social Change in Belgic Gaul: copper working at the Tittelberg, Luxembourg,*

*125 BC-AD 300*. Masca Research Papers Vol. 13. University of Pennsylvania.

Hook. D. R., and P.T. Craddock, P.T. (1996). The Scientific Analysis of the Copper-Alloy Lamps: Aspects of Classical Alloying Practices. In D. M. Bailey (Ed). *A Catalogue of the Lamps in the British Museum, Part 4. Lamps of Metal and Stone, and Lampstands.* pp.144-163. London: British Museum Press.

Hughes, M. J., Cowell, M.R.and Craddock, P.T. (1976). Atomic Absorption Techniques in Archaeology. *Archaeometry* **18**:19-37.

Josephus, Flavius.Bellum Judaicum. Translated by G. A. Williamson. Penguin books, 1981.

Merkel, J. F.(1990). Experimental Reconstruction of Bronze Age Copper Smelting Based on Archaeological Evidence from Timna. In B. Rothenburg, (Ed). *The Ancient Metallurgy of Copper.* pp. 78-120 London: IAMS.

Millar, F.(1993). *The Roman Near East; 31 BC-AD* 337. Cambridge: Harvard University Press.

Ponting, M. J.(1998). East meets West in Post-Classical Bet She'an: the archaeometallurgy of culture change. *Journal of Archaeological Science* **26**; 1311-1321.

Ponting, M. J. (forthcoming). Compositional Analysis of copper-alloy artefacts from Ein Gedi excavations. In Y. Hirschfeld. (Ed). *Excavations at Ein Gedi.* Jerusalem: Israel Exploration Fund.

Ponting, M. J. (forthcoming). Compositional Analysis of copper-alloy artefacts from excavations at Gamla. *In Excavations at Gamla*, D. Syon. 'Atiqot, *Journal of the Israel Antiquities Authority.*

Ponting, M. J., and Segal, I. (1998). ICP-AES Analyses of Roman Military Copper-Alloy Artefacts from the Excavations of Masada, *Israel. Archaeometry* **40**(1), 109-123.

Schweizer, F. (1994). Aspect Metallurgique Des Quelques Objets Byzantins et Omeyyades Decouverts Recemment en Jordanie. In L'Oevre d'Art Sous le Regard Des Sciences, pp. 191-208.

# Very-Realistic visualisation of the sculpted bas-reliefs from Cap Blanc

Kate Robson Brown[1] Alan Chalmers[2] Francesco d'Errico[3]

[1] Centre for Human Evolutionary Research, Department of Archaeology,
[2] Department of Computer Science,
University of Bristol, Bristol BS8 1UB, United Kingdom.
[3] UMR 5808 of the CNRS, Institut de Préhistoire et de Géologie du Quaternaire, Av. des Facultés, 33405 Talence, France.

## Abstract

Three-dimensional structure is a key feature of Upper Palaeolithic rock art. Subtle irregularities of the contours of an art surface may indeed have had a significance to the interpretation of the archaeological feature. Furthermore, this artwork would have been viewed in the Upper Palaeolithic, not under modern electric lights as we do today, but rather under some form of flame-lit conditions. Advances in image synthesis techniques allow us to simulate the distribution of light energy in a scene with great precision, while modern laser scanning techniques enable detailed 3D models of a rock surface to be acquired in a non-invasive manner.

This paper describes how such detailed laser-scanned 3D models, computer graphics and archaeology can be combined to produce very realistic reconstructions of how the Upper Palaeolithic site of Cap Blanc in south-west France may have appeared to our ancestors some 15,000 years ago.

## Introduction

Computer graphics techniques are increasingly being used to reconstruct and visualise features of archaeological sites that may otherwise be difficult to appreciate. While this new perspective may enhance our understanding of the environments used by our ancestors, if we are to avoid misleading impressions of a site, then the computer generated images should not only look "real", but must simulate accurately all the physical evidence for the site being modelled. Before the advent of modern lighting, illumination within ancient environments was dependent on daylight and flame. The fuel used for the fire directly affects the visual appearance of the scene. Thus any realistic flame-lit environment should incorporate the accurate spectral profile of the fuel being burnt. The aim of realistic image synthesis is the creation of such accurate, high quality imagery that faithfully represents a physical environment, the ultimate goal being to create images that are perceptually indistinguishable from an actual scene.

The use of laser range measurement, has been shown to have great potential for surveying the detailed contours of architectural structures, natural phenomena such as caves, or sections produced as a result of excavation of archaeological sites (Rouzaud 1993; Heinz 1998; Ng et al 1998; Levoy 1999a, b). Several types of laser, and measurement mechanisms, can be used to calculate the location of points on a surface (Atkin, 1987; Letellier 1995). For instance, the lasers may differ in colour or strength, and the measurement mechanism may rely on calculating time-of-flight or waveform. These variables will determine the speed and accuracy of the method, the type of data collected, and the optimum distance over which a recording may be made, and clearly they have financial and logistical implications for archaeology.

## The Prehistoric Site

The rock shelter site of Cap Blanc, overlooking the Beaune valley in the Dordogne, contains perhaps the most dramatic and impressive example of Upper Palaeolithic haut relief carving. A frieze of horses, bison and deer, some overlain on other images, was carved some 15,000 years ago into the limestone as deeply as 45cms, covers 13m of the wall of the shelter. Since its discovery in 1909 by Raymond Peyrille several descriptions, sketches, and surveys of the frieze have been published, but they appear to be variable in their detail and accuracy (Leroi-Gourham et al 1972; Roussot, 1972). In 1999, a team from the University of Bristol undertook a laser scan of part of the frieze, Figure 1, at 20mm precision. It was obviously of utmost importance that an "eye safe" laser was used to ensure there was no damage at all to the site.

**Figure 1: Part of the frieze from Cap Blanc**

Some 55,000 points were obtained in two scans of the upper and lower part of the selected area, Figure 2 (the MDL laser scanner used did not have sufficient memory to store all the points in a single scan). These points were stitched together, converted into a triangular mesh and imported into the lighting simulation software, Radiance (Ward Larson and Shakespeare, 1998).

Detailed photographs of the frieze were taken, each one of which included a standard colour chart, just visible in Figure 1. As the exact spectral data for the colour chart is known, this enabled us to compensate for the lighting in the photograph and thus obtain approximate "illumination free" textures to include with the wire-frame model to produce the final reconstructed model, Figure 3.

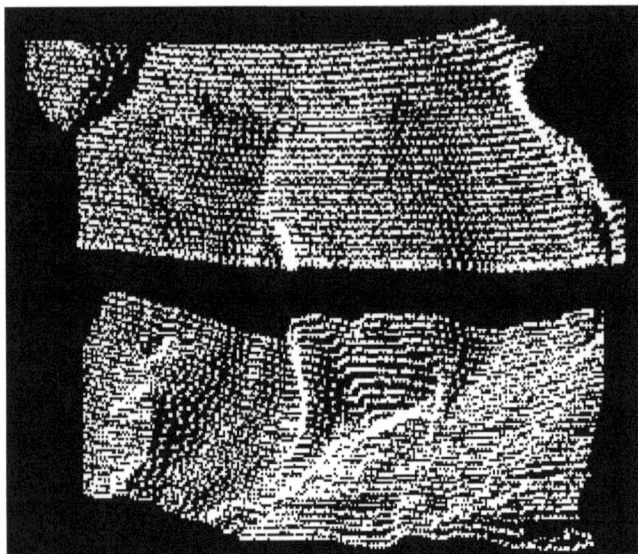

**Figure 2: Clouds of points from the scan**

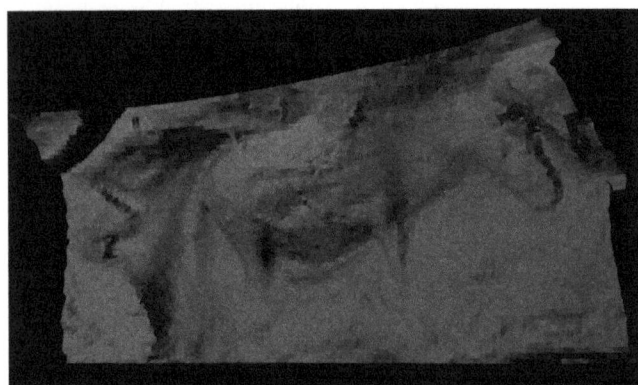

**Figure 3: The reconstructed horse**

## Luminaires

The luminosity of flame is due to glowing particles of solids in laminar flux, the colour of which is primarily related to the emission from incandescent carbon particles. A typical fuel/air wick flame consists of three distinct zones: the inner core, blue intermediate zone and the outer cone (Gaydon and Wolfard 1979). The different zones of the flame produce different emissions depending on the fuel type and environment conditions.

Previous work on modelling flame has focussed on large-scale flames such as fires (Gardner, 1994), fireballs and explosions (Reeves, 1983, Perlin and Hoffert, 1989) or more generic flames, for example (Rushmeier 1995, Sakas 1993, Stam and Fiume 1993). Inakage introduced a simplified candle flame model (Inakage 1990), which Raczkowski extended to include the dynamic nature of the flame (Raczkowski 1996).

The acquisition of valid experimental data was of vital importance to this project as the material used may have had a significant influence on the perception of the ancient environment. The first stage was to build a reconstruction of a rendered animal fat lamp, such as may have been used in the Upper Palaeolithic, Figure 4.

**Figure 4: Experimental archaeology: reconstructing ancient light sources**

Detailed spectral data was gathered using a spectoradiometer. This device is able to measure the emission spectrum of a light source from 380nm to 760nm, in 5nm wavelength increments. This gives an accurate breakdown of the emission lines generated by the combustion of a particular fuel. This data can be used to create an RGB colour model for use in rendering the scene.

## Discussion

Images were rendered using Radiance (Ward Larson and Shakespeare, 1998). Figure 5 (upper) shows the horse illuminated by a simulated 55W incandescent bulb (as in a low-power floodlight), which is how visitors view the actual site today. In Figure 5 (lower) the horse is now illuminated

**Figure 5: Frieze lit by 55W incandescent bulb (upper) and animal fat candle (lower)**

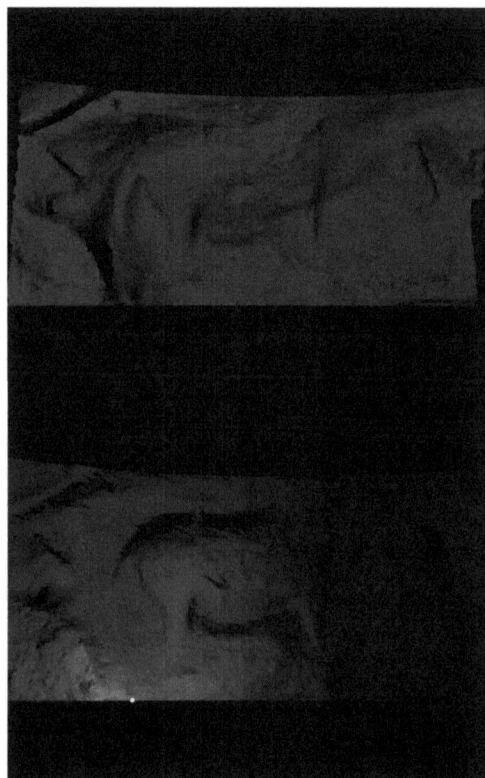

by a simulated animal fat tallow candle as it may have been viewed 15,000 years ago. As can be seen the difference between the two images is significant with the candle illumination giving a "warmer glow" to the scene as well as more shadows.

We will of course never know for certain how people in the Upper Palaeolithic viewed their artwork. What these results do show is that it is important for archaeologists to view such artwork under (simulated) original conditions rather than under modern lighting. It is of course impossible to investigate these sensitive sites with real flame sources.

Future work will investigate the high fidelity reconstructions of other painted (rather than carved) sites in the region.

## Acknowledgements

We would like to thank Jean Archambeau, the owner of Cap Blanc, for his permission to work at the site and his interest and Chris Green, Ian Roberts and Michael Hall for their input to this project. Many thanks also to the Bristol/Bordeaux Twinning Association and the ALLIANCE / British Council programme (Action integrée franco-britanique) for their financial support.

## References

Atkin, B. and Gill, M. and Newton, S. (1987). *CAD Techniques: Opportunities for chartered quantity surveyors.* Royal Institute of Chartered Surveyors, London.

Gardner G.Y. (1994). Modeling Amorphous Natural Features. in SIGGRAPH'94 Course Notes 22, 1994.

Gaydon, A.G. and Wolfard, H.G (1979). *Flames: Their structure, radiation and temperature.* London: Chapman and Hall.

Heinz, G. (1998) Comparison of different methods for sculpture recording. *Abstract in Hakodate Symposium, The ISPRS Commission V Symposium on Real-Time Imaging and Dynamic Analysis, June 2-5 1998:* Hakodate, Japan. http://www.planner.t.u-tokyo.ac.jp/ISPRS/postsym/index.htm

Inakage M. (1990). A Simple Model of Flames. *Computer Graphics Around the World*, ed. T.S.Chua, T.L.Kunii, Proc. of Computer Graphics International, Springer-Verlag, p.71-81.

Leroi-Gourhan, A. and Graziozi, P. and Roussot, A. and Anati, E. (1972). Coloquio sobre la comunicación "Contribution à l'étude de la frise pariétale du Cap Blanc". *Santander Symposium. Actas del Symposium Internacional de Arte Prehistórico 1972*, pp115-116.

Letellier, R.: (1995). *Recording, Documentation and Information Management Guidelines for World Heritage Sites* .ICCROM, UNESCO, ICOMOS. Heritage Recording Services of Public Works Canada: Hull.

Levoy, M (1999a) The Digital Michaeolangelo Project. Abstract in Electronic Imaging and the Visual Arts (EVA '99).

Levoy, M (1999b). *The Digital Michaelangelo Website.* http://www.graphics.stanford.edu/projects/mich/

Ng, K. and Sequeira, V. and Butterfield, S. and Hogg, D. and Gonçalves, J. G. M. (1998)). An integrated multisensory system for photo-realistic 3D scene reconstruction. *Abstract in Hakodate Symposium, The ISPRS Commission V Symposium on Real-Time Imaging and Dynamic Analysis, June 2-5 1998:* Hakodate, Japan. http://www.planner.t.u-tokyo.ac.jp/ISPRS/postsym/index.htm

Perlin K., Hoffert E.M. (1989). "Hypertexture", Proc. SIGGRAPH'89, vol.23, no.4, pp.253-262.

Raczkowski, J. (1996). Visual Simulation and Animation of a laminar Candle Flame. *International conference on Image Processing and Computer Graphics*, Poland 1996.

Reeves W.T. (1983). Particle Systems - A Technique for Modeling a Class of Fuzzy Objects. Proc. SIGGRAPH'83, vol.17, no.3, pp.359-376.

Roussot, A. (1972). Contribution à l'étude de la frise pariétale du Cap Blanc. *Santander Symposium. Actas del Symposium Internacional de Arte Prehistórico 1972*, pp87-113.

Rouzaud, F. (1993). Topographie interne. Le levé topographique. In Grapp (Ed.) *L'art parietal paléolithique. Techniques et méthodes d'étude.* Paris: CTHS, pp. 39-48

Rushmeier, H.E. (1995). Rendering Participating Media: Problems and Solutions from Application Areas. *Proceedings of the Fifth Eurographics Rendering Workshop Darmstadt, Germany June 13-15, Photorealistic Rendering Techniques*, Springer-Verlag.

Sakas G. (1993). Cloud modeling for visual simulators. In *Optics for protection of man and environment against natural and technological disasters* ed. G. von Bally and H.I. Bjelkhagen, Elsevier Science Publishers B.V., pp.323-333.

Stam J., & Fiume E. (1993). Turbulent Wind Fields for Gaseous Phenomena. Proc. SIGGRAPH'93, pp.369-376, 1993.

Ward Larson, G. and Shakespeare, R. (1998). *Rendering with RADIANCE: The art and science of lighting simulation.* New York: Morgan Kauffman.

# Identification of a malaria epidemic in antiquity using ancient DNA

Robert Sallares*, Susan Gomzi, Abigail Bouwman, Cecilia Anderung and Terry Brown

Dept. of Biomolecular Sciences, UMIST, PO Box 88, Manchester, M60 1QD, U.K.
* to whom correspondence should be addressed

## Introduction

In 1988-1992 a team of archaeologists from the University of Arizona, led by David Soren, excavated a very unusual site at Poggio Gramignano near the modern town of Lugnano in Teverina in the Terni province of Umbria in Italy, about seventy miles north of Rome (Soren and Soren 1997). In one corner of an abandoned Roman villa, which had been occupied from the end of the first century BC to the second century AD, was discovered an infant cemetery dating to the fifth century AD. This is the largest cemetery exclusively used for infant burials which has been found so far in Roman Italy. Forty-seven burials were uncovered and more would probably be found if the excavations were to be resumed one day. The mere fact of finding a cemetery solely for infants by itself indicates an unusual situation, since infants rarely received proper burials in classical antiquity and are frequently heavily under-represented in archaeological excavations, judging by likely mortality profiles of ancient populations based on comparative evidence from better documented populations in more recent times.

The details of the finds also indicate an unusual situation. The lack of stratification and joins between pottery sherds from all parts of the fill used for the burials suggest that all the burials occurred within a short space of time, perhaps a month or so. The pattern of the burials indicates an increasing mortality rate during this short period of time. The evidence of plant remains suggests that this short period of burials occurred during the summer of one year in the fifth century AD. Many details of the individual burials, such as the presence of twelve puppies and one dog (many of them decapitated or otherwise dismembered) provide evidence for strange rituals. Ancient authors associate some of these rituals with disease. For example, B (burial) 33 contained the skeleton of a toad. The Roman author Pliny the Elder reports that the Magi claimed that toads were a useful remedy for quartan fevers caused by *Plasmodium malariae*, the most easily recognisable of the three species of human malaria which were active in Mediterranean countries in the past, and for other fevers.

"*hoc (sc. ossiculum) et quartanas sanari adalligato in pellicula agnina recenti aliasque febres, amorem inhiberi*" - a small bone (from the right side of the toad) is said to cure quartan and other fevers if worn in fresh lamb's skin, but it inhibits love! (Pliny *Natural History* XXXII. xviii.52).

The evidence yielded by the excavations suggests that the infant burials were produced by an epidemic of some disease. The sheer number of burials suggests that this disease, whatever it was, swept through the whole local population, since the number of burials in the cemetery is larger than the number of young children in the population of the town of Lugnano nearby today. If the burials were contemporaneous, as appears to have been the case, the local population must have contained at least forty women who were all either pregnant at the same time or had recently given birth (allowing for the possibility of twins). From this statistic it is possible to make some inferences about the minimum size of the local population in the fifth century AD, by using model life tables, and it is surprisingly large, of the same order of magnitude as the modern population. Of course fertility rates were much higher in the past than they are today. During pregnancy, cell-mediated immunity to many diseases is weakened, especially during the final trimester (Weinberg 1984). No fewer than twenty-two of the burials were premature births. To explain the observed phenomena a disease is required which produces not only a high rate of infant mortality but also a high rate of premature deliveries in pregnant women.

The archaeologists who excavated the cemetery consulted specialists in medicine and came up with several possibilities. One possibility is brucellosis, a zoonosis generally transmitted to humans by consumption of milk from infected goats. The area of distribution of brucellosis certainly included Mediterranean countries. Brucellosis can cause abortions in pregnant women. However, the fact that there are no cases on record of it being transmitted to nursing infants, according to the standard textbook *Manson's Tropical Diseases* (Wilcocks and Manfred-Bahr 1972, 483), militates against its involvement in this particular epidemic. Brucellosis has not been certainly identified on any ancient human skeletal remains yet. Many bones, which have lesions that are rather atypical of tuberculosis and have been suggested as possible cases of brucellosis, have always yielded evidence for tuberculosis only, not for brucellosis, when subjected to ancient DNA analysis (Mike Taylor, personal communication). Other possible causes of the epidemic at Lugnano are *Listeria* and *Toxoplasma*. However, neither of these two diseases explains all the observed phenomena. They have rarely been known to sweep through entire populations in the way in which the pathogen which struck Lugnano appears to have done.

There remains one outstanding possibility. The most dangerous species of human malaria, *Plasmodium falciparum*, was certainly endemic in many parts of central and southern Italy in the past, especially in coastal wetlands which generated very large populations of the vector mosquito species *Anopheles labranchiae* and *An. Sacharovi*. However, malaria also occurred far inland along river valleys, since periodic floods created temporary breeding sites for mosquitoes in the vicinity of rivers. With regard to the possibility of malaria at Lugnano in antiquity, it is important to note that the archaeological site is situated about 3 ½ km from the river Tiber, which is visible from the site down a gently sloping hill. *P. falciparum* malaria is capable of producing very high levels of both infant and adult mortality, especially among those with no inherited immunity. Recent studies by Italian demographers have shown that the population of Grosseto on the coast of Tuscany, which was severely affected by malaria in the nineteenth century AD, had levels of adult life expectancy lower than any of those given in even the worst model life tables used by modern demographers (Sallares and Scheidel, forthcoming*). P. falciparum* malaria also produced premature abortion rates sometimes as high as 50-60% among pregnant women in Mediterranean populations until recently (Barbosa and Arjona 1935). In Italy it was a seasonal disease which only occurred in the summer and autumn because of the temperature requirements of the parasites for the completion of the cycle of sporogony in the vector mosquito species. *P. falciparum* malaria has all the characteristics required to produce the observed phenomena at the Roman infant cemetery. Consequently the excavators, David Soren and his colleagues, devised the hypothesis that the infant burials at Lugnano were produced by an epidemic of *P. falciparum* malaria in the summer of one year sometime during the fifth century AD (Soren, Fenton and Birkby 1995; Soren and Soren 1997). They invited the current authors to attempt to test their hypothesis using ancient DNA.

This is being done in two ways: firstly, by attempting to extract malarial DNA itself from the human bones; secondly, an indirect approach is also being tried searching for evidence of human genetic mutations which are associated with resistance to malaria. Finding such evidence in the DNA extracted from an ancient skeleton would not prove that the individual in question had ever been infected with malaria, but it would suggest that his or her ancestors had a population history of contact with endemic *P. falciparum* malaria, the most dangerous species of human malaria.

In the search for human genetic mutations associated with malaria, we decided to focus on the glucose-6-phosphate dehydrogenase gene. Mutations which reduce G6PD levels in erythrocytes or eliminate it altogether are believed to confer some resistance to *P. falciparum* malaria because such erythrocytes are more vulnerable to lysis following oxidant-induced stress before the parasites have completed their development inside the cell (Greene and Danubio 1997). Since G6PD deficiency does not create any obvious pathology on human bones, biomolecular techniques are the only way of directly tracing its evolution and history in ancient human populations. This then is a good example of a medical condition in respect of which biomolecular techniques have the potential to take us a long way beyond traditional palaeopathology, based on bone morphology. No previous work has been done on G6PD in ancient populations. Since G6PD is an X-linked gene, G6PD deficiency may have different effects in female homozygotes, female heterozygotes and male hemizygotes. Consequently it may be of interest to undertake sex determination for these infant skeletons, and so work in this area is also being performed. The sex of infants and foetuses cannot be determined from bone morphology. Some of the preliminary results of this research, which is still in progress, are reported here.

## Materials and Methods

### DNA Extraction

The bones (mainly ribs, but an intact long bone in the case of B36) were UV irradiated (254 nm) prior to the removal of the outer surface with bleach-cleaned scalpel blades. They were then pulverised with a lead weight. About 0.5g of bone powder was subjected to a standard silica extraction method with extraction buffer (6M guanidinium thiocyanate, 0.1M Tris-HCl pH 6.4, 0.02M EDTA pH 8.0 and 1.3% Triton X-100) and wash buffer (10M guanidinium thiocyanate and 0.1M Tris-HCl pH6.4) (Höss and Pääbo 1993). The extraction and wash buffers were prepared with autoclaved MilliQwater, aliquoted into 1.5 ml Eppendorf tubes, and UV irradiated for 10 minutes at 5000 joules to eliminate contamination. The bone powder was incubated with the extraction buffer for 48 hours. Two extract blanks accompanied each batch of bone samples throughout the extraction process. 10 microlitres of extract were used in each PCR. Extractions were performed in a room dedicated solely to ancient DNA extraction work.

### PCR

PCRs were also set up in a room reserved for this purpose. All oligos were obtained from Oswel DNA Service. In the initial stages of this project, reported here, to try to detect *P. falciparum* malaria itself, the hemi-nested PCR system for plasmodial 18S ribosomal DNA of Taylor *et al.* (1997) was used, with oligonucleotide primers R1 (5' TTACCGCGGCTGCTGGCAC 3'), R2 (5' CTG GCACCAGACTTGCCC 3') and F1 (5' TAAATTACCCAATTCTAAADAAGAGAG 3', where D= A+G+T), yielding PCR products 135-138 bp in length, depending on the species of malaria, after the second stage of the hemi-nested PCR. For more details of the PCR set up and reaction conditions see Gomzi (1998).

As far as G6PD is concerned, the initial target was the C>T mutation at nucleotide position 563 of exon 6 of the human G6PD gene. This is the so-called Mediterranean variant, which is one of the two commonest G6PD mutations in modern Italians (Vulliamy *et al.* 1989). We are searching for other mutations as well in work which is still in progress. To amplify the Mediterranean variant the following primers were used to amplify a 127bp segment of the gene: 5' CATCATCGTGGAGAAGC 3' and 5' CACCATCTCCTTGCCCA 3' (Hirono and Beutler 1989). The mutated sequence can be detected by the restriction enzyme *MboII* (New England Biolabs). For futher details of the PCR setup, reaction conditions, and restriction digests see Richards (1999).

For sex identification the amelogenin PCR system was used, which yields 112 and 106 bp bands from males, but only the 106bp band from females. The following primers were used: 5' CCCTGGGCTCTGTAAAGAATAATG 3' AND 5' ATCAGAGCTTAAACTGGGAAGCTG 3'. For further details of the PCR setup and reaction conditions see Anderung (1999).

## Electrophoresis

Various types of gels were used, including 4% MetaPhor agarose (FMC BioProducts) and 3% ordinary agarose gels on horizontal gel apparatuses, and 10% polyacrylamide gels on a vertical minigel apparatus (Atto Corp.). Gels were stained with either ethidium bromide or with SYBR Gold nucleic acid stain (Molecular Probes). Again for more details see Anderung (1999), Gomzi (1998) and Richards (1999).

## Sequencing

PCR products were sequenced directly using the Cyclist *Pfu*$^{(-)}$ kit (Stratagene) and autoradiography with (alpha-$^{35}$S)dATP.

## Results

The initial work searching for DNA from *P. falciparum* itself focused on the seven oldest infants from the cemetery. Of these seven infants one, by far the oldest, was aged 2-3 years at the time of death, while the others were all no more than five or six months old at the time of death. It was decided to concentrate on infants who actually survived birth for some time because it was not very likely (although possible) that transplacental transmission of malarial parasites will occur in the womb. Thus, although the mothers of the premature infants may well have been infected themselves with malaria, it is unlikely that most of the foetuses were actually infected themselves, although maternal malaria may well have been the direct cause of their premature deliveries and indirect cause of their deaths. Consequently the foetuses are unlikely to yield plasmodial DNA themselves (Sallares and Gomzi, forthcoming).

So far one infant, the oldest, B36, has yielded positive evidence for *P. falciparum* DNA. There were two successful PCR amplifications from separate extractions in respect of which the identity of the PCR products was confirmed by sequencing. The following sequences were obtained. They correspond to the 18S gene sequences of *P. falciparum*, which are not expressed in asexual parasite stages.

5'
AGAAATAACAATACAATATCGAAAAATGATTTTGTA
ATTGGAATGATAGGATTGACAAGGTTCCTAGAGAA
ACAATTGGAGGGCAAGT 3'

5'
AGAAATAACAATACAATATCGAAAAATGATTTTGTA
ATTGGAATGATAGGATTTACAAGGTTCCTAGAGAAA
CCATTGGAGGGCAAGT 3'

Both B36 and other burials from this site have also yielded other, definitely non-malarial sequences, using the same primers. These other sequences, which appear to belong to fungi or bacteria, will be discussed elsewhere (Sallares and Gomzi, forthcoming).

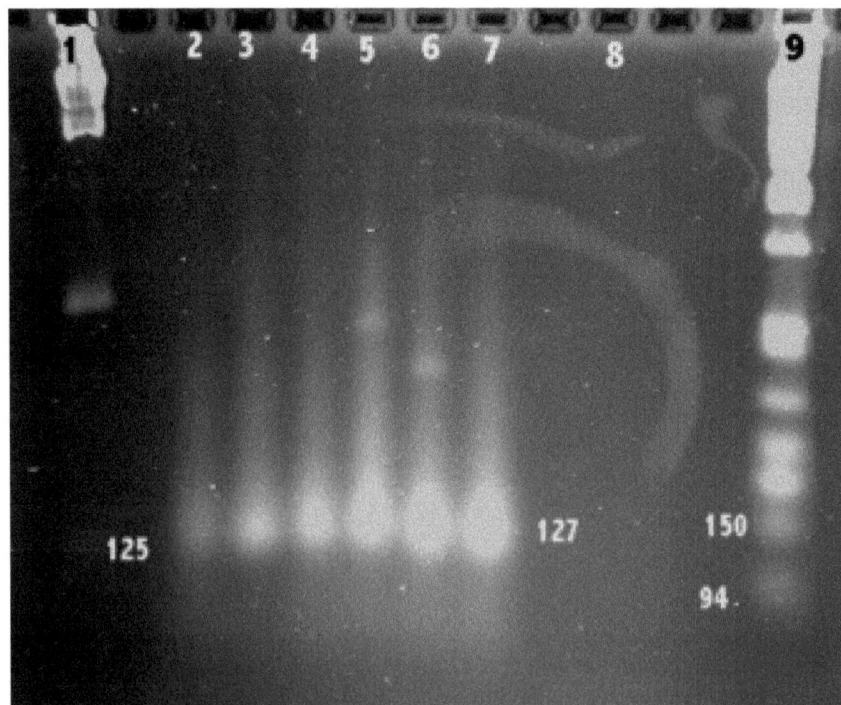

**Fig. 1. Lane 1 = *HindIII*-lambda DNA, 2 = B6, 3 = B14, 4 = B21, 5 = B22, 6 = B32, 7 =B33, 9 = *PstI*-lambda DNA, other lanes = controls. 3% agarose, stained with EtBr.**

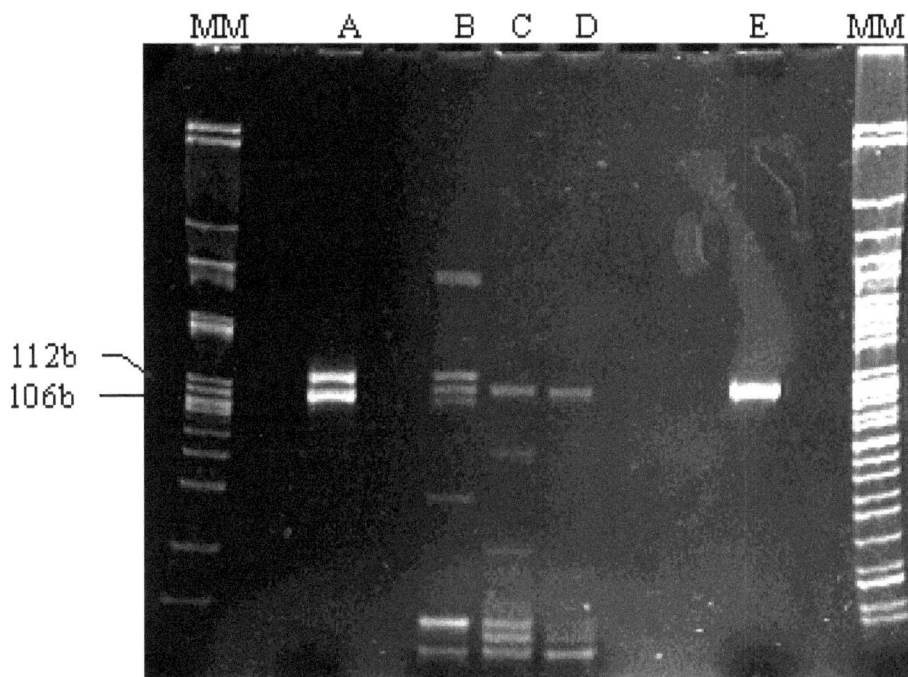

**Fig. 2. Lane 1 = molecular marker, 3 = modern male DNA, 5 = B22, 6 = B32, 7 = B33, 10 = modern female DNA, 12 = molecular marker. Polyacrylamide gel.**

A number of the infants have yielded amplifications of the target sequence in the G6PD gene (Fig. 1). This part of the work is still in progress. However, one of the infants, namely B22, has produced the characteristic 73 bp DNA fragment expected after restriction of the mutant sequence with the restriction enzyme *MboII*. This result was obtained from PCR products derived from two separate DNA extractions, confirming the result (Richards 1999). All individuals working in the laboratory where these ancient DNA extractions were performed were also tested for this mutation. Since the results were negative in all cases laboratory contamination can be categorically excluded.

Since G6PD is an X-linked gene, it is interesting to try to determine the sex of the individual when a mutation is found, since this may affect the expression of G6PD deficiency. In the case of B22, one PCR produced a male result, with the expected bands at 112 and 106 bp (Fig. 2). However, it proved to be difficult to reproduce this result, and reproducibility is always desirable in ancient DNA research. Problems were also encountered with the formation of spurious bands in these experiments, using the amelogenin PCR system. Nevertheless it is possible that the male result may be genuine, since the person who performed these experiments was female (C. Anderung). If this result is valid, then B22, a late foetus or neonate, was a male hemizygote for the 563 C>T mutation in G6PD exon 6. In all, attempts at sex identification have been made on fifteen of the burials. Six of them have not yielded any results so far. Of the nine which did, five (B2, B28, B32, B33 and B39) were probably female (taking account of the possibility of allelic dropout which is always inherent in this particular PCR system) and four (B6, B14, B22 and B25) were male. Thus these results suggest

that this ancient population had a normal 50:50 sex ratio, insofar as it can be determined. There is no evidence for selective female infanticide or any other practice, which could have skewed the sex ratio.

**Discussion**

The results obtained so far tend to confirm the hypothesis proposed by the excavators that the burials in the infant cemetery at Lugnano were produced by an epidemic of *P. falciparum* malaria. One of the infants – the oldest, B36 – has produced conclusive evidence for infection by *P. falciparum*. Since malarial DNA is rapidly removed from the blood circulation after the death of parasites, the results reported here indicate an active infection at the time of death. Consequently it is reasonable to conclude that *P. falciparum* malaria was the cause of death of this 2-3 year old infant. This proves that the most dangerous species of human malaria was present and active in the area at the time when the burials took place. Given that *P. falciparum* malaria is known to produce a very high rate of miscarriages in pregnant women, especially in primigravidae who do not yet have any acquired immunity, and given that this is particularly true of geographical regions (like Italy in the past) with a highly seasonal climate in which malaria is seasonal and epidemic in character, rather than active all the year round as in tropical countries in which the effects of *P. falciparum* malaria on pregnant women take the form of reductions in average birth weight of infants rather than premature deliveries, it is extremely likely that infections of pregnant women with *P. falciparum* malaria caused the numerous premature abortions recorded in the Lugnano cemetery. However, this cannot be proved directly since foetuses are unlikely to become infected themselves in the womb and are consequently unlikely to yield ancient DNA from malaria themselves. In view of the geographical location of the archaeological site, it is probable that *P. falciparum* malaria had an epidemic rather than an endemic character in that region in the past. This is entirely consistent with the finds in the cemetery.

Since infection with malaria has only been verified in the case of one individual, it remains quite possible that other diseases or other causes of death may have played a role in the other mortalities of older infants found in the cemetery. However, this possibility does not in any way invalidate the malaria hypothesis because the effects of malaria in terms of mortality are frequently produced by synergistic interactions with other diseases in any case (Sallares and Scheidel, forthcoming). In the case of infants in the summer in a Mediterranean country such as Italy in the past, these other diseases were most likely to have been diarrhoeal infections caused by the rotaviruses and a variety of other micro-organisms. Infants born prematurely as a result of maternal malaria would have been particularly susceptible to diarrhoeal diseases. It is doubtless not coincidence that the positive results, which have been obtained so far, came from the oldest infant in the cemetery, because that infant provided by far the best preserved skeletal material which was available for study. Other recent work on ancient human skeletal remains from central Italy has also concluded that the success rate of ancient DNA amplifications varies widely depending on the state of preservation of the bones (Vernesi *et al*. 1999).

The excavators' hypothesis to explain the cemetery is also indirectly supported by the results of the second approach, namely searching for human genetic mutations associated with malaria. The results from B22 establish that the so-called Mediterranean variant of G6PD deficiency existed by the fifth century AD and prove that the maternal ancestors of that infant had a history of contact with endemic *P. falciparum* malaria. It is possible that the mother of that infant could have mitigated to Umbria in the fifth century AD from another region with a history of endemic malaria, but malaria did exist in Umbria in the early modern period and G6PD deficiency occurs with a low frequency (0.5-1%) in the modern population today. Consequently the experimental result is not unexpected. In Roman times malaria may well have been more widespread than it was in the early modern period, since the climate was warmer in the first few centuries AD and malaria is a temperature-dependent disease (Sallares and Scheidel, forthcoming).

The results reported here constitute an independent test of a hypothesis about the cause of an ancient epidemic which was originally proposed on other grounds by people who are not specialists in molecular biology. Consequently the research design here avoids the problem of circularity in the design of ancient DNA experiments in relation to palaeodisease research to which attention has been drawn (Roberts and Manchester 1995, 198). These results also illustrate the potential great value of biomolecular techniques in the archaeology of disease. Firstly, the use of ancient DNA

permits the identification of a disease, namely malaria, which does not affect the hard tissues of bones (although it does affect bone marrow – Gandapur *et al*. 1997). In this way it is possible to extend the scope of palaeopathology to diseases which do not leave any traces on bone. Secondly, the use of ancient DNA makes possible investigation of the human genetic response to disease. This cannot be done at all by traditional osteology. In this particular case, we have identified for the first time in ancient human remains a genetic condition, G6PD deficiency, which affects large numbers of people in many human populations with a history of contact with malaria, but which is ignored in textbooks on palaeopathology because it does not leave any visible traces on bones. Thirdly, the human population under study here consisted entirely of infants and foetuses (no corresponding adult cemetery has been discovered yet). Conventional osteology cannot determine even the sex of such young infants, but sex determination is possible through the application of the techniques of molecular biology. The human population which was buried in the Lugnano cemetery is a population about which hardly anything can be said by conventional osteological techniques. However, the application of biomolecular techniques to study ancient DNA facilitates the recovery of a great deal of information about this population which could not be obtained in any other way. This study demonstrates the value of ancient DNA to archaeology. In conclusion, we suggest that the view that "perhaps in another 150 years there will have been some major advances in this field" (Roberts and Manchester 1995, 199) is unduly pessimistic.

## References

Anderung, E. G. C. (1999). *Sex identification of infant archaeological remains: amplification of the amelogenin gene* (Unpublished MSc dissertation, UMIST, Manchester).

Barbosa, A. and Arjona, B.L. (1935). *El paludismo en el primer año de la vida*. Sáez Hermanos, Madrid..

Gandapur, A. S., Malik, S. A. and Raziq, F. (1997). Bone marrow changes in human malaria: a retrospective *study Journal of the Pakistan Medical Association* **47**, 5, 137-139.

Gomzi, S. M. (1998). *Hemi-nested PCR for detection of malaria parasites in ancient skeletal remains* (Unpublished MSc dissertation, UMIST, Manchester).

Greene, L. S. and Danubio, M. E. (Eds) (1997) *Adaptation to malaria: the interaction of biology and culture. Amsterdam:* London: Gordon and Breach Publishers.

Hirono, A. and Beutler, E. (1989). Alternative splicing of human glucose-6-phosphate dehydrogenase messenger RNA in different tissues. *Journal of Clinical Investigation* **83**, 343-346.

Höss, M. and Pääbo, S. (1993). DNA extraction from Pleistocene bones by a silica-based purification method. *Nucleic Acids Research* **21**, 3913-3914.

Richards, A. S. (1999). *Biological adaptation to malaria: ancient DNA survey of a fifth century Italian infant cemetery.* (Unpublished MSc dissertation, UMIST, Manchester)

Roberts, C. and Manchester, K. (1995). *The archaeology of disease* (2nd Ed). Ithaca: Cornell University Press.

Sallares, R. and Gomzi, S. (forthcoming) 'Palaeopathology: malaria' *Ancient Biomolecules.*

Sallares, R. and Scheidel, W. (forthcoming book) *Disease and demography in the Roman world.*

Soren, D., Fenton, T. and Birkby, W. (1995). 'The late Roman infant cemetery near Lugnano in Teverina, Italy: some implications' *Journal of Palaeopathology* 7,13-42.

Soren, D. and Soren, N. (1997). *Excavation of a late Roman villa and late Roman infant cemetery near Lugnano in Teverina, Italy* 2 volumes, Rome: University Press.

Taylor, G. M., Ruthland, P. and Molleson, T. (1997). A sensitive polymerase chain reaction method for the detection of *Plasmodium* species DNA in ancient human remains. *Ancient Biomolecules* 1, 193-203.

Vernesi, C., Caramelli, D., Carbonell i Sala, S., Ubaldi, M., Rollo, F. and Chiarelli, B. (1999). Application of DNA sex tests to bone specimens from three Etruscan (VII-III century B.C.) archaeological sites. *Ancient Biomolecules* 2, 295-305.

Vulliamy, T. J. *et al.* (1989). Diverse point mutations in the glucose-6-phosphate dehydrogenase gene cause enzyme deficiency and mild or severe haemolytic anaemia. *Proceedings of the National Academy of Sciences, USA* 85, 5171-5175.

Weinberg, E. D. (1984). Pregnancy-associated depression of cell-mediated immunity. *Reviews of Infectious Diseases* VI.6, 814-831.

Wilcocks, C. and Manson-Bahr, P. E. C. (1972). *Manson's Tropical Diseases* (17th. Ed). London: John Wiley.

www.ingramcontent.com/pod-product-compliance
Lightning Source LLC
Chambersburg PA
CBHW061002030426
42334CB00033B/3328